ETHICAL JOURNALISM

This book makes the case for the news media to take the lead in combatting key threats to American society including racial injustice, economic disparity and climate change by adopting an "ethics of care" in reporting practices.

Examining how traditional news coverage of race, economics and climate change has been dedicated to straightforward facts, the author asserts that journalism should now respond to societal needs by adopting a moral philosophy of the "ethics of care," opening the door to empathetic yet factual and fair coverage of news events, with a goal to move public opinion to the point that politicians are persuaded to take effective action. The book charts a clear path for how this style of ethics can be applied by today's journalists, tracing the emergence of this empathy-based ethics from feminist philosophy in the 1980s. It ultimately urges ethical news organizations to adopt the ethics of care, based on the human emotion prioritized by Scottish Enlightenment philosopher David Hume, and to pursue a more proactive, solutions-seeking coverage of current events.

This is an invaluable text for students and academics in the fields of journalism ethics, media ethics and media law, as well as for media professionals looking for a fresh perspective on practicing ethical journalism.

Joe Mathewson covered the Supreme Court for *The Wall Street Journal* and practiced law in Chicago. Since 1997, he has taught business journalism and journalism law and ethics at the Medill School of Journalism, Media, Integrated Marketing Communications at Northwestern University. He's the author of *Law and Ethics for Today's Journalist: A Quick Guide* (Routledge) and *The Supreme Court and the Press: The Indispensable Conflict*.

ETHICAL JOURNALISM

Adopting the Ethics of Care

Joe Mathewson

LONDON AND NEW YORK

First published 2022
by Routledge
2 Park Square, Milton Park, Abingdon, Oxon OX14 4RN

and by Routledge
605 Third Avenue, New York, NY 10158

Routledge is an imprint of the Taylor & Francis Group, an informa business

© 2022 Joe Mathewson

The right of Joe Mathewson to be identified as author of this work has been asserted by him in accordance with sections 77 and 78 of the Copyright, Designs and Patents Act 1988.

All rights reserved. No part of this book may be reprinted or reproduced or utilised in any form or by any electronic, mechanical, or other means, now known or hereafter invented, including photocopying and recording, or in any information storage or retrieval system, without permission in writing from the publishers.

Trademark notice: Product or corporate names may be trademarks or registered trademarks, and are used only for identification and explanation without intent to infringe.

British Library Cataloguing-in-Publication Data
A catalogue record for this book is available from the British Library

Library of Congress Cataloging-in-Publication Data
Names: Mathewson, Joe, 1933- author.
Title: Ethical journalism : adopting the ethics of care/Joe Mathewson.
Description: London; New York: Routledge, 2022. | Includes
    bibliographical references and index. |
Identifiers: LCCN 2021009421 | ISBN 9780367690762 (hardback) | ISBN
    9780367690779 (paperback) | ISBN 9781003140337 (ebook)
Subjects: LCSH: Journalistic ethics--United States.
Classification: LCC PN4756 .M326 2022 | DDC 174.9097--dc23
LC record available at https://lccn.loc.gov/2021009421

ISBN: 978-0-367-69076-2 (hbk)
ISBN: 978-0-367-69077-9 (pbk)
ISBN: 978-1-003-14033-7 (ebk)

DOI: 10.4324/9781003140337

Typeset in Bembo
by SPi Technologies India Pvt Ltd (Straive)

CONTENTS

Introduction	1

SECTION I
This is unacceptable | 5

1	Twentieth-century journalism ethics were good for America, but no longer suffice	7
2	Racial inequity is still pervasive and ominous	11
3	Economic disparity grows and grows	22
4	Climate change advances on us	33
5	Democracy itself hangs in the balance	44
6	Politicians today won't compromise, producing government gridlock	63

vi Contents

SECTION II
Discomfiting realities are also opportunities 69

7   The ethics of care nicely complements existing codes of ethics   71

8   Current codes of ethics render high professional standards
    that endure, and should   87

9   The bright side of the financial pressure on the media   104

10 Not-for-profit journalism makes sense (if not money)   112

SECTION III
The road to success redefined 125

11 Ethical media continue to drive public discourse   127

12 Coverage of conscience coincides with journalists' motivations   140

13 The caring newsroom: Diverse, purposeful, committed to results   154

    Conclusion   166

Appendix   170
Bibliography   172
Index   177

INTRODUCTION

> Moral decisions are qualitatively different from the solution of geometry problems.
>
> —Nel Noddings

American society and democracy have long been beset by three fundamental threats to the nation's future: climate change, racial inequity and economic disparity. In 2020, those threats were highlighted by the Covid-19 pandemic, the ensuing recession and the explosive racial furor ignited first by the police killing of George Floyd. Americans had to wonder what would be the enduring impacts of these powerful forces. Journalists, especially, had to question their own prospective role in the nation's transition to an undoubtedly "new normal."

Should the ethical news media simply chronicle how the tumultuous events of 2020 exacerbated and magnified racial inequity and income disparity? Should they take more than passing notice that the damage of climate change is aggravated by forest fires raging in the West, and conversely, carbon discharge is ameliorated by a contraction of commercial and social life?

Though coverage of the year's tumult could be carried out quite professionally in conformity with the prevailing, century-old ethics of journalism reflective of moral philosophy—honestly, truthfully, factually, fairly, sensitively, transparently—that simply does not measure up to the needs of our twenty-first-century society. Ethical journalism may be under attack and mistrusted by much of our divided population, but it still is the principal provider of verifiable facts—as opposed to unsupported emotion or malicious propaganda—to voting-age Americans. If substantial societal enhancement is to occur as a result of these historic moments, it will be led by authoritative, factual, ethical news media.

This book recognizes, with admiration, the high professional standards formulated and generally practiced by the ethical news media in the twentieth century. Truth

DOI: 10.4324/9781003140337-1

2 Introduction

and facts, the foundations of ethical journalism since they were adopted in the 1890s by *The New York Times* and *The Wall Street Journal*, served both journalism and society well for more than a century. Now, as society is ominously threatened, as truth is assailed as "fake news" and ethical journalism as "the enemy of the people," the old standards, however fine, no longer suffice.

Why? Because so much is at stake. The pandemic, the recession, and the scandals erupting over police mistreatment of black Americans cannot simply be dismissed as temporary, passing hiccups on the way back to "normal." They have spotlighted and aggravated systemic dangers of racial inequities and economic disparities. Then there's climate change, an acknowledged danger to the entire planet, not just America.

It's apparent to all—America and the entire world—that U.S. policymakers have not coped well with these systemic threats. Democracy itself is at issue. Band-aids won't do. Imaginative, vigorous and decisive action is necessary. And how will American elected officials, business leaders and other policy influencers, often cautious or even hostile to amelioration, be persuaded to take such bold steps? By an aroused public. And that arousal won't happen without an aroused press. The press must do more, much more, than simply report problems, no matter how factually and truthfully.

The answer presented here is for the news media to embrace the ethics of care. A relatively new but profound approach to human morality, the ethics of care takes issue with the venerated, rational philosophical standards of duty, utility and rights or justice. The ethics of care declares a moral standard based on human empathy, calling for an active response to the needs of others, rather than on cool, detached reason. Though not grounded in our market economy or in any profession, it has something to say to journalism.

Does this mean that the ethics of care also challenges journalism's codes of ethics, which are based—implicitly if not explicitly—largely on the rational moral philosophy at odds with the ethics of care? Not at all.

The codes are set forth by most major news organizations, such as *The New York Times*, the parent of *The Wall Street Journal*, the Associated Press, the *Washington Post*, the *Los Angeles Times* and TEGNA Corp., a major owner of television stations. These organizations insist that their staff members take the codes seriously, and it appears that they genuinely strive to do so. The codes set important, indeed admirable, professional standards. They call for journalism that is truthful, factual, accurate, honest, fair and sensitive—noble qualities all. They represent the ethical epitome of twentieth-century journalism, no mean achievement. But they are defensive, intended to avoid error or embarrassment—and not incidentally, libel, invasion of privacy or other legal entanglements.

The ethics of care takes no issue with journalism's worthy standards of truth, facts, honesty, fairness, sensitivity and transparency. It simply asks more of the human species. Could that include journalists?

This book argues that it should. Recent events in the United States and worldwide tell us that we are at a turning point in human history—maybe more than one.

Ethical journalism simply must respond. Just as the profession turned an historic page at the advent of the twentieth century, meeting the information needs of

American democracy in the Golden Age economy, America's insular empire, the Great War, the Great Depression, World War II and on through the twentieth century, so now must journalism once again elevate its sights and its ambition. Still the major conduit of truth to the American public, journalism must not only point the way, but in fact *lead* the way, to a better, more equitable and more secure future. It's quite clear that climate change, racial inequity and economic disparity are not simply going to fade away, ever.

An embrace of the ethics of care can provide a moral, philosophical underpinning for journalists to initiate greater, continuing, persistent but still truthful and factual coverage and commentary on the climate and racial and economic ills that beset us. Ethical journalism has the potential influence, indeed the power, to persuade the public that vigorous government action is mandatory to alleviate these systemic threats, and that an engaged (or perhaps enraged) public opinion will finally persuade America's leaders that they must act decisively or face removal.

We will also explore specific ideas and examples to illustrate how the ethical news media can lead.

Because this undertaking is addressed to ethical journalists and all who care about journalism's role in our democracy, it will be developed in large part through the best source: the news.

Let us proceed.

SECTION I

This is unacceptable

1

TWENTIETH-CENTURY JOURNALISM ETHICS WERE GOOD FOR AMERICA, BUT NO LONGER SUFFICE

Journalism in the late nineteenth century, notably in New York, was characterized by a race for circulation among many daily newspapers, with Joseph Pulitzer's racy *New York World* running to the fore in 1890 with a stunning circulation of six-hundred thousand in a city of 2.7 million. But that began to change in the 1890s with the purchase of *The New York Times* by a self-made Chattanooga newspaper owner named Adolph Ochs, and the creation of the nascent *Wall Street Journal* by reporters Charles Dow, Edward Jones and Charles Bergstresser. Instead of striving for the most sales, these newcomers introduced a higher priority: accuracy. It caught on.

Whether you called it truth, facts, honesty, fairness, sensitivity or transparency, the quest for accuracy served both the nation and the journalism profession well through the Golden Age of industrial capitalism, the creation of the American island empire, the Great War, the Twenties, the Great Depression, World War II and beyond. Facts mattered. There were exceptions, of course, notably a chain of two dozen flashy newspapers featuring scandal and sex published by an ambitious upstart named William Randolph Hearst. Nevertheless, as time went on many of the biggest, most reputable newspapers, such as *The Times, The Journal, Washington Post, Los Angeles Times* and *Chicago Tribune* codified their admirable professional standards in wide-ranging codes of ethics intended to avoid error and embarrassment, and, not incidentally, legal entanglements such as libel and invasion of privacy. The news services Associated Press and Bloomberg News have their own statements, as do principal professional associations the Society of Professional Journalists and the Radio Television Digital News Association. These codes endure, and they have substantial commonalities, such as commitments to truth, accuracy, fairness, sensitivity and transparency.

It's not explicit, but we must note that these codes of ethics inherently draw intellectual validity from rational principles of duty, utility (or usefulness) and human rights or justice enunciated by venerated moral philosophers. Their expression of

DOI: 10.4324/9781003140337-3

8 This is unacceptable

standards of moral behavior is now being challenged, so it's necessary to take a closer look at them.

Perhaps most notably, at least for our purpose, German philosopher Immanuel Kant (1724–1804) posited an obligation, or duty, to govern human decision-making. Kant argues that sound personal decisions, or maxims, should be tantamount to a law that would govern everyone: "There is therefore but one categorical imperative, namely this: Act only on that maxim whereby thou canst at the same time will that it should become a universal law." The phrase "categorical imperative" is indelibly Kant's.

He gives this example: "A man reduced to despair by a series of misfortunes feels weary of life" and contemplates suicide…

> [H]e inquires whether the maxim of his action could become a universal law of nature…. Now we see at once that a system of nature of which it should be a law to destroy life by means of the very feeling whose special nature it is to impel to the improvement of life would contradict itself and, therefore, could not exist as a system of nature; hence that maxim cannot possibly exist as a universal law of nature and consequently, would be wholly inconsistent with the supreme principle of duty.[1]

Echoes of Kant's conception of duty in contemporary journalism codes of ethics are not hard to find. Clearly, ethical journalists today have their own duty, or categorical imperative. As the SPJ Code of Ethics puts it: "Ethical journalism should be accurate and fair. Journalists should be honest and courageous in gathering, reporting and interpreting information." And the RTDNA Code of Ethics: "Ethical decision-making should occur at every step of the journalistic process, including story selection, news-gathering, production, presentation and delivery."

Another rational ethical principle is called utility or utilitarianism. That's a belief that a proper course of action is one that maximizes human happiness. It began with a Kant contemporary, an English philosopher and jurist named Jeremy Bentham (1748–1832). Bentham was a man before his time. He advocated individual legal rights, economic freedom, separation of church and state, decriminalization of homosexual acts, and abolition of slavery and capital punishment. Bentham writes in his seminal work: "By utility is meant that property in any object, whereby it tends to produce benefit, advantage, pleasure, good, or happiness … or to prevent the happening of mischief, pain, evil, or unhappiness" to an individual or to the community.[2]

Bentham focuses particularly on acts of government, declaring that "An action … may be said to be conformable to the principle of utility … when the tendency it has to augment the happiness of the community is greater than any it has to diminish it."[3]

This philosophy of utility, especially as to its impact on government, is reflected today in the personal motivation of many working journalists and in the Preamble to the SPJ Code of Ethics, echoing a Bentham concern for informed policy-making: "Members of the Society of Professional Journalists believe that public enlightenment is the forerunner of justice and the foundation of democracy." Similarly, in the RTNDA Code of Ethics:

"Journalism empowers viewers, listeners and readers to make more informed decisions for themselves; it does not tell people what to believe or how to feel." A long-standing journalism testament, now in its third edition, by veteran journalists and educators Bill Kovach and Tom Rosenstiel, reiterates this emphasis on the import of the profession:

> The elements of journalism are the ingredients that allow people to know the facts and context of events, to understand how they should react to that information, and to work on compromises and solutions that make their communities better. Journalists didn't create these needs—they simply developed a series of concepts and methods for meeting them.[4]

Finally, John Locke (1632–1704), an English physician-philosopher, conceives of ethics based on individual rights and a quest for maximum human happiness, all in the context of the community. Locke believes that recognition of individual rights leads to collective decisions for "the greater good" and "the removing of pain as long as we have any left, as the first and necessary step toward happiness." His conception of community and individual rights, Locke emphasizes, requires enforcement:

> Since it would be utterly in vain to suppose a rule set to the free actions of men, without annexing to it some enforcement of good and evil to determine his will we must, wherever we suppose a law, suppose also some reward or punishment annexed to that law.[5]

Today, individual rights are respected by both the SPJ and RTDNA codes of ethics, in almost the same sense as a Lockean reference to rights jeopardized by a criminal prosecution, but leavened now by the guarantee of the Sixth Amendment to the U.S. Constitution of the "right to a speedy and public trial, by an impartial jury." The SPJ states: "Balance a suspect's right to a fair trial with the public's right to know." RTDNA: "the right to a fair trial ... deserve[s] consideration and to be balanced against the importance or urgency of reporting." The RTDNA code also mentions, in another context, "the rights of citizenship." So it's appropriate to observe that respect for individual rights, especially when threatened by criminal prosecution, though first formulated nearly four centuries ago, is indeed an aspect of ethical journalism today.

So, you may ask, what's the problem here? Why are these reason-based philosophical standards of human morality being questioned? And who says so anyway?

It begins with women philosophers writing in the 1980s. One of the foremost pioneers, Nel Noddings (1929–), expresses a distinctly feminine view: "It represents an alternative to present views, one that begins with the moral attitude or

10 This is unacceptable

longing for goodness and not with moral reasoning."[6] She adds in the preface to the 2013 edition:

> In care ethics ... we are not much interested in moral credit. We are, rather, interested in maintaining and enhancing caring relations—attending to those we encounter, listening to their expressed needs, and responding positively if possible. Ethical caring ... derives its strength from natural caring. This is clearly a reversal of Kantian priorities.[7]

Do the proponents of the ethics of care reject all the venerated philosophers? No. In fact, they have their own philosopher hero: David Hume (1711–76). A pillar of the Scottish Enlightenment and a friend of political economist Adam Smith, Hume sees reason as subordinate to emotion in human action: "Reason is, and ought only to be the slave of the passions, and can never pretend to any other office than to serve and obey them."[8]

We will explore the ethics of care in greater detail as we go along, but suffice it to say here that Noddings and other proponents of the ethics of care, while taking issue with traditional moral reasoning, do not clash with journalism codes of ethics despite their conformity with cool reason.

So, let's consider what ethical journalists—and American democracy—are up against in the twenty-first century.

Notes

1 Immanuel Kant, *Groundwork of the Metaphysics of Morals*, trans. Thomas Kingsmill Abbott, Monee, IL, 2020; originally published 1785, 36, 38, 39.
2 Jeremy Bentham, *An Introduction to the Principles of Morals and Legislation*, Dumfries & Galloway: Anodos Books, 2019; originally published 1780, 7.
3 Ibid. 8.
4 Bill Kovach and Tom Rosenstiel, *The Elements of Journalism, Revised and Updated*, New York: Three Rivers Press, 2014, x–xi.
5 John Locke, *An Essay Concerning Human Understanding*, quoted in A. John Simmons, *The Lockean Theory of Rights*, Princeton: Princeton University Press, 1992, 131.
6 Nel Noddings, *Caring: A Relational Approach to Ethics and Moral Education*, 2013 edition, Berkeley and Los Angeles: University of California Press, 2013, 1. First published 1984, original title *Caring: A Feminine Approach to Ethics and Moral Education*.
7 Ibid., preface.
8 David Hume, *A Treatise of Human Nature*, in *The Essential Philosophical Works: David Hume*, Ware, Hertfordshire: Wordsworth Editions Limited, 2011, 360.

2

RACIAL INEQUITY IS STILL PERVASIVE AND OMINOUS

The history of American racism is baleful. Slavery was unashamedly embraced for more than two centuries, and after it was officially abolished by the Civil War and the Thirteenth Amendment to the Constitution in 1865, "Jim Crow" legislation and blatant cruelty continued to subjugate and humiliate African Americans well into the twentieth century. Historian Jon Meacham describes that period as "bleak, and violence remained a fact of life…. By the 1890s and into the first years of the twentieth century, Jim Crow laws were prevalent in the South, and black voters were systematically disenfranchised."[1] The Supreme Court was indifferent to the Bill of Rights, but finally, the Court under Chief Justice Earl Warren in the 1950s and 1960s recognized civil rights, among other historic decisions. "They changed the law, and they changed society," as Constitutional scholars Geoffrey R. Stone and David A. Straus put it.[2] President Lyndon Johnson persuaded Congress to enact major civil rights legislation in the 1960s. But these advances in law did little to relieve black segregation and poverty in the cities, which erupted in angry, violent protests from 1964 to 1967. In response, President Johnson formed a National Advisory Commission on Civil Disorders headed by Governor Otto Kerner Jr. of Illinois. The 1968 report of the Kerner Commission declared, "Our nation is moving toward two societies, one black, one white—separate and unequal." It famously recommended massive, costly federal programs to respond to black poverty and unrest, including improvements of police-community relations, administration of justice under emergency conditions, compensation for property damage, and employment, education, welfare and housing initiatives.[3] But the sweeping recommendations were mostly ignored by the government. Then, just months later, the Democratic National Convention was memorably marred by violent confrontations between civil rights demonstrators and the Chicago police.

DOI: 10.4324/9781003140337-4

12 This is unacceptable

Black lives, white lives

Huge, unacceptable differences between white and black lives persist. As *The New York Times* reported in mid-2020, "Only eight miles apart, the Streeterville and Englewood neighborhoods of Chicago have a life-expectancy gap of roughly 30 years." The story, a photo essay, went on to explain,

> Streeterville is a neighborhood of mostly white, affluent, college-educated families living in townhomes and high-rise condominiums along the shore of Lake Michigan. A baby born there in 2015 could expect to live to 90. In nearby Englewood, a poor, predominantly black neighborhood of low-rise apartments in the shadow of Interstate 94, a baby born in 2015 could not expect to reach 60. There are many reasons for such extreme differences in life expectancy between rich and poor in the United States, including access to health care, environmental factors such as pollution and the chronic stress associated with poverty.

The story appeared in the midst of the epic Covid-19 pandemic, which the story took note of: "The pandemic is likely to have only widened the gap. The poorer Englewood had one confirmed death from the coronavirus for every 559 residents, while in Streeterville there was just one confirmed death for every 8,107 residents." The median household income in Streeterville was given as one-hundred three thousand five hundred fifty-two dollars, and in Englewood, only twenty thousand nine hundred ninety-one dollars.[4]

Violent crime, in impoverished Englewood as well as in several other predominantly African American neighborhoods on Chicago's south and west sides, is rampant. In the twelve months to October 20, 2020, the Englewood police district (which covers adjacent West Englewood as well as Englewood) recorded sixty murders, up from thirty-seven a year earlier, and two hundred fifty-three shooting incidents versus one hundred forty-one. Sharply different, in the same year-long period the lakefront police district encompassing Streeterville and adjacent upscale neighborhoods recorded nine murders, up from four, and twenty-nine shooting incidents compared with nineteen.[5]

High unemployment in Chicago's black neighborhoods, aggravated by the Covid-19 pandemic and its concomitant deep depression, precipitated mindless outbreaks of violence in 2020. "[O]n the first official summer weekend of the year, it was 106 people shot, 14 of them fatally—including a 3-year-old boy," the *Chicago Tribune* reported grimly in June.

> The tally between Friday afternoon and early Monday marked the most people shot in one weekend here since at least 2012, and the violence took a particular toll on children. Twelve of those shot were younger than 18 years old. Five of them died, including two walking into their backyard after going to get candy at a corner shop.... The Austin District, where 3-year-old Mekhi James was fatally shot Saturday afternoon, had the most shooting victims: 18.[6]

That district, on the city's beleaguered West Side, is majority black.

Forlorn Englewood, a once-vibrant working class South Side neighborhood of sixty thousand residents shrunken to less than thirty thousand, is emblematic of Chicago segregation and need. An earlier study of Chicago neighborhoods by Harvard sociologist Robert J. Sampson found that the dire conditions of Englewood and other black neighborhoods on Chicago's South Side were aggravated by the forced displacement of twenty-seven thousand low-income people, given housing vouchers, caused by demolition of a nearby gigantic public housing project called Robert Taylor Homes, and by the Great Recession of 2008–09. "According to the 2009 data," Sampson finds,

> Englewood and [neighboring] West Englewood represent the third- and fifth-highest foreclosure rates in Chicago, respectively. Moreover, because of their cheap housing to begin with, many CHA [Chicago Housing Authority] voucher holders are moving south and east to communities like Englewood, Washington Park, and South Shore.... poor communities with the least resources are taking on added burdens disproportionately, in turn reinforcing preexisting inequality.[7]

Commencing in the mid-twentieth century American businesses and universities, prodded by street demonstrations, governments at all levels, and reinforced by the Supreme Court, undertook significant efforts to remedy the nation's racial inequity. Perhaps the best known effort, then and now, is "affirmative action," intended to assist minorities' admission to higher education and access to good jobs. A study of affirmative action notes appropriately, "The discrimination faced by African Americans is perhaps the best known—slavery, then Jim Crow, and then an endemic racism that still permeates much of American life." The author, Melvin I. Urofsky of Virginia Commonwealth University, finds that

> Affirmative action has worked in that hundreds of thousands of people who would have been barred from colleges or from the workplace have gotten in, have gotten an education or a job, and while there is still much too great an economic gulf between whites on the one hand and African Americans and Hispanics on the other, that gulf would be even greater without preferential programs.[8]

However, Urofsky goes on,

> African American students in many schools are not finishing their undergraduate degree in six years; many are at finishing at all. It is also beyond doubt that racism and sexism are still very much with us, as events during the 2016 presidential campaign and the first two years of the Trump administration have clearly shown.

In short, the goals of affirmative action "have not been achieved; sexism and racism are still with us; and whether one reads an old-fashioned newspaper or

14 This is unacceptable

gets information on a handheld device, affirmative action stories are still with us."[9] Historian Meacham declares that "the Civil War was only a chapter in the perennial contest between right and wrong in the nation's soul," and "it is correct … to say that color in some ways remains the problem of American democracy as a whole."[10]

An op-ed contributor to *The New York Times*, a Michigan State economist named Lisa D. Cook, wrote in 2020 that the damage done by racial discrimination is not limited to racial minorities. "Discrimination," she stated,

> inflicts a staggering cost on the entire economy, reducing the wealth and income of millions of people, including many who do not customarily view themselves as victims.… Recent research calculates the effects of the discriminatory practice of placing highly skilled African-American workers, who might have flourished as, say, doctors, into lower-skilled occupations …. Such practices 50 years ago — which linger, to a lesser extent, today — have cost the economy up to 40 percent of aggregate productivity and output today. Similarly, other research estimates that aggregate economic output would have been $16 trillion higher since 2000 if racial gaps had been closed. To put that total in context, the gross domestic product of the United States in 2019 was $21.4 trillion.[11]

Racial inequity in the news

The news media are fully aware of U.S. racial inequity, as is the general public. Coverage of the problem is profuse, and it was greatly magnified in 2020 by the Covid-19 pandemic, the deep recession it caused, and blatant, on-camera killings of several unarmed African Americans by local policemen. The most prominent of those crimes was committed in Minneapolis, Minnesota, where four policemen pulled from his car a black man suspected of passing a counterfeit bill at a convenience store. They handcuffed him, thrust him face-down to the pavement, and one officer knelt on his neck for more than eight minutes as he gasped that he could not breathe. He expired soon after. His image and name, George Floyd, were immediately and repeatedly flashed in angry demonstrations that erupted throughout the country.[12] The uproar was aggravated again and again in 2020, by the Louisville police killing of an innocent young black woman, Breonna Taylor, in her own bed (a drug raid gone wrong; no drugs or cash were found);[13] the point-blank shooting by Kenosha, Wisconsin, police of an unarmed black man, leaving him paralyzed from the waist down;[14] the killing in Georgia of an unarmed black jogger, Ahmaud Arbery, by a former policeman and his son;[15] the killing by a Texas officer of an unarmed black man, Jonathan Price, as he walked away;[16] the killing by a Waukegan, Illinois policeman of a black man in his car;[17] the killing by Philadelphia policemen of a black man brandishing a knife, on a street in full view of bystanders including his mother, who said afterward he had a mental problem.[18] The first killing, that of George Floyd in Minneapolis, caused the governor of Colorado to call for review of the case of Elijah McClain, a young black man who died in August 2019 after being forcefully apprehended by police officers in Aurora, Colorado, as he walked home.[19]

Steven Levitzky and Daniel Ziblatt, Harvard professors and authors of *How Democracies Die*, saw great significance in the nationwide protests, often pockmarked by frenzied looting of stores, that were triggered by these killings. "America's emerging multiracial democratic majority was visible this summer in the aftermath of the police killing of George Floyd in Minneapolis," they wrote in a *New York Times* opinion piece.

> The killing set off what may be the biggest wave of protest in United States history. An estimated 15 million to 26 million Americans took to the streets, and protests extended into small-town and rural America. Three-quarters of Americans supported the protests in June, and large majorities — including 60 percent of whites — supported the Black Lives Matter movement. These numbers declined over the course of the summer. As of September, however, 55 percent of Americans (and 45 percent of white Americans) continued to support Black Lives Matter, levels that were considerably higher than ever before in the movement's history.[20]

Broader news response

The shock of this repeated cruelty, often caught on camera phones by passers-by, combined with the simultaneous devastation of the Covid-19 pandemic,

> stimulated many news reports about racial inequity. The Associated Press reported that "African Americans still earn barely 60 cents for every $1 in white income. They have 10 cents in wealth for every $1 whites own. They remain more than twice as likely to live in poverty. And they're about as likely to own a home as they were when Richard Nixon was president." The story went on: "Now, demonstrators are out in the streets again, this time to protest what happened in Minneapolis to George Floyd, dead after a police officer pressed a knee into his neck for eight minutes and 46 seconds. Once again, racial inequality underlies rage and despair, especially because the unrest coincides with an economic and health calamity, one that's falling hardest, yet again, on African Americans.[21]

ProPublica, the muscular, investigative not-for-profit, reported, "No, the coronavirus is not an 'equalizer.' Black people are being infected and dying at higher rates. Here's what Milwaukee is doing about it — and why governments need to start releasing data on the race of COVID-19 patients."[22] *The New York Times*, after suing to obtain revealing data from the Centers for Disease Control, reported that

> Latino and African-American residents of the United States have been three times as likely to become infected as their white neighbors, according to the

16 This is unacceptable

new data, which provides detailed characteristics of 640,000 infections detected in nearly 1,000 U.S. counties. And Black and Latino people have been nearly twice as likely to die from the virus as white people, the data shows.[23]

Later, the not-for-profit Marshall Project reported: "New data shows deaths from all causes—COVID and otherwise—have gone up 9 percent among White Americans, but more than 30 percent in communities of color."[24] The *Chicago Tribune* found that "the highest rates of infection are happening in communities that also have high rates of crime and violence, such as Garfield Park, Austin, West Englewood and Lawndale."[25]

Another ProPublica reporter, Lizzie Presser, spent months in Mississippi reporting a powerful story about the disproportionately high number of diabetes-related leg amputations among blacks. "Nobody knew it in January," she wrote later,

> but within months, the new coronavirus would sweep the United States, killing tens of thousands of people, a disproportionately high number of them black and diabetic. They were at a disadvantage, put at risk by an array of factors, from unequal health care access to racist biases to cuts in public health funding. These elements have long driven disparities, particularly across the South. One of the clearest ways to see them is by tracking who suffers diabetic amputations, which are, by one measure, the most preventable surgery in the country.

Her pen was like a hammer:

> Diabetics undergo 130,000 amputations each year, often in low-income and underinsured neighborhoods. Black patients lose limbs at a rate triple that of others. It is the cardinal sin of the American health system in a single surgery: save on preventive care, pay big on the backend, and let the chronically sick and underprivileged feel the extreme consequences.[26]

This avalanche of stories on discrimination against blacks and Latinos should not be taken to ignore stories about other minorities. A tiny, online not-for-profit, the San Francisco Public Press, reported in August 2020 that

> Nearly 2,500 cases of verbal and physical attacks against Asian Americans were reported between March 19 and July 22 to a tracking project called Stop AAPI Hate, a group representing Asian Americans and Pacific Islanders. In San Francisco, an Asian American bus driver was assaulted by passengers after an argument over proper mask wearing. A woman reported getting verbally assaulted and a drink thrown at her by a passenger who told her and her brother to 'go back to their country.' Another man reported being shoved on the stairs, trampled and kicked in the head.[27]

The often-neglected Native American minority was accorded at least occasional attention. ProPublica reported that the federal Bureau of Indian Education

Racial inequity is still pervasive and ominous **17**

produces some of the lowest academic results in the country and has allowed school buildings to go years in disrepair. But perhaps one of its biggest failures has been a history of repeatedly neglecting warnings that it is not providing a quality education for the 46,000 students who attend its schools, which operate primarily on reservations and are often the only available option in rural communities.[28]

The Wall Street Journal told of an Indian Health Service doctor in Browning, Montana, accused of pedophilia, "But the Indian Health Service didn't fire Mr. Weber. Instead, it transferred him to another hospital in Pine Ridge, S.D. He continued treating Native American children there for another 21 years, leaving behind a trail of sexual-assault allegations."[29]

Chicago journalists reminded their audience that the city still owned its reputation as one of America's most segregated cities. A collaborative investigation by National Public Radio station WBEZ and a new, nonprofit newsroom, City Bureau, examined mortgage lending throughout the city and found

gaping disparities in the amount of money lent in Chicago's white neighborhoods compared to black and Latino areas — a pattern that locks residents out of home ownership, deprives communities of desperately needed capital investment and threatens to exacerbate racial inequities between neighborhoods.... 68.1% of dollars loaned for housing purchases went to majority-white neighborhoods, while just 8.1% went to majority-black neighborhoods and 8.7% went to majority-Latino neighborhoods.[30]

As a result of these cascading events and stories, racial inequity was the second most important issue in the 2020 election, according to nationwide exit polling of three thousand eight hundred forty-five voters by Edison Research for the National Election Pool; 20 percent of voters rated it number one (after the economy), and they voted 92 percent for Joe Biden against only 7 percent for Donald Trump.

What's missing?

If the above stories—just a few examples of abundant, continuous coverage of the nation's racial inequity, heightened by the Covid-19 pandemic and the resulting severe recession—seem to be repeating pre-2020 stories that sounded pretty much the same. In fact they are. The pandemic and recession just made things worse— even worse—for America's disadvantaged racial minorities. And the police brutality exposed by citizen videos, all capturing incidents victimizing unarmed black men, made one wonder how commonly such outrages might have occurred clandestinely in years past.

Such conditions are simply unacceptable in a democratic republic that, as James Madison emphasized over and over again in the Federalist Papers, is designed to serve "justice and the public good," "the good of the whole," "both the public good

18 This is unacceptable

and the rights of other citizens," to be a "force directed to any object which the public good requires."[31] Alexander Hamilton, Madison's leading collaborator in the Federalist, heartily concurred:

> The republican principle demands that the deliberate sense of the community should govern the conduct of those to whom they intrust the management of their affairs … It is a just observation that the people commonly *intend* the PUBLIC GOOD.[32]

The post-World War II Hutchins Commission, bristling with an awesome prestige of illustrious membership, upped the ante. The press "can advance the progress of civilization or they can thwart it…. These instruments can spread lies faster and farther than our forefathers dreamed when they enshrined the freedom of the press in the First Amendment to our Constitution." But the Commission ceded little discretion to the press; it has a *duty*, a "responsibility with regard to the values and goals of our society as a whole." Almost eerily prescient, the Commission lectured the press about coverage of our

> many groups which are partially insulated from one another and which need to be interpreted to one another. Factually correct but substantially untrue accounts of the behavior of members of one of these social islands can intensify the antagonisms of others toward them. A single incident will be accepted as a sample of group action unless the press has given a flow of information and interpretation concerning the relations between two racial groups such as to enable the reader to set a single event in its proper perspective.[33]

The New York Times sets an admirable example of rat-a-tat-tat coverage of racial inequity, and many other news organizations are commendable, too. Nevertheless, as the experience of 2020 too graphically demonstrates, there remains a painful—perhaps widening—gulf between the white majority and racial minorities of the United States. Listen to Madison, Hamilton and the Hutchins Commission. American news organizations *do* have a duty, a responsibility to go beyond chronicling unjust events and conditions that belie democracy. As we will assert later, their duty and responsibility is to right wrongs, to inform, incite and actually mobilize the public to take private action and especially to demand that government take effective action to realize the true promise of our democratic republic.

Racial inequity undermines our social fabric. It is a fundamental threat to realization of the full promise of our society and democracy. Centuries of experience testify that, despite civil rights laws and other progressive actions, racial inequity prevails. "Democracy requires more than majority rule," professors Levitsky and Ziblatt declared in *The New York Times*. "But without majority rule, there is no democracy. Either we become a truly multiracial democracy or we cease to be a democracy at all."[34]

Without the news media, the status quo will persist. With the news media leading, the promise of significant change may be realized. Madison and Hamilton expect it. The Hutchins Commission demands it. So does conscience.

Notes

1 Jon Meacham, *The Soul of America: The Battle for Our Better Angels*, New York: Random House, 2018, 68.
2 Geoffrey R. Stone and David A. Straus, *Democracy and Equality: The Enduring Constitutional Vision of the Warren Court*, New York: Oxford University Press, 2020, 3.
3 *Report of the National Advisory Commission on Civil Disorders: Summary of Report*, 1968, Homeland Security Digital Library, https://www.hsdl.org/?abstract&did=35837
4 Alec Soth, "The Great Divide," *The New York Times*, September 5, 2020, https://www.nytimes.com/interactive/2020/09/05/opinion/inequality-life-expectancy.html?action=click&module=Opinion&pgtype=Homepage
5 Chicago Police Department crime statistics by police district, https://www.google.com/search?client=safari&sxsrf=ALeKk01l1DShJZ4ebntu8Oq3tULtrWut7g%3A1603127041891&source=hp&ei=AceNX9WbM9jbtQb1sIW4AQ&q=chicago+crime+statistics+by+police+district&oq=&gs_lcp=CgZwc3ktYWIQARgAMgcIIxDqAhAnAnMgcIIxDqAhAnMgcIIxDqAhAnMgcIIxDqAhAnMgcILhDqAhAnMgcIIxDqAhAnMgcILhDqAhAnMgcIIxDqAhAnMgcIIxDqAhAnMgcIIxDqAhAnUABYAGCHPmgBcAB4AIABAIgBAJIBAJgBAKoBB2d3cy13aXqwAQo&sclient=psy-ab
6 Annie Sweeney and Jeremy Gorner, "Chicago's Violent Weekend Renews Search for Answers in a Tense City, Points Again to Entrenched Problems," *Chicago Tribune*, June 23, 2020, https://www.chicagotribune.com/news/criminal-justice/ct-chicago-weekend-violence-analysis-20200623-bucz3ynr3rcazemol4663fhtqy-story.html
7 Robert J. Sampson, *Great American City: Chicago and the Enduring Neighborhood Effect*, Chicago and London: University of Chicago Press, 2012, 401.
8 Melvin I. Urofsky, *The Affirmative Action Puzzle: A Living History from Reconstruction to Today*, New York: Pantheon Books, 2020, 465.
9 Ibid. xvii, xiii.
10 Jon Meacham, op. cit. 52, 15.
11 Lisa D. Cook, "Racism Impoverishes the Whole Economy," *The New York Times*, November 22, 2020, BU12, https://www.nytimes.com/2020/11/18/business/racism-impoverishes-the-whole-economy.html?searchResultPosition=1 Cook was a member of the Biden-Harris transition team.
12 Amy Forliti and Tim Sullivan, "Officer Charged with George Floyd's death as protests flare," Associated Press, May 30, 2020, https://apnews.com/article/e27cfce9464809aa8c91afd74c930bb5
13 WSJ Staff, "What Happened to Breonna Taylor? What We Know about the Case and Her Death," *The Wall Street Journal*, October 2, 2020, https://www.wsj.com/articles/what-happened-to-breonna-taylor-louisville-settles-over-police-shooting-11600185062
14 "Kenosha Shooting: Protests Erupt after US Police Shoot Black Man," *BBC*, August 24, 2020, https://www.bbc.com/news/world-us-canada-53886070
15 Rich McKay, "Three to Face Judge in Fatal Shooting of Black Jogger in Georgia," Reuters, July 17, 2020, https://www.reuters.com/article/us-usa-georgia-shooting/three-to-face-judge-in-fatal-shooting-of-black-jogger-in-georgia-idUSKCN24I1JQ
16 Joe Sutton, Eliott C. McLaughlin and Carma Hassan, "Texas Officer Charged with Murder after Shooting a 31-Year-Old Black Man Who Tried to Intervene in a Dispute,

20 This is unacceptable

Attorney Says," CNN, October 7, 2020, https://www.cnn.com/2020/10/06/us/jonathan-price-police-shooting-texas/index.html

17 Michael Levenson, "Police Killing of Black Man Sets Off Protests in Illinois," *The New York Times*, October 22, 2020, https://www.nytimes.com/2020/10/22/us/waukegan-police-shooting-protests.html

18 Frances Stead Sellers, Katie Shepherd, Griff Witte, Maura Ewing and Mark Berman, "Protests Grip Philadelphia, Leaving Officers Injured and Stores Damaged, after Police Kill a Black Man," *Washington Post*, October 27, 2020, https://www.washingtonpost.com/nation/2020/10/27/philadelphia-police-shooting-walter-wallace/

19 Katie Shepherd, "An Unarmed 23-Year-Old Black Man Died after police stopped him. The Colorado Governor Wants a New Probe," *Washington Post*, June 25, 2020, https://www.washingtonpost.com/nation/2020/06/25/colorado-elijah-mcclain-death/

20 Steven Levitzky and Daniel Ziblatt, "Let's End Minority Rule," *The New York Times*, October 25, 2020, https://www.nytimes.com/2020/10/23/opinion/sunday/disenfranchisement-democracy-minority-rule.html?searchResultPosition=1

21 Paul Wiseman, Associated Press, "Coronavirus Deaths, George Floyd Protests Spotlight Persistent Racial Gap: Black Americans Have 10 Cents in Wealth for Every $1 Whites Own," *Chicago Tribune*, June 9, 2020, https://www.chicagotribune.com/coronavirus/ct-nw-coronavirus-george-floyd-economic-gap-20200608-jy5efvnnpvdvbmeypfai45qvbu-story.html

22 Akilah Johnson and Talia Buford, "Early Data Shows African Americans Have Contracted and Died of Coronavirus at an Alarming Rate," ProPublica, April 3, 2020, https://www.propublica.org/article/early-data-shows-african-americans-have-contracted-and-died-of-coronavirus-at-an-alarming-rate

23 Richard A. Oppel Jr., Robert Gebeloff, K.K. Rebecca Lai, Will Wright and Mitch Smith, "The Fullest Look Yet at the Racial Inequity of Coronavirus," *The New York Times*, July 5, 2020, https://www.nytimes.com/interactive/2020/07/05/us/coronavirus-latinos-african-americans-cdc-data.html?campaign_id=56&emc=edit_cn_20200707&instance_id=20074&nl=on-politics-with-lisa-lerer&regi_id=12942352&segment_id=32789&te=1&user_id=7d0e5105b76418ac21466ea00fa29497

24 Anna Flagg, Damini Sharma, Larry Fenn and Mike Stobbe, "COVID-19's Toll on People of Color Is Worse Than We Knew," The Marshall Project, August 21, 2020, https://www.themarshallproject.org/2020/08/21/covid-19-s-toll-on-people-of-color-is-worse-than-we-knew

25 Annie Sweeney, Joe Mahr and Jeremy Gorner, "COVID-19 Hitting Hardest in Chicago ZIP Codes Already Struggling with Deadly Threat of Gun Violence," *Chicago Tribune*, May 15, 2020, https://www.chicagotribune.com/coronavirus/ct-covid-crime-zipcodes-20200515-7oggwt5csbbt7pmojewnp4ruo4-story.html

26 Lizzie Presser, "The Black American Amputation Epidemic," ProPublica, May 19, 2020, https://features.propublica.org/diabetes-amputations/black-american-amputation-epidemic/

27 Laura Wenus, "Professor: Governments, Residents Must Address Racist Attacks against Asians," San Francisco Public Press, August 6, 2020, https://www.sfpublicpress.org/professor-governments-residents-must-address-racist-attacks-against-asians/#

28 Alden Woods, ProPublica, "The Federal Government Gives Native Students an Inadequate Education, and Gets Away with It," *Arizona Republic*, August 6, 2020, https://www.propublica.org/article/the-federal-government-gives-native-students-an-inadequate-education-and-gets-away-with-it?utm_source=sailthru&utm_medium=email&utm_campaign=majorinvestigations&utm_content=feature

Racial inequity is still pervasive and ominous **21**

29 Christopher Weaver, Dan Frosch and Gabe Johnson, "A Pedophile Doctor Drew Suspicions for 21 Years. No One Stopped Him," *The Wall Street Journal*, February 8, 2019, https://www.wsj.com/articles/a-pedophile-doctor-drew-suspicions-for-21-years-no-one-stopped-him-11549639961
30 Linda Lutton, WBEZ; Andrew Fan, City Bureau; Alden Loury, WBEZ, "Where Banks Don't Lend," WBEZ and City Bureau, June 3, 2020, https://interactive.wbez.org/2020/banking/disparity/
31 James Madison, Federalist 10 and 14, *The Federalist Papers*, New York and London: Penguin Books, 1961, 77, 80, 100–01.
32 Alexander Hamilton, Federalist 71, Ibid. 432.
33 *A Free and Responsible Press: A General Report on Mass Communication: Newspapers, Radio, Motion Pictures, Magazines, and Books,* The Commission on Freedom of the Press, Chicago: The University of Chicago Press, 1946, 3, 4, 27.
34 Levitsky and Ziblatt, op. cit.

3

ECONOMIC DISPARITY GROWS AND GROWS

The numbers don't lie. The rich get richer. The Pew Research Center reported in 2020,

> The wealth gap between upper-income and lower- and middle-income families has grown wider this century. Upper-income families were the only income tier able to build on their wealth from 2001 to 2016, adding 33% at the median. On the other hand, middle-income families saw their median net worth shrink by 20% and lower-income families experienced a loss of 45%.[1]

The trend is not good—for the people struggling at the bottom, or for American democracy and its original focus on the "public good."

This is not a new notion. Supreme Court Justice Louis Brandeis fretted about economic disparity during the Great Depression of the 1930s. "There is a widespread belief," he wrote in a case challenging a state tax law that favored independent local retailers over chain-store companies,

> that the existing unemployment is the result, in large part, of the gross inequality in the distribution of wealth and income which giant corporations have fostered ... and that only through participation by the many in the responsibilities and determinations of business can Americans secure the moral and intellectual development which is essential to the maintenance of liberty.[2]

French economist Thomas Piketty, in his surprise best-seller *Capital in the Twenty-first Century*, published in translation in 2017, declares that since 1980

> income inequality has exploded in the United States.... The upper decile's [2010 income greater than one hundred fifty thousand dollars] share

DOI: 10.4324/9781003140337-5

increased from 30–35 percent of national income in the 1970s to 45–50 percent in the 2000s,

on track to reach 60 percent in 2030. "The bulk of the growth of inequality," he went on, "came from 'the 1 percent' [income exceeding three hundred fifty-two thousand dollars], whose share of national income rose from 9 percent in the 1970s to about 20 percent in 2000–2010."[3]

Paul Krugman, Nobel Prize winner in economics who writes a regular column for *The New York Times*, declared in 1992 that

> During the mid-1980s, economists became aware that something unexpected was happening to the distribution of income in the United States.... there had been a dramatic change ... 70 percent of the rise in average family income has gone to the top 1 percent of families.... What does this tell us? Since the 1970s median income has failed to keep up with average income or, to put it differently, the typical American family has seen little gain in spite of rising productivity.[4]

Wall Street's greedy infatuation with mortgage-backed securities of dubious validity and value led to the disastrous Great Recession of 2007–8, and the recovery from it—particularly static average wages (although unemployment dropped to near-record lows)—endured to the sudden pandemic-induced recession of 2020, when unemployment soared to as high as 14 percent and thirty million lost their jobs. In late 2020, twenty million Americans were still out of work and dependent on state unemployment compensation, which typically lasts only thirty-nine weeks.

According to a 2014 report of the Economic Policy Institute, a Washington, D.C., think tank whose mission is "to defend and promote the interests of workers in economic policy debates," the

> median worker's wages and benefits grew just 7.9 percent between 1979 and 2013. This exceptionally slow pay growth is shocking considering that economic growth and productivity—up 64.9 percent in that same time period—were robust enough to support strong pay growth for all Americans. The break between productivity and pay means a disproportionate share of income growth is going to corporate profits, the returns to financial assets, and the pay of those at the upper end of the pay scale. In other words, economic growth is benefiting those at the top, not ordinary workers.

The average annual inflation-adjusted earnings of all workers, the EPI stated, increased by a very modest 0.9 percent, down from 2.1 percent between 1947 and 1979.[5] In a more recent report, the EPI stated, "In 2017, middle-wage workers earned just 16.8 percent more than their counterparts almost four decades earlier. This corresponds to an annualized inflation-adjusted growth rate over the 38-year period of just 0.4 percent per year." Furthermore, "For workers with less than a

24 This is unacceptable

four-year college degree (over 60 percent of the workforce in 2017), real wages for the typical (median) worker were *lower* in 2017 than they had been in 1979."[6]

The EPI cites three factors behind these sobering figures:

> The first is the long-term decline in manufacturing employment, which has traditionally been the sector of the economy that pays relatively high wages to the non-college-educated workers who still make up a large majority of the U.S. workforce. The second countervailing force is the long-term decline in union membership, which has had a negative effect on the pay and benefits of both union and nonunion workers. The third factor is the persistent failure to run the economy at full employment, which has undermined the important leverage workers have in tight labor markets.[7]

In still another report, the EPI finds that 2019 compensation of chief executive officers rose 14 percent to an average 21.3 million dollars, three hundred twenty times the wages of a typical worker.

> Corporate boards running America's largest public firms are giving top executives outsize compensation packages that have grown much faster than the stock market and the pay of typical workers, college graduates, and even the top 0.1%. In 2019, a CEO at one of the top 350 firms in the U.S. was paid $21.3 million on average (using a 'realized' measure of CEO pay that counts stock awards when vested and stock options when cashed in rather than when granted). This 14% increase from 2018 occurred because of rapid growth in vested stock awards and exercised stock options tied to stock market growth.[8]

Other scholars concur about this alarming imbalance in income. In its 2020 report, Pew Research Center stated,

> Over the past 50 years, the highest-earning 20% of U.S. households have steadily brought in a larger share of the country's total income. In 2018, households in the top fifth of earners (with incomes of $130,001 or more that year) brought in 52% of all U.S. income, more than the lower four-fifths combined, according to Census Bureau data .... In 1968, by comparison, the top-earning 20% of households brought in 43% of the nation's income, while those in the lower four income quintiles accounted for 56%.[9]

Another measure of economic disparity is household wealth. In that respect, the difference between white and black families is most striking. In 2020, the Brookings Institution reported

> staggering racial disparities.... At $171,000, the net worth of a typical white family is nearly ten times greater than that of a Black family ($17,150) in 2016 .... The Black-white wealth gap reflects a society that has not and does not afford equality of opportunity to all its citizens.[10]

The New York Times reported in mid-2020 that a Federal Reserve study showed rising household net worth of 18 percent between 2016 and 2019, but, "despite the progress, massive gaps persisted — the share of wealth owned by the top 1 percent of households was still near a three-decade high."[11]

As Harvard professors Steven Levitsky and Daniel Ziblatt note, "For many Americans, the economic changes of the last few decades have brought decreased job security, longer working hours, fewer prospects for upward mobility, and, consequently, a growth in social resentment."[12] This is the resentment that Donald Trump astutely recognized and capitalized on to win the election of 2016, notably in southern and rural states, where hourly wages were comparatively low. According to EPI, 2015–17 median hourly wages in a seven-state "manufacturing Southeast" region (excluding Florida) were only 16.20 dollars, and in a six-state, mostly rural "other Midwest" region 16.71 dollars, compared with the top 20.25 dollars in the "other Northeast" region (excluding New York), 19.00 dollars in the four-state "other Pacific" region (excluding California), and 18.69 dollars in California.[13] Trump swept all fourteen states comprising the two lowest-wage regions, the "manufacturing Southeast" and "other Midwest." (Although Trump won only 46 percent of the popular vote in 2016, he carried thirty of the fifty states to win the electoral college vote, 304 to 227.)

The stark differences in personal finances are also reflected in a rise in what another economics Nobelist and his wife, both Princeton economists, call "deaths of despair"—suicides and deaths from drug overdoses and alcoholism. They examine the surprising recent decline of mortality in the United States, focusing in particular on white mortality in the age group forty-five to fifty-four. "In 2017," Angus Deaton and Anne Case write,

> those with a bachelor's degree or more earned twice as much as those without, which speaks to the advantage of the more educated in life. Their risk of dying in midlife is only a quarter of that seen for those with a bachelor's degree speaks to their advantage in death.... it was the rise in deaths of despair among those with less than a bachelor's degree that largely accounts for the widening of the all-cause mortality gap.... [T]hose in the less educated group were three times more likely to succumb to these deaths.... The march of death from arteries and lungs to minds, livers, and veins is largely confined to those who have not been to college.[14]

And, they note, "The most obvious advantage of having gone to college is that you earn more, and with more money, you can live a better life." America suffers from a "flawed democracy," the two economists declare.[15]

Although *The New York Times* probably devoted as much space to stories about poverty and economic disparities as any major news organization, its public editor, Margaret Sullivan, found the coverage "of high quality but insufficient in volume, and dwarfed by stories meant to appeal to the rich, or at least those aspiring to be so."[16]

26 This is unacceptable

Pandemic aggravation

The worrisome trends in personal finances were exacerbated by the Covid-19 pandemic and the resulting recession as they struck in 2020. "Economists worry," *The New York Times* reported in September,

> that progress for disadvantaged workers has probably reversed in recent months as the pandemic-related shutdowns threw millions of people out of work. The crisis has especially cost minority and less-educated employees, who are more likely to work in high-interaction jobs at restaurants, hotels and entertainment venues. Many economists expect the crisis to worsen inequality as lower earners fare the worst.[17]

Most immediately, the pandemic highlighted and aggravated the economic disadvantage of low-income workers such as those in restaurants, groceries and some health services, and in basic public services like sanitation and mass transportation. As upper-income Americans cut back their spending and worked from home during the pandemic and recession, the impact fell most heavily on the less fortunate. The CNN reported,

> Rich Americans who curtailed their spending during the pandemic ended up costing a lot of low-wage workers their jobs, a trend that could hinder economic recovery, according to Harvard University research released Wednesday. The top 25% of the wealthiest US households accounted for two-thirds of the declines in credit card spending from the beginning of January to the end of May, whereas the bottom 25% kept their spending patterns the same, researchers found, noting that the high-income individuals reduced their spending primarily because of health concerns — not loss of jobs.[18]

Differences in the cost of health care became more apparent, and more painful. *The Wall Street Journal* reported that

> some patients, such as Medicare beneficiaries who don't carry supplemental insurance, are falling through the cracks. And the uninsured are required to seek financial assistance and sometimes fill out labyrinthine paperwork to cover their bills, a tall task for many patients still suffering from the illness's long-term effects.[19]

The New York Times found that many families that had been affluent enough to buy a car—even expensive cars—were struggling from unemployment during the pandemic to find enough food to subsist. *The Times* pointed to one California mother roaming mile after mile in San Diego County,

> first to one food giveaway and then to another and then to more .... gathering food for her four children as well as neighbors in need. She pulls her packed

silver Volkswagen van alongside the BMWs and Mercedeses as they edge their way through the long, snaking lines.[20]

Long-standing poverty

To be clear, it wasn't as if the excruciating pain and perils of poverty hadn't been noticed by the press before the pandemic and the recession. In 2018, a *Los Angeles Times* editorial described the city's skid row as a "Dickensian dystopia" and a "national disgrace" where

> men and women sleep in rows, lined up one after another for block after block in makeshift tents or on cardboard mats on the sidewalks — the mad, the afflicted and the disabled alongside those who are merely down on their luck. Criminals prey on them, drugs such as heroin and crystal meth are easily available, sexual assault and physical violence are common and infectious diseases like tuberculosis, hepatitis and AIDS are constant threats.

This hideous scene, the editorial went on,

> is only the ugly epicenter of a staggering homelessness problem that radiates outward for more than 100 miles throughout Los Angeles County and beyond. There are now more than 57,000 people who lack a 'fixed, regular or adequate place to sleep' on any given night in the county, and fewer than 1 in 10 of them are in skid row.[21]

The online not-for-profit San Francisco Public Press worried about the lack of social distancing, among other problems, in that city's crowded Tenderloin district. "In a pandemic that mandates physical distancing," reporter Christopher D. Cook wrote,

> survival in the poverty-suffused Tenderloin is endangered by relentlessly overcrowded conditions, a dearth of open public spaces and limited mobility. Every corner of life here is packed tight: sidewalks, streets, homeless tent encampments, apartment buildings and single-room-occupancy hotels, where residents have their own rooms but typically share bathrooms and kitchens. By far the most densely populated neighborhood in San Francisco, the Tenderloin is home to 45,587 people per square mile, almost 2.5 times the citywide density of 18,939 people per square mile. Neighborhood residents suffer the city's second-highest rate of COVID-19 infections — eclipsed only by the Bayview — and five times that of neighboring Nob Hill.[22]

A fundamental defect

Former Chicago Mayor Rahm Emanuel considers income inequality "perhaps the most pressing issue in the United States and maybe even the world today .... and the gap between the haves and the have-nots has been getting wider over the last

28 This is unacceptable

four decades." Furthermore, Emanuel declares in his memoir, "Income inequality and access to opportunity are issues that affect everyone," notably the business community.[23] On the other hand, according to a *The New York Times* business reporter, the surge in upper-upper incomes is so great that it has created an extraordinarily privileged economy catering to the ultra-rich, exemplified by expensive stadium club memberships and private jets. The reporter, Nelson D. Schwartz, calls it the "velvet rope economy." He dates the beginning of persistent flat incomes for everyone else to the 1970s; since then

> incomes for all but the top 10 percent of American households have remained flat. Within the top 10 percent, however, salaries have been rising, and nowhere has the surge in pay been as great as among the top one percent. The top one tenth of one percent have done the best of all. Gains in disposable income, which drive consumer spending and in turn corporate profits, have been similarly confined to the very top of the income scale.[24]

Another journalist, Adam Cohen, argues that the Supreme Court, after the retirement of Chief Justice Earl Warren in 1969, aggravated the inequality by repeatedly ruling "often cruelly, against the poor.... The Supreme Court has played a critical role in building today's America, in which income inequality is the largest it has been in nearly a century." Cohen, formerly of *The New York Times* and *Time* magazine, points to "a landmark decision rejecting a poor family's constitutional challenge to a cap on welfare benefits that pushed them far below the poverty level." He warns that "[e]xtreme inequality puts democracy at risk: the concentration of wealth in the top 1 percent—and, to a striking degree, the top 0.1 percent—is pushing the nation toward plutocracy." In particular, he asserts, the American dream "of upward mobility is unraveling as a growing share of the nation's wealth is arrogated by a small number of very wealthy people at the top."[25]

What to do?

The New York Times in mid-2020 voiced strong editorial support for a raft of federal legislative proposals to ease the pain of economic disparity, including:

> Create a federal savings account for every newborn child.
> Eliminate single-family zoning, as Minneapolis did in 2018.
> Provide universal prekindergarten for 4-year-olds.
> Spend more on the education of lower-income children.
> Increase the minimum wage to $15 an hour.
> Double the earned-income tax credit.
> Require employers to pay for family and medical leave.
> Extend federal labor protections to domestic workers.
> Provide housing vouchers to all eligible families.

Reward cities that allow more housing construction.
Expand the program to end homelessness among veterans to all Americans.
Restore federal funding for public health agencies.[26]

In Chicago, for one, the economic battle was joined even before the pandemic and recession hit. Mayor Lori Lightfoot, a black woman who grew up poor in an Ohio industrial town, confronted city business leaders at a luncheon in early 2020 with what the *Chicago Tribune* termed a "stark declaration:" "Poverty is killing us. All of us. Literally and figuratively." The story elaborated:

> Lightfoot ran through a number of everyday scenes in the city that she said illustrate the problem: children relying on school for food, a life expectancy rate that's 17 years lower for black and brown residents in one neighborhood compared with the life span of other mostly white neighborhoods, and the high costs of Chicago's gun violence.

She served advance notice that she would call on the City Council—and, by implication, the business leaders—to support ordinances that would ensure that "renters get more than 30 days to find a new place to live during no-fault evictions, to end housing discrimination against people with arrest records," and a pilot program in the low-income Woodlawn neighborhood, on the city's South Side, "giving qualified community buyers the right of first refusal to purchase certain multifamily buildings when an owner puts a building up for sale." The story quoted the mayor as challenging the business leaders: "Am I making you uncomfortable? I mean to."[27] Chicago was then experiencing a shortage of affordable rental units, contributing to "the city's large affordability gap, exacerbating housing cost burdens and limiting housing opportunities for lower-income renter households," according to a report of the Institute for Housing Studies at DePaul University. The report continued, "Affordability pressures rooted in a shrinking affordable rental stock may also undermine neighborhood diversity, contribute to growing inequities, and heighten displacement risk."[28] However, in Chicago as elsewhere, the pandemic recession put landlords under severe pressure, caught in the middle between their mortgage-holders and their utilities providers on the one hand, and government exhortations to go easy on evictions (temporarily prohibited by legislation) on the other—just one of the many painful economic dislocations caused by the pandemic.

The pandemic and recession hit minorities hardest. "The coronavirus pandemic," *The Wall Street Journal* reported in August 2020, "risks widening the financial gap in Buffalo, N.Y., between white and Black workers, who entered this year's economic downturn with less financial security and are disproportionately employed in sectors more vulnerable to layoffs and exposure to Covid-19." *The Journal* interviewed George Winfield, a fifty-four-year old college graduate and a father of six, who had earned thirty dollars an hour until his factory closed in 2007, then was furloughed in March 2020 from his thirteen-dollars-an-hour job washing dishes and cooking at a University of Buffalo cafeteria. He told *The Journal*, "There's a level of being disheartened, of course, but I'm a bit inured to it." Winfield said he had never found a job that made use of his degree.[29]

The pandemic and recession made apparent the large number of Americans, even those employed, who were living on the brink of a financial abyss. Week after week in 2020, more than one million applied for first-time state unemployment benefits (twenty-six weeks) or for temporary federal pandemic benefits for the uninsured, such as gig workers (thirteen weeks). In the summer of 2020, more than thirty million were receiving benefits or awaiting benefits at any one time—out of a pre-pandemic work force of one hundred sixty-four million.[30] When the weekly benefits ran out, people were desperate. Many had little or no savings to fall back on. "Once my money finally came in from unemployment, then I had to put it toward my three months of late rent," a sixty-one-year-old Army veteran named Barbara Eckes in Eau Claire, Wisconsin, told the *Eau Claire Leader-Telegram* in September. She was subsisting on a military pension of three hundred twenty-seven dollars a month until she found part-time work stocking shelves at a local store. "I worked at Michaels today," she told the newspaper in October,

> and now I don't work until Friday. I get about four and a half hours a day when I work. Once the holidays start coming round we'll get more hours, but then in January it will drop back off to eight or nine hours a week.[31]

It's appropriate to recall, again, that the Federalist writers said the democratic republic they created was to serve the "public good." The public good is woefully underserved when much of the population is struggling to survive day by day—or just to survive at all.

Notes

1 Juliana Menasche Horowitz, Ruth Igielnik and Rakesh Kochhar, "Most Americans Say There Is Too Much Economic Inequality in the U.S., But Fewer Than Half Call It a Top Priority," Pew Research Center, January 9, 2020, https://www.pewsocialtrends.org/2020/01/09/trends-in-income-and-wealth-inequality/
2 *Louis K. Liggett Co. v. Lee*, 288 U.S. 517, 580 (1933), Brandeis, J., dissenting in part.
3 Thomas Piketty, *Capital in the Twenty-First Century*, Cambridge, Massachusetts: Harvard, 2014, 369, 371.
4 Paul Krugman, "The Rich, the Right, and the Facts," *The American Prospect*, Fall 1992, in Paul Krugman, *Arguing with Zombies: Economics, Politics, and the Fight for a Better Future*, New York: W.W. Norton & Company, 2020, 261, 267.
5 Economic Policy Institute, "Raising America's Pay," June 4, 2014, https://www.epi.org/publication/raising-americas-pay-summary-initiative/
6 Economic Policy Institute, "Raising America's Pay, Wage Data," June 4, 2014, italics added, https://www.epi.org/publication/raising-americas-pay-data/
7 Ibid.
8 Lawrence Mishel and Jori Kandra, "CEO Compensation Surged 14% in 2019 to $21.3 Million. CEOs Now Earn 320 Times as Much as a Typical Worker," Economic Policy Institute press release, August 18, 2020, https://www.epi.org/publication/

Economic disparity grows and grows **31**

ceo-compensation-surged-14-in-2019-to-21-3-million-ceos-now-earn-320-times-as-much-as-a-typical-worker/

9 Katherine Schaeffer, "The Highest-Earning 20% of Families Made More Than Half of all U.S. Income in 2018," Pew Research Center, February 7, 2020, https://www.pewresearch.org/fact-tank/2020/02/07/6-facts-about-economic-inequality-in-the-u-s/

10 Kriston McIntosh, Emily Moss (both of The Hamilton Project), Ryan Nunn (Federal Reserve Bank of Minneapolis), and Jay Shambaugh, "Examining the Black-White Wealth Gap," The Brookings Institution, February 27, 2020, https://www.brookings.edu/blog/up-front/2020/02/27/examining-the-black-white-wealth-gap/

11 Jeanna Smialek, "U.S. Household Wealth Rose Before the Pandemic, but Inequality Persisted," *The New York Times*, September 28, 2020, https://www.nytimes.com/2020/09/28/business/economy/coronavirus-pandemic-income-inequality.html

12 Steven Levitsky and Daniel Ziblatt, *How Democracies Die*, New York: Broadway Books, 2018, 228.

13 EPI, op. cit. "Manufacturing South" is Alabama, Georgia, Kentucky, Mississippi, North Carolina, South Carolina, Tennessee." Other Midwest" is Iowa, Kansas, Missouri, Nebraska, North Dakota, South Dakota. "Other Northeast" is Connecticut, Delaware, District of Columbia, Maine, Maryland, Massachusetts, New Hampshire, New Jersey, Rhode Island, Vermont. "Other Pacific" is Alaska, Hawaii, Oregon, Washington.

14 Anne Case and Angus Deaton, *Deaths of Despair and the Future of Capitalism*, Princeton: Princeton University Press, 2020, 57, 58, 49.

15 Ibid. 50, 14.

16 Margaret Sullivan, *Ghosting the News: Local Journalism and the Crisis of American Democracy*, New York: Columbia Global Reports, 2020, 93.

17 Jeanna Smialek, op. cit. https://www.nytimes.com/2020/09/28/business/economy/coronavirus-pandemic-income-inequality.html

18 CNN Wire, "Harvard Researchers: Rich Americans Cut Their Spending, Hurt Low-Income Jobs,'" Fox40, https://fox40.com/news/business/harvard-researchers-rich-americans-cut-their-spending-hurt-low-income-jobs/

19 Robbie Whelan, "Who Pays for Covid-19 Medical Care? That Depends on How (or if) You Are Insured; Pandemic has put a spotlight on the vast differences in affordability of health care across the country," *The Wall Street Journal*, September 14, 2020, https://www.wsj.com/articles/who-pays-for-covid-19-medical-care-that-depends-on-how-or-if-you-are-insured-11600075801

20 Tim Arango, photographs by Brenda Ann Kenneally, "'Just Because I Have a Car Doesn't Mean I Have Enough Money to Buy Food,'" *The New York Times*, September 3, 2020, https://www.nytimes.com/2020/09/03/us/food-pantries-hunger-us.html?searchResultPosition=1

21 Editorial, "Los Angeles' Homelessness Crisis Is a National Disgrace," *Los Angeles Times*, February 25, 2018, https://www.latimes.com/opinion/editorials/la-ed-homeless-crisis-overview-20180225-htmlstory.html

22 Christopher D. Cook, "What Crowding Looks Like During a Pandemic: Dismal Days in the Tenderloin," San Francisco Public Press, August 28, 2020, https://sfpublicpress.org/what-crowding-looks-like-during-a-pandemic-dismal-days-in-the-tenderloin/?utm_content=Contact&utm_source=VerticalResponse&utm_medium=Email&utm_term=Neighborhood%20residents%20suffer%20the%20city%26rsquo%3Bs%26nbsp%3Bsecond-highest%26nbsp%3Brate%20of%20COVID-19%20infections%20%26mdash%3B%20eclipsed%20only%20by%20the%20Bayview%20%26mdash%3B%20and%20five%20times%20that%20of%26nbsp%3Bneighboring%20Nob%20Hill&utm_campaign=What%20Crowding%20

32 This is unacceptable

Looks%20Like%20During%20a%20Pandemic%3A%20Dismal%20Days%20in%20 the%20Tenderloin

23 Rahm Emanuel, *The Nation City: Why Mayors Are Now Running the World*, New York: Alfred A. Knopf, 2020, 15, 28.

24 Nelson D. Schwartz, *The Velvet Rope Economy: How Inequality Became Big Business*, New York: Doubeday, 2020, 10.

25 Adam Cohen, *Supreme Inequality: The Supreme Court's Fifty-Year Battle for a More Unjust America*, New York: Penguin Press, 2020, xv, xxiv, xxv, xxviii, xxix.

26 Editorial, "America Needs Some Repairs. Here's Where to Start. This nation began as a set of promises that it has yet to keep," *The New York Times*, July 2, 2020, https://www. nytimes.com/2020/07/02/opinion/sunday/income-inequality-solutions.html

27 Gregory Pratt, "Mayor Lori Lightfoot Calls on Well-Heeled City Club of Chicago Audience to Help Fight Poverty:'We the People Must Solve It'," *Chicago Tribune*, February 14, 2020, https://www.chicagotribune.com/politics/ct-lightfoot-chicago-poverty-city-club-20200215-wttabmphffhcjcpk24ezlvvada-story.html

28 "Policy Interventions to Respond to the Housing Impacts of COVID-19," Institute for Housing Studies at DePaul University, June 5, 2020, https://www.housingstudies.org/ blog/covid-policy-interventions/

29 Kim Mackrael, photographs by Malik Rainey, "Black Workers in Buffalo Face Bigger Share of Coronavirus Impact; Fewer factory jobs in western New York factor in outsize employment loss for Black residents," *The Wall Street Journal*, August 16, 2020, https:// www.wsj.com/articles/black-workers-in-buffalo-face-bigger-share-of-coronavirus-impact-11597570201

30 Heidi Shierholz, "Many Workers Have Exhausted Their State's Regular Unemployment Benefits," Economic Policy Institute, September 24, 2020, https://www.epi.org/blog/ many-workers-have-exhausted-their-states-regular-unemployment-benefits-the-cares-act-provided-important-ui-benefits-and-congress-must-act-to-extend-them/

31 "Before, I would sometimes go out for dinner or grab an ice cream cone, but you can't do that if you don't have any money," *Eau Claire Leader-Telegram*, leadertelegram.com, in "Out of work in America," A Special Section, *The New York Times*, October 23, 2020, https://www.nytimes.com/interactive/2020/10/22/us/pandemic-unemployment-covid.html?searchResultPosition=1

4
CLIMATE CHANGE ADVANCES ON US

Our planet is warming. It's a fact. Its deleterious effects are already becoming apparent, to the detriment of human life, not to mention plants and animals. Remedial efforts have been proposed, and some undertaken. But global warming continues. It threatens the future of mankind, meaning our children's and grandchildren's very existence. Aggravated by human activity, especially the burning of fossil fuels, climate change is caused by heat from the sun that warms the earth and then is trapped in the earth's atmosphere by greenhouse gases such as carbon dioxide and methane, as well as agriculture practices, industrial processes and clearcutting of forests.

This chapter does not attempt to prove a point. It's universally known. "To be honest," writes *The New York Times* columnist and Nobel prize winner Paul Krugman,

> sometimes I wonder whether I'm wasting my time talking about any issue other than climate change. I mean, civilization faces an existential threat; if we don't take action to limit emissions of greenhouse gases, in the long run nothing else—not health reform, not income inequality, not even financial crisis—will matter.[1]

So we'll summarize what scientists and common sense tell us. We'll look at the multiplicity of recommendations, ideas, intentions and remedies already before us. But for caring, ethical journalism, the question is: how do we—and the nations of the world—respond? Can ethical journalism be satisfied simply to report the facts—the changing weather and climate patterns, the catastrophic storms and wildfires, the hunger caused by altered agricultural conditions, the drought of water shortages, the flooding of seacoasts and entire Pacific isles, the many plans and insufficient efforts to respond? Hardly. As in dealing with the systemic corrosion of democracy by racial inequities and economic disparities, ethical journalists must again assume

DOI: 10.4324/9781003140337-6

34 This is unacceptable

responsibility to care—to mobilize the citizenry to alter our ways and to pressure our politicians and business leaders to take action that is bold, remedial and effective. It won't happen without active, ethical, caring journalism. Because it hasn't, despite worldwide awareness of the threats to human life as we know it. If journalists fail in this, the future of journalism itself is in jeopardy, too. The culprit is clear. As one climate journalist-activist puts it, "Scientists are now certain that our use of fossil fuels and our destruction of the planet's ecosystems are quickly bringing the future of human civilization into doubt."[2] Burning carbon-based fuels, as all the world knows now, releases carbon dioxide (CO_2), the principal "greenhouse gas," into the atmosphere. The journalist-activist, Eric Holthaus, goes on to declare that "We have reached a point at which all weather, in every season, and in every country on Earth, is directly connected to the changes we've inflicted on our planet's atmosphere." He cites numerous examples, including Hurricane Maria's calamitous strike against housing, fresh water supplies, electricity, hardwood trees and most human life on Puerto Rico in 2017: "A 2019 study in the journal Geophysical Research Letters found that global warming made Maria's disastrous floods nearly five times more like than it would have been in 1956, when high-quality rainfall record keeping began in Puerto Rico."[3]

Significantly, Holthaus faults his fellow journalists, too. Pointing to the catastrophic devastation of the Abaco Islands in the Bahamas by Hurricane Dorian in 2019, he asserts that

> the American press largely ignored Dorian and its aftermath, deciding to cover with great fervor President Trump's use of a black Sharpie to alter an official National Hurricane Center forecast to make it seem as if it were in line with his erroneous tweet stating the storm threatened Alabama instead. But this is how the press often behaves, as if the people enduring the worsening climate emergency are irrelevant, as long as the disasters do not land on US soil.[4]

The Paris Agreement

Fortunately, we have an accepted baseline for measuring and countering climate change. In 2015, five thousand delegates representing one hundred ninety-five nations capped years of negotiations by enthusiastically adopting the Paris Agreement, intended to guide national and international efforts to thwart climate change for the next four decades. (Perversely, in 2019, President Donald Trump announced his intention to withdraw the United States, a major contributor to global warming, from the Paris Agreement, significantly undermining its efficacy; he contended that it would damage the nation's economy.[5]) The agreement calls on the subscribing nations to halve their greenhouse gas emissions by 2030 and further limit emissions by 2050 to what the earth can naturally absorb, thus "carbon neutrality." This commitment, two United Nations negotiators of the treaty declare, means "our global greenhouse gas emissions must be clearly on the decline

Climate change advances on us **35**

by the early 2020s and reduced by at least 50 percent by 2030."[6] The negotiators, Christiana Figueres and Tom Rivett-Carnac, warn, ominously, that

> We are too far down the road of destruction to be able to 'solve' climate change.... We cannot bring back the extinct species, the melted glaciers, the dead coral reefs, or the destroyed primary forests. The best we can do is keep the changes within a manageable range, staving off total calamity ...

In their optimistic view,

> We can have more efficient and cheaper transportation resulting in less traffic; we can have cleaner air, supporting better health and enhancing the enjoyment of city life; and we can practice smarter use of natural resources, resulting in less pollution of land and water.[7]

Other writers emphasize humane aspects of the global warming problem. Darrel Moellendorf, a German professor of philosophy and political theory, declares that global poverty is "central to climate change policy.... It should be scandalous that nearly half the world's population lives in desperate poverty, especially while many lavish in such plenty." As it is, he avers,

> large climate impacts are expected to be experienced in tropical regions where there are a great many poor people. Another is that the poor will have fewer resources to cope with droughts, inundation by oceans, rivers flooding, tropical storms, and disease.... Poor people living in drought-prone regions and in large mega deltas will be made especially vulnerable by climate change.

For instance, in regions without electricity, indoor pollution caused by burning biomass "is likely to become a bigger threat to human health than either HIV or tuberculosis, resulting in more than 4,000 premature deaths each day by 2030."[8] Already, according to the Paris negotiators Figueres and Rivett-Carnac, burning of fossil fuels "pollutes the local ambient air with particulate matter" that damages "lungs, hearts and brains" so egregiously that "more than 7 million people die from air pollution each year."[9]

The goals of the Paris Agreement are expressed in degrees of global temperature rise. It recognizes, according to the negotiators, that "we have already warmed the planet by 0.9 degrees Celsius more than the average temperature before the Industrial Revolution," and commits the nations

> to limit warming to "well under 2 degrees Celsius" and ideally no more than 1.5 degrees Celsius (2.7 degrees Fahrenheit) through national emissions-reduction efforts that substantially increase every five years. To start the process, in 2015, 184 countries registered details of what they would do in the first five years and agreed to come back every five years to make stronger commitments.

36 This is unacceptable

Realistically, the authors continue,

> Scientists have been extremely clear that the 1.5-degree-Celsius-warmer scenario is still attainable but that the window is rapidly closing. To have at least a 50 percent chance of success (which in itself is an unacceptably high level of risk), we must cut global emissions to half their current levels by 2030, half again by 2040, and finally to net zero by 2050 at the very latest.[10]

The challenge to journalism

So, what is a caring, ethical journalist to do? These are monumental admonitions, requiring monumental actions—by individuals, businesses and especially by governments.

First, of course, it's incumbent on conscientious journalists to do what they always strive to do: report the facts. Admirably, in recent times global warming and climate change stories are abundant—in all media. *The New Yorker* magazine and *The New York Times* are exemplary. *The New Yorker* traces its proud environmental legacy back to its issue of June 23, 1962, when it published Rachel Carson's "Silent Spring," soon to become a book-length, blockbuster pioneer work that warned presciently of the dangers of DDT and other widely used pesticides. More recent examples of *New Yorker* conscience are "A Grand Plan to Clean the Great Pacific Garbage Patch," by Carolyn Kormann, about a young entrepreneur's dream of vacuuming plastic wastes from the ocean (February 4, 2019); "How Extreme Weather Is Shrinking the Planet," by Bill McKibben, exploring how wildfires and rising sea levels threaten to make large regions of the world uninhabitable (November 26, 2018); and "Greenland Is Melting," by Elizabeth Kolbert, explaining how the shrinking of that ice sheet is exacerbating the worldwide climate crisis (October 24, 2016).

Continuous waving of the climate-change red flag by *The New York Times* is truly a formidable public service. Even in the midst of covering (very well) the pandemic and recession in 2020, *The Times* mounted powerful illuminations of the threat of climate change. Vast, uncontrollable wildfires raging for weeks in California and Oregon caused ProPublica reporter Abrahm Lustgarten, a resident of Marin County, near San Francisco, to acknowledge out loud in a cover story of *The New York Times Magazine*, "Like the subjects of my reporting, climate change had found me, its indiscriminate forces erasing all semblance of normalcy. Suddenly I had to ask myself the very question I'd been asking others: Was it time to move?" Lustgarten went on,

> I am far from the only American facing such questions. This summer has seen more fires, more heat, more storms—all of it making life increasingly untenable in larger areas of the nation. Already, droughts regularly threaten food crops across the East, while destructive floods inundate towns and fields from the Dakotas to Maryland, collapsing dams in Michigan and raising the shorelines of the Great Lakes. Rising seas and increasingly violent hurricanes are making thousands of miles of American shoreline nearly uninhabitable.

Citing scientific and demographic data, he predicted significant population moves from the South toward the North, the West and Northwest.

> Such a shift is likely to increase poverty and widen the gulf between the rich and the poor. It will accelerate rapid, perhaps chaotic, urbanization of cities ill-equipped for the burden, testing their capacity to provide basic services and amplifying existing inequities,

while also creating, for instance, "a renaissance" in cities like Detroit, Rochester, Buffalo and Milwaukee, "with their excess capacity in infrastructure, water supplies and highways," a "new breadbasket along the Canadian border," and a "megalopolis of Seattle, which by then has nearly merged with Vancouver to its north." As a result, Lustgarten declared, "Half of Americans now rank climate change as a top political priority, up from roughly one-third in 2016."[11] Just two weeks after the Lustgarten opus, *The Times* produced a lavishly illustrated, fourteen-page special "Opinion" section, totally devoid of advertising, "The Amazon Has Seen Our Future." Several articles described threats of fires and deliberate deforestation to the peoples of the Amazon River basin in Brazil, while one, asking "Could the Amazon Save Your Life?", reported that "Scientists are looking at the medicinal potential of the region's plants and animals." The article, by ethnobotanist and rainforest defender Mark J. Plotkin, asserted,

> The entire world pays a price if the continuing destruction of the rainforest proceeds unabated, not just in terms of the very real disruptions and economic costs of climate change, but also in cures forgone as the forest burns, just so that the world can have more cheap beef and soy.[12]

The Times frequently published enterprise climate-change stories during the pandemic and recession of 2020. Some samples: "The Climate Legacy of Racist Housing Policies: Measures like redlining leave communities of color more vulnerable to a warming world," focused on housing patterns in Richmond, Virginia;[13] an opinion piece by Stuart A. Thompson and Yaryna Serkez of *The Times* declaring that "climate droughts now lengthen fire season" and therefore the raging western wildfires should be called "climate fires," in the words of Governor Jay Inslee of Washington state, also afflicted by the summer's fires;[14] an article referring to California droughts and floods as well as the wildfires, finding that "The same manufactured landscapes that have enabled California's tremendous growth, building the state into a $3 trillion economy that is home to one in 10 Americans, have also left it more exposed to climate shocks, experts say;"[15] and a five-reporter, finely illustrated article stating that, judging by NASA heat-detecting satellites, "2020 fire activity on the West Coast has already eclipsed even the worst previous years," explaining that "outdated forest management practices and climate change—which brings hotter, drier conditions—have provided the kindling for infernos of such immense scale."[16]

38 This is unacceptable

Continuing its impressive climate-change coverage, *The Times* reported yet-another aspect of the 2020 Western wildfires: "experts are focusing more attention on what happens to municipal water systems after a fire, when released toxic chemicals can get pulled into plumbing systems, and other damage can linger in pipes for years," explaining that benzene and "many other compounds that end up in water after a fire can also create health risks."[17]

Public and political response to climate change

In the midst of a hotly contested 2020 U.S. presidential campaign, there was inevitably, and necessarily, attention given to public attitudes and public policy in regard to climate change. Among other publications, *The Economist* weighed in heavily, and thoughtfully. While knocking economic lockdowns as "blunt instruments that can cause immense harm," the paper saw the Covid-19 crisis as

> a unique chance to enact government policies that steer the economy away from carbon at a lower financial social and political cost than might otherwise have been the case. Rock-bottom energy prices make it easier to cut subsidies for fossil fuels and to introduce a tax on carbon.[18] ... The harm from climate change will be slower than the pandemic but more massive and longer lasting. If there is a moment for leaders to show bravery in heading off that disaster, this is it. They will never have a more attentive audience.[19]

Separately, but in the same issue, *The Economist* addressed governments of the world, referring to the goal of limiting global warming to 2°C, declared that enormous new public and private investments are needed every year and "governments need to make the signals clear... If policy choices show that the road away from fossil fuels is right, private capital will follow."[20] *The Economist* also addressed a very specific message to the American Midwest, urging the area to anticipate climate-change opportunities:

> If coastal places face worsening tornadoes, hurricanes and forest fires, the American middle may look appealing. But that depends, at least, on cities building better infrastructure—such as big, expensive storm drains, or stronger and higher bridges—to protect themselves. Voters in the region also need to get behind a fast switch to cleaner forms of energy

and support easier immigration than the "misguided national policy under Mr Trump that chokes off inflows of foreigners."[21]

Although the notion of a carbon tax wasn't front and center in 2020—neither party advocated one in the presidential election campaign—*The Times* published an informative opinion piece by Cornell University economics professor Robert H. Frank supporting such a tax. He described it as "a fee on the carbon content of fossil fuels" and called it "the classical remedy" for climate change, in part, he said, because it would encourage beneficial personal behavior such as installing solar panels and consuming less meat (which would become more expensive). Frank argued that political opposition to such a tax could be allayed by requiring that "all revenue from the tax would be returned to consumers in the form of monthly rebate checks."[22] Previously, economists and even oil companies had voiced support for a carbon tax. Axios reported in May 2019 that "Companies across virtually all sectors of the economy, including big oil producers, are beginning to lobby Washington, D.C., to put a price on carbon dioxide emissions." The story named Shell, BP, EDF Renewables, ExxonMobil and ConocoPhillips as contributing to one particular lobbying effort for such a tax, and Microsoft and Tesla as supporting another.[23]

The Wall Street Journal gives frequent attention to climate change, often in its Opinion pages. In early 2019, it published a call for a carbon tax signed by a most impressive array of economists: twenty-seven recipients of the Nobel Memorial Prize in Economic Sciences, four former chairs of the Federal Reserve, twelve former chairs of the U.S. president's Council of Economic Advisers, and two former secretaries of the Treasury. They declared:

> A carbon tax offers the most cost-effective lever to reduce carbon emissions at the scale and speed that is necessary. By correcting a well-known market failure, a carbon tax will send a powerful price signal that harnesses the invisible hand of the marketplace to steer economic actors towards a low-carbon future.

Further, the former officials went on, "all the revenue should be returned directly to U.S. citizens through equal lump-sum rebates. The majority of American families, including the most vulnerable, will benefit financially by receiving more in 'carbon dividends' than they pay in increased energy prices."[24]

Nevertheless, *The Wall Street Journal* is cautious about the need for other corrective action. In early 2020, it published an opinion piece by Ted Nordhaus, founder and executive director of the Breakthrough Institute, an environmental research center, and a co-author of "An Ecomodernist Manifesto," panning both climate deniers and climate zealots, and acknowledging the need for fossil-fueled industrialization of much of the world.

> For this and other reasons, the world is unlikely to cut emissions fast enough to stabilize global temperatures at less than 2 degrees Celsius above pre-industrial levels, the long-standing international target, much less 1.5 degrees, as many activists now demand,

Nordhaus declared. But, he argued, growing adoption of natural gas, wind and solar energy, even nuclear in parts of Asia, is moderating the use of fossil fuels, and "All of this suggests that continuing political, economic and technological modernization,

40 This is unacceptable

not a radical remaking of society, is the key to both slowing climate change and adapting to it." Thus, he concluded,

> The world will tackle this problem the way that it tackles most other problems, partially and incrementally, by taking up the challenges that are right in front of us—adaptation, economic development, energy modernization, public health—and finding practical ways to address them.[25]

A "100% solution"

In sharp contrast, one young but determined former state legislator put forth in 2020, a remarkably detailed plan to achieve *negative* emissions of greenhouse gases by 2050. Solomon Goldstein-Rose, elected in 2016 to a term in the Massachusetts legislature at the age of twenty-two, proclaimed his thinking as *The 100% Solution: A Plan for Solving Climate Change*. His book derides "conventional" climate remedies as addressing less than half of global emissions, instead identifying his targets as *all* greenhouse gas emissions: electricity generation (27 percent of the problem), agriculture and deforestation (18 percent), transportation (15 percent), industry fuel use (12 percent), on down to industry process emissions, building heating, escaped methane, fossil fuel processing, waste and "other."

Goldstein-Rose offers a comprehensive plan built on five "pillars": clean generation of electricity; electrify equipment than can be electrified; create synthesized fuels for equipment that can't be electrified; implement various "non-energy shifts" such as altering agricultural practices (e.g., tax beef to discourage cattle raising; limit tropical deforestation for farming); and make up for any remaining emissions by sequestration of carbon dioxide, which means removing it from the atmosphere and storing it

> in some way that it will not be released again for a long time, if ever. CO_2 can be locked into the wood, soil, and other plant matter in forests; mixed into farm soils by microorganisms and crops; pumped as a gas into underground caverns; or chemically converted into plastics or other goods that lock the carbon inside their materials.[26]

Goldstein-Rose acknowledges that his ambitious plan calls for great technological innovation. He urges industrialized countries' governments to sponsor major research initiatives, to adopt carbon pricing, to subsidize "clean technologies that are still slightly more expensive than fossil options," and to foster "international pressure to speed each country in reducing emissions."[27] He looks to the United States or China to lead the way.

Also looking ahead, though less practically, journalist-activist Eric Holthaus presents a fantasy version of 2020 and the new 2021 Congress, envisioning prompt nationalization of all utilities, an end to all fossil fuel subsidies and a ban on fossil fuel advertising, new investments in rural regions and "regenerative agriculture,"

Climate change advances on us **41**

a car buyback program and commencement of city redesigns "aimed to completely eliminate cars by 2040," a four-day workweek, "universal guarantees for housing, health care and employment," and climate reparations—"all of which would help transform the current economic system into a completely circular economy by 2050"—and all of the great cost financed by "a wealth tax on billionaires."[28] No details provided.

The commitment of caring journalism

Even discounting the Holthaus dream world, the complexity and costs of reversing global warming and climate change are, to say the least, daunting. Still, the extensive coverage of the problem over many years by *The New York Times* and virtually all other news organizations has certainly made the populace aware of the threat. The Paris Agreement and the Intergovernmental Panel on Climate Change have established goals and targets for 2030 and 2050, also now well known to all. But the necessary drastic, specific, expensive actions, such as those envisioned by Solomon Goldstein-Rose, are not in sight. It will take more than public awareness. Call it public resolve, public determination, public mobilization, maybe public anger, but that's the measure of public pressure that will be required to move our government and business leaders to take real action—action that will make a difference, action that will measure up to the threat to our democratic society, and overcome it—by 2030 and 2050. As Goldstein-Rose says, a sufficient response will require immediate steps in the first two years of the 2020s to set the process—particularly government-financed research and planning—in motion.

Existing government programs, even currently popular ideas and proposals, are clearly inadequate to meet the climate-change challenge. This means that the challenge of caring journalism now is to cover both climate-change problems and climate-change solutions so thoroughly, so intensely, so continuously that the voters will rise up and demand amelioration—not just cosmetics—but actual remedies to the many, many aspects of this long-advancing threat to our society and our democracy. The status quo may seem tolerable in the moment. But it is not. And the necessary seismic shift in public opinion and political and business action will not happen without caring journalism in action.

Notes

1 Paul Krugman, *Arguing With Zombies: Economics, Politics, and The Fight for a Better Future*, New York: W.W. Norton & Company, 2020, 327.
2 Eric Holthaus, *The Future Earth: A Radical Vision for What's Possible in the Age of Warming*, New York: Harper One, 2020, 5.
3 Ibid. 4.
4 Ibid. 4, 9.
5 Lisa Freedman, "Trump Serves Notice to Quit Paris Climate Agreement," *The New York Times*, November 4, 2019, https://www.nytimes.com/2019/11/04/climate/trump-paris-agreement-climate.html. Mayors of eighty cities worldwide pushed back in a

42 This is unacceptable

special Chicago conference by subscribing to the Paris goals. "It has worked, too," former Chicago mayor Rahm Emanuel writes in his 2020 memoir. "More than half of the cities that signed the pledge have reduced their greenhouse gas emissions … " *The Nation City: Why Mayors Are Now Running the World*, New York: Alfred A. Knopf, 2020, 72.

6 Christiana Figueres and Tom Rivett-Carnac, *The Future We Choose: Surviving the Climate Crisis*, New York: Borzoi Books, Alfred A. Knopf, 2020, xxii. From 2010 to 2016 Figueres, a Costa Rican, was executive secretary of the United Nations Framework Convention on Climate Change, and Rivett-Carnac, an American, was her chief political strategist. They describe themselves as "Architects of the 2015 Paris Agreement."

7 Ibid. xx, xxi.

8 Darrel Moellendorf, *The Moral Challenge of Dangerous Climate Change: Values, Poverty, and Policy*, Cambridge and New York: Cambridge University Press, 2014, 1, 17. He refers to a 2010 report of the twenty-eight-member, Paris-based International Energy Agency, *Energy Poverty: How to Make Modern Energy Access Universal?* http://www.globalbioenergy. org/uploads/media/1009_IEA_-_Energy_poverty.pdf

9 Figueres and Rivett-Carnac, op. cit. xxv.

10 Ibid. 6, 7. They refer to a 2018 report of the Intergovernmental Panel on Climate Change, *Special Report: Global Warming of 1.5°C*, https://www.ipcc.ch/sr15/

11 Abrahm Lustgarten, "How Climate Change Will Remap Where Americans Live," *The New York Times Magazine*, September 20, 2020, 34 et. seq., https://www.nytimes.com/ interactive/2020/09/15/magazine/climate-crisis-migration-america.html? searchResultPosition=1

12 Mark J. Plotkin, "How the Amazon Could Save Your Life," special "Opinion" section, "The Amazon Has Seen Our Future," *The New York Times*, October 4, 2020, 12-13, https://www.nytimes.com/2020/10/02/opinion/amazon-novel-species-medicine. html?searchResultPosition=1

13 Brad Plumer, Nadja Popovich and Brian Palmer, "The Climate Legacy of Racist Housing Policies," *The New York Times*, August 29, 2020, A22-A24, https://www. nytimes.com/interactive/2020/08/24/climate/racism-redlining-cities-global-warming. html?searchResultPosition=1

14 Stuart A. Thompson and Yaryna Serkez, "Just Call Them Climate Fires," *The New York Times*, September 20, 2020, SR9, https://www.nytimes.com/interactive/2020/09/18/ opinion/wildfire-hurricane-climate.html?searchResultPosition=1

15 Christopher Flavelle, "Mankind's Feats Place California At Climate Risk," *The New York Times*, September 21, 2020, 1, https://www.nytimes.com/2020/09/20/climate/califor- nia-climate-change-fires.html?searchResultPosition=1

16 Nadja Popovich, Blacki Migliozzi, Tim Wallace, Allison McCann and Scott Reinhard, "In a Ruinous Stretch, the Worst Fire Season on Record," *The New York Times*, September 26, 2020, A12, https://www.nytimes.com/interactive/2020/09/24/climate/fires-worst- year-california-oregon-washington.html?searchResultPosition=1

17 Max Horberry, "Wildfires Also Threaten Drinking Water," *The New York Times*, October 6, 2020, D1, https://www.nytimes.com/2020/10/02/science/wildfires-water-toxic. html?searchResultPosition=1

18 "The Cure and the Disease," *The Economist*, May 23, 2020, 8, https://www.economist. com/weeklyedition/2020-05-23

19 "Seize the Moment," *The Economist*, May 23, 2020, 7, https://www.economist.com/ weeklyedition/2020-05-23

20 "Not-So-Slow Burn," *The Economist*, May 23, 2020, 49–50, https://www.economist.com/ schools-brief/2020/05/23/the-worlds-energy-system-must-be-transformed-completely

Climate change advances on us **43**

21 "Don't Be the Next Cahokia," *The Economist*, July 23, 2020, 11–12, https://www.economist.com/special-report/2020/07/23/dont-be-the-next-cahokia

22 Robert H. Frank, "Behavioral Contagion Could Spread Carbon Tax Benefits," *The New York Times*, August 23, 2020, BU5, https://www.nytimes.com/2020/08/19/business/behavioral-contagion-carbon-tax.html?searchResultPosition=2

23 Amy Harder, "The Big Corporate Shift on Climate Change," axios.com, May 20, 2019, https://www.axios.com/the-big-corporate-shift-on-climate-change-1edea61e-ca43-4df9-a293-d42e00f08caa.html

24 "Economists' Statement on Carbon Dividends," *The Wall Street Journal*, January 16, 2019, https://www.wsj.com/articles/economists-statement-on-carbon-dividends-11547682910#:~:text=By%20correcting%20a%20well-known,towards%20a%20low-carbon%20future.&text=A%20consistently%20rising%20carbon%20price,and%20large-scale%20infrastructure%20development.

25 Ted Nordhaus, "Ignore the Fake Climate Debate," *The Wall Street Journal*, January 23, 2020, https://www.wsj.com/articles/ignore-the-fake-climate-debate-11579795816

26 Solomon Goldstein-Rose, *The 100% Solution: A Plan for Solving Climate Change*, Brooklyn and London: Melville House, 2020, 59, 52.

27 Ibid. 259.

28 Eric Holthaus, op. cit. 106, 107.

5

DEMOCRACY ITSELF HANGS IN THE BALANCE

There is no dearth these days of threats to American democracy perceived by reputable observers. The demise of many local newspapers, says Margaret Sullivan of the *Washington Post*, means that democracy "loses its foundation" because citizens are less likely to vote, to stay politically informed, or to run for office.[1] A 2020 book titled *Twilight of Democracy: The Seductive Lure of Authoritarianism*, by Anne Applebaum, won the Pulitzer Prize. Another current book, by Malcolm W. Nance, is *The Plot to Destroy Democracy: How Putin and His Spies Are Undermining America and Dismantling the West*. Andrew Marantz wrote in *The New Yorker* that "democracy hangs in the balance" so "activists are drawing lessons from the study of civil resistance."[2] Even former President Barack Obama weighed in, soberly telling *The Atlantic*, "America is the first real experiment in building a large, multiethnic, multicultural democracy. And we don't know yet if that can hold."[3]

If personal safety can be seen as an essential protection provided by democracy, booming gun sales in 2020 constituted a resounding vote of no-confidence. CNN reported "an unprecedented year for the firearms industry, which has seen a steady, pandemic-related surge in sales since Covid-19-related lockdowns began in March." The network added that

> this year's sales spike is different because it's being driven by a rise in first-time gun buyers, especially among African Americans and women.... Gun sales among Black Americans are up 58% through September, according to the NSSF [National Shooting Sports Foundation].[4]

A Brookings Institution report, saying "[w]hen Americans are concerned about their personal security, they buy firearms," attributed the sales surge in part to the "social unrest in June that followed George Floyd's killing." The report, in July 2020,

DOI: 10.4324/9781003140337-7

estimated that "almost three million more firearms have been sold since March than would have ordinarily been sold during these months."[5]

In the midst of such pessimism and gloom about democracy, the three ominous threats to American society described in previous chapters still stand out. They are of much longer standing than current politics, and in 2020, they loomed increasingly into sharper focus. The understated question for the nation was how—or whether—the government and business would confront and eventually overcome them. Why was the question understated? Was it because Americans simply assumed that our leaders, despite inordinate torpor, would some day, finally, do the right thing? Or was it understated because no one had an answer? In any event, if timorous politicians and profit-obsessed business executives shy away from these threats, the ethical news media cannot. For the sake of America's democracy, and for the nation's future, the news media must take the lead, simply must rise to this challenge. It will require, as we have noted, more than the traditional truth and accuracy and fairness and transparency.

What is this "democracy"?

If asked what the nation's political system is, Americans will invariably respond, a democracy. But that's not quite right, as the authors of *The Federalist* papers pointed out. *The Federalist*—eighty-five erudite but clear essays—were written and published in colonial newspapers to help Americans understand, and support, the new Constitution, which had just been drafted in the summer of 1787, after the colonists' victory in the War of Independence. The Constitution was laboriously fashioned over six months by intelligent, articulate, opinionated men, and it was controversial. Its fate was now in the hands of the thirteen states, with ratification by at least nine required to make the document effective. The Constitution had required a great deal of hard-fought compromise between representatives of large states and small, between proponents and opponents of a bill of rights, and between advocates of a strong central government and defenders of the existing state-centered Articles of Confederation. The Confederation was an unwieldy loose amalgam adopted during the war and requiring unanimous agreement of the states to take any action.

In fact, the Constitutional Convention of 1787 had been convened for the explicit purpose of reviewing and confirming the Articles of Confederation as defining the government of the new United States of America. But most delegates balked. They called for a strong central government, though with its power shared with the states, in several ways: each state, large and small, would have two seats in the Senate of the new Congress; treaties and important presidential appointments such as justices of the Supreme Court would be subject to ratification by the Senate; the senators would be appointed by the state legislatures, not directly elected by the people like members of the House of Representatives, who would be apportioned by population; and the central government was endowed with certain enumerated powers, such as conducting foreign affairs and regulating interstate commerce, with all other powers reserved to the states.

46 This is unacceptable

After the Constitution was drafted and signed by thirty-nine delegates (it was not unanimous), Alexander Hamilton of New York and James Madison of Virginia (history remembers him as the "Father of the Constitution"), who both had argued in the Convention for a strong national government, promptly took pen in hand and with remarkable speed produced scores of persuasive essays to explain the new Constitution and solicit public support for it. Their essays—Hamilton and Madison wrote eighty of the eighty-five *Federalist* papers—were published in newspapers; they were profound and forceful, invoking both logic and prior human experience back to antiquity. They still stand today as extraordinary expositions of political philosophy. And they emphasized that this new, indeed revolutionary, government was not a democracy. It was a republic.

Both Madison and Hamilton made the distinction: a democracy, as in ancient Greece, is governed directly by the decisions and votes of the governed, while a republic is governed by elected representatives of the populace. Both men preferred the republican form. "The republican principle," Hamilton wrote,

> demands that the deliberate sense of the community should govern the conduct of those to whom they intrust the management of their affairs; but it does not require an unqualified complaisance to every sudden breeze of passion, or to every transient impulse which the people may receive from the arts of men, who flatter their prejudices to betray their interests.[6]

For his part, Madison worried about opposing factions—citizens with property against those without, debtors versus creditors, "a manufacturing interest, a mercantile interest, a moneyed interest"—and "concluded that a pure democracy, by which I mean a society consisting of a small number of citizens, who assemble and administer the government in person, can admit of no cure for mischiefs of faction." But a republican system, he went on, is better able

> to refine and enlarge the public views by passing them through the medium of a chosen body of citizens, whose wisdom may best discern the true interest of their country and whose patriotism and love of justice will be least likely to sacrifice it to temporary or partial considerations.[7]

As we proceed to consider democracy and what it imports, let us assume, therefore, that we mean a democratic republic.

From Scotland and David Hume

However, let's hesitate at this point to consider why Hamilton, Madison and the other Founding Fathers, the authors of the Constitution, were so taken by the idea of a democratic republic—a form that did not exist at the time, a government from the ground up rather than a top-down monarchy or aristocracy, from which all the founders were descended. According to an artful, present-day "journal" of the Constitutional Convention, in its early days "James Madison of Virginia warned the delegates that unless a republican government is held out to the people they might, in despair, incline toward a monarchy."[8] Despite the Convention's interminable delays and frustrations, that never happened. Why not? Why did the delegates, especially their most prominent and persuasive leaders, place so much faith in the people?

One reason—or perhaps several—may be found in Scotland, in particular in the Scottish Enlightenment. The Enlightenment, which was in full flower in the eighteenth century, was a protracted time of religious, philosophical, literary, commercial and industrial creativity in tiny Scotland. Among its intellectual leaders were Adam Smith, who preached the benefits of free enterprise, and David Hume, who challenged the prevailing rational moral philosophies that extended from Aristotle to Immanuel Kant, John Locke, John Stuart Mill and other contemporary Europeans; Hume contends instead that human behavior is driven more by emotions than reason, and properly so.

According to historian Arthur Herman, the Scottish Enlightenment started with a religious conversion:

> Just as the German Reformation was largely the work of a single individual, Martin Luther, so the Scottish Reformation was the achievement of one man of heroic will and tireless energy, John Knox. Like Luther, Knox left an indelible mark on national culture. Uncompromising, dogmatic, and driven, John Knox was a prolific writer and teacher of truly terrifying power.... Beginning in 1559, Knox single-handedly inspired, intimidated, and bullied Scotland's nobility and urban classes into overthrowing the Catholic Church of their forebears and adopting the religious creed of Geneva's John Calvin.[9]

Among other changes wrought by Knox, Herman states, "he and his followers scoured away not only Scottish Catholicism but all its physical manifestations.... [T]he idols disappeared from southern Scotland, and the Scottish Kirk rose up to take their place."

This new church rejected the top-down authority of bishops. "The congregation was the center of everything. It elected its own board of elders or presbyters; it even chose its ministers." So it became the Presbyterian Church. A Knox follower, George Buchanan, "turned it into a full-fledged doctrine of popular sovereignty, the first in Europe."[10] When Charles I tried to crush this incendiary creed, the Scots rioted and affixed their names to a National Covenant, "the Presbyterian version of democracy in action," which "challenged the king's prerogative to make laws without consent." The Covenanters raised an army, fought the crown in the Bishops' War, and encouraged Parliament in London to join in opposition to Charles. The rest is history: "A civil war ensued, which culminated in the king's execution in 1649 and the emergence of Oliver Cromwell as Lord Protector." The movement was "the enemy of public tyranny. It empowered individuals to defy authority when it crossed a certain line." Philosopher David Hume

48 This is unacceptable

saw this quality in the Covenanters of 1638. The religion of John Knox "consecrated ... every individual," he explained to readers in 1757, "and, in his own eyes, bestowed a character on him much superior to what forms and ceremonious institutions alone could confer."[11]

Staking out a position as the leading philosopher of the Scottish Enlightenment, Hume rejected the venerated rational moral philosophers, who had declared various forms of reason—duty, utilitarianism, rights, justice—to be the proper guides for resolving human difference or conflicts. Instead, Hume declared, "Reason is, and ought only to be the slave of the passions, and can never pretend to any other office than to serve and obey them."[12] He emphasized: "reason alone can never be a motive to any action of the will; and ... it can never oppose passion in the direction of the will."[13] When the Americans revolted, Hume's "sympathies lay entirely with the colonists. 'I am an American in my principles,' he told Benjamin Franklin in 1775, 'and wish we would let [them] alone to govern or misgovern themselves as they think proper.'"[14]

Scottish influence imported

Though his parents never married, Alexander Hamilton's father, James Hamilton, was the son of a Scottish laird and grew up in a castle in Ayrshire, southwest of Glasgow. As the fourth son, not destined to inherit, he decided to seek his fortune in the West Indies. It did not go well there. He took a common-law wife who had abandoned a previous, unhappy marriage but was not legally divorced so could not marry again. They had two sons, but in time James deserted his family. At that time, Alexander, born on the British island of Nevis, was only ten years old. The youngster had a "pronounced religious bent," states biographer Ron Chernow, without elaborating.[15] Three years later, Alexander's mother succumbed to a virulent fever, so at thirteen, he went to work as a clerk in a busy export-import firm on the nearby island of St. Croix. "Like Ben Franklin, Hamilton was mostly self-taught and probably snatched every spare moment to read. The young clerk aimed to be a man of letters."[16] At sixteen, he began submitting touching poems, at first amorous, to the local newspaper. Then another Scot entered his life, more auspiciously than his absent father.

> The next year, Hamilton published two more poems in the paper, now recreating himself as a somber religious poet. The change in heart can almost certainly be attributed to the advent in St. Croix of a Presbyterian minister named Hugh Knox,

who was "born in northern Ireland of Scottish ancestry."[17] Knox had studied divinity at the College of New Jersey (later Princeton); he became the pastor of the Scotch Presbyterian Church on the island. "Knox threw open his library to this prodigious youth, encouraged him to write verse, and prodded him toward scholarship.... Knox had an accurate intuition that this exceptional adolescent was fated to accomplish great deeds." After a hurricane struck the island, Hamilton published a flowery, sophisticated letter in the newspaper, characterizing the storm, according to Chernow, as "a divine rebuke to human vanity and pomposity." The teenager wrote: "Despise thyself and adore thy God .... O ye who revel in affluence see the afflictions of humanity and bestow your superfluity to ease them." Impressed by the letter, and probably at the instance of Hugh Knox, local businessmen took up a fund "to send this promising youth to North America to be educated."[18]

Upon his arrival in New York, Hamilton carried letters from Hugh Knox that introduced him to prominent Presbyterian clergymen and soon wafted him into a prominent Presbyterian preparatory school across the Hudson River in New Jersey. Hugh Knox's letters gave him instant access to men at the pinnacle of colonial society in New Jersey. He met William Livingston and Elias Boudinot, well-heeled lawyers and luminaries in the Presbyterian political world, who exposed him to the heterodox political currents of the day.

Hamilton became close to both men and their families. Boudinot later became president of the Continental Congress; and "such was his piety that he became the first president of the American Bible Society." As for Livingston, a founder of the New York Society Library, "[l]ike many Presbyterians, Livingston had gravitated to political dissent while opposing Tory efforts to entrench the Church of England in America." Chernow surmises about Hamilton's political leaning at this time: "Mingling with Presbyterians may ... have influenced his politics. The denomination was associated with the Whig critique of the British Crown, while Anglicans tended to be Tories and more often supported British imperial policy toward the colonies and an established church."[19]

Despite his Presbyterian affections, when the recently installed president of the College of New Jersey, the prominent Scottish clergyman John Witherspoon, turned down Hamilton's request to hurry through the college at his own speed, the ambitious youth opted to attend King's College (later Columbia) in New York. King's was decidedly Anglican, with obligatory morning chapel and evening prayers.

> His friends were struck by his religious nature ... [One friend] was convinced that Hamilton's religious practice was driven by more than duty. He 'was attentive to public worship and in the habit of praying on his knees night and morning.... I have often been powerfully affected by the fervor and eloquence of his prayers.'[20]

At King's, Chernow speculates, a Glasgow-trained tutor, Professor Robert Harpur, "probably introduced his new pupil to the writings of David Hume and other worthies of the Scottish Enlightenment."[21] That notion, in Chernow's thinking, was apparently confirmed by several scholarly pamphlets Hamilton wrote, anonymously,

50 This is unacceptable

while still a student, in which he aggressively supported colonists' complaints about taxation without representation. Chernow declares:

> Clearly, Hamilton was reading the skeptical Scottish philosopher David Hume, and he quoted his view that in framing a government "*every man* ought to be supposed a *knave* and to have no other end in all his actions but *private interests.*" … Hamilton was spurred by Hume's dark vision of human nature, which corresponded to his own.[22]

Hamilton's nationalist colleague in the Constitutional Convention, James Madison of Virginia, did not share his immersion in the Scottish church and its bottom-up governance. He was from a prominent Episcopalian family. However, he *did* attend the College of New Jersey, where President Witherspoon "was instrumental in delivering Scots philosophy and education to the new American republic," according to James Buchan.[23] Herman states that Madison

> became deeply attached to President Witherspoon, and even delayed graduation in order to continue special work with him. This included tutoring in Hebrew, and exposure to the most advanced of the Scottish thinkers, from [Francis] Hutcheson and [Lord] Kames to Adam Smith and David Hume. It was above all to Hume, Witherspoon's avowed nemesis, that Madison found himself drawn…. Hume represented a new kind of intellectual persona that Madison admired and cultivated.[24]

Madison apparently took particular note of Hume's theorizing that a "perfect commonwealth," especially a large one with many divergent interests, might well be a democratic republic. The elected governors of such a territory, Hume opined, would find it "very difficult, either by intrigue, prejudice, or passion, to hurry … into any measures against the public interest."[25] Thus, as noted at the outset of this chapter, Madison, too, expressed concern in *The Federalist* papers about the inevitable but potentially destructive influence of factions—financial, religious, social, commercial or other—in the governance of the expansive United States, concluding that the elected leaders of a democratic republic would successfully resolve them to "secure the public good." This would occur, Madison believed, by passing the

> public views … through the medium of a chosen body of citizens, whose wisdom may best discern the true interest of their country and whose patriotism and love of justice will be least likely to sacrifice it to temporary or partial considerations.

The proposed system would still leave room for local issues to be considered, "the great and aggregate interests being referred to the national, the local and particular to the State legislatures."[26]

Yet another influential delegate to the Constitutional Convention was Pennsylvania lawyer James Wilson. Born and educated in Scotland, he, too, studied Scottish Enlightenment thinkers including Francis Hutcheson, David Hume and Adam Smith. Wilson emigrated to Philadelphia as a young man, read law under a prominent lawyer and commenced what proved to be a lucrative practice of his own. Termed a "serious Christian thinker" by a modern student of the intersection of religion and politics, Wilson believed that an individual has a "natural right to his property, to his character, to liberty, and to safety," and "because rights are based upon God's universal and absolute law, they must always be respected."[27] His church affiliation wasn't always clear, though for years he rented a pew in the First Presbyterian Church of Philadelphia.

The convention

At the Constitutional Convention Wilson was deeply engaged, an extremely active speaker. Sounding quite Presbyterian, he was a strong proponent of popular sovereignty. He "was led to embrace democracy with more consistency than any other major founder," favoring direct election of members of Congress and the president, and was largely responsible for drafting the final language of the four-thousand-word Constitution.[28] He advocated creation of a Supreme Court, believing that

> a judge is someone who makes judgments about the world, in matters of fact, of right and wrong, and of truth and falsehood. Wilson's idea also reflected the role of the judge in Scottish law, whose job in court was not just to be a legal referee, but to find out what happened.[29]

One colleague in the Constitutional Convention remarked of Wilson that

> Government seems to have been his peculiar Study, all the political institutions of the World he knows in detail, and can trace the causes and effects of every revolution from the earliest stages of the Grecian commonwealth down to the present time. No man is more clear, copious, and comprehensive than Mr. Wilson.[30]

Of the fifty-five men who had agreed in May to serve as delegates to the Constitutional Convention, only forty-two were present at the end in mid-September, the others having abandoned the assignment, and three of the remaining forty-two declined to sign, objecting to some aspects of the final document. What form of government had they created? As Ben Franklin famously put it, when confronted with that question by a curious citizen, "A Republic, if you can keep it."[31] After ratification in mid-1978 by the ninth state (New Hampshire; the remaining four came on board by mid-1790), the Constitution became effective on March 4, 1789.

Democracy in America

Having laboriously crafted this new government, what, exactly, did the delegates now expect their creation to do? The writers of *The Federalist* papers didn't elaborate; Madison stated simply that the object was "the public good."[32] Perhaps the founders' purpose was best stated in their preamble to the Constitution:

> We the people of the United States, in Order to form a more perfect Union, establish Justice, insure domestic Tranquility, provide for the common defence, promote the general Welfare, and secure the Blessings of Liberty to ourselves and our Posterity, do ordain and establish this Constitution for the United States of America.

It took nearly half a century, but the best elaboration on this broad statement of purpose came not from an American, but a perceptive French count, Alexis de Tocqueville, who visited the United States for ten months in 1831–1832, when a population of thirteen million spread out over twenty-four states. Ostensibly, he came to study prisons. In fact, he never reported on prisons, but Tocqueville did write a remarkable, multi-volume work called *Democracy in America*, published in 1835, in which he observed and assessed every imaginable aspect of American life and society, including the government. He mostly liked what he saw. "Amongst the novel objects that attracted my attention during my stay in the United States," he declared,

> nothing struck me more forcibly than the general equality of conditions..... it creates opinions, engenders sentiments, suggests the ordinary practices of life, and modifies whatever it does not produce.... [T]he equality of conditions is the fundamental fact from which all others seems to be derived, and the central point at which all my observations constantly terminated.[33]

Addressing the "purport of society and the aim of government," Tocqueville posited that if your objectives are "the production of comfort," the "acquirement of the necessities of life," creation of "habits of peace" and "prosperity around you," ensuring "the greatest degree of enjoyment and the least degree of misery to each of the individuals," then "you can have no surer means of satisfying them than by equalizing the conditions of men, and establishing democratic institutions."[34]

Significantly, Tocqueville did not contend that democracy would inevitably bring forth the best possible leadership. *Au contraire.*

> On my arrival in the United States I was surprised to find so much distinguished talent among the subjects, and so little among the heads of Government. It is a well-authenticated fact, that at the present day the most able men in the United States are very rarely placed at the head of affairs; and it must be acknowledged that such has been the result in proportion as democracy has

Democracy itself hangs in the balance **53**

outstepped all its former limits. The race of American statesmen has evidently dwindled most remarkably in the last fifty years.[35]

Andrew Jackson was then president.

Seeking an explanation why such a "vast number of very ordinary men … occupy public stations," Tocqueville puckishly reasoned that

> The pursuit of wealth generally diverts men of great talents and of great passions from the pursuit of power, and it very frequently happens that a man does not undertake to direct the fortune of the State until he has discovered his incompetence to conduct his own affairs.[36]

Nevertheless, even though "Democracy does not confer the most skilful kind of government upon the people," Tocqueville affirmed,

> it produces that which the most skilful governments are frequently unable to awaken, namely, an all-pervading and restless activity, a superabundant force, and an energy which is inseparable from it, and which may, under favorable circumstances, beget the most amazing benefits. These are the true advantages of democracy.[37]

He observed that when things go awry, "the great advantage of the Americans consists in their being able to commit faults which they may afterward repair."[38]

The benefits that Tocqueville perceived were, he repeatedly pointed out, economic. The democratic advantage was not in "favoring the prosperity of all, but simply in contributing to the well-being of the greatest possible number." He frequently compared America to Europe, noting that differences between people with property and those without in Europe did not similarly materialize in the United States "because in America there are no paupers." "[T]he dissemination of wealth brings the notion of property within the reach of all the members of the community." "Democratic laws generally tend to promote the welfare of the greatest possible number."[39]

Democracy needs income

Tocqueville is not alone in tying the success of democracy to the economic benefits it confers on the citizenry. Modern scholars agree. Brandeis University political scientist Robert Kuttner writes, "Sages since Aristotle have pointed out that gross inequity in income and wealth is incompatible with democracy." In their recent, highly praised book, *Deaths of Despair*, Princeton economists Anne Case and Angus Deaton (he's a Nobel Prize winner) declare pessimistically: "Working class whites do not believe that democracy can help them."[40]

This needs unraveling.

A persuasive explanatory thesis is set forth by Harvard economist Benjamin M. Friedman in *The Moral Consequences of Economic Growth*, published in 2005. He declares,

54 This is unacceptable

Countries where living standards improve over sustained periods of time are more likely to seek and preserve an open, tolerant society, and to broaden and strengthen their democratic institutions. But where most citizens sense that they are not getting ahead, society instead becomes rigid and democracy weakens.[41]

As evidence, Friedman cites several periods in American history—some periods where economic growth and rising incomes opened the door to enhancements of American life and society, and other periods where economic and wage stagnation wrought regressive spirits and actions, against minorities and immigrants, for instance. He states:

It is not hard to see that a strong economy, where opportunities are plentiful and jobs go begging, helps break down social barriers. Bigoted employers may still dislike hiring members of one group or another, but when nobody else is available discrimination most often gives way to the sheer need to get the work done. The same goes for employees with prejudices about whom they do and do not like working alongside.[42]

Moreover,

[t]he difference between economic growth and stagnation likewise affects how the society divides its available resources between what people spend on their own private activities—for food, clothes, cars, houses, entertainment, vacations—and what they devote to more public undertakings like parks, sports facilities, orchestras, libraries and the like.[43]

Friedman delineates periods of economic growth and expansion in which unemployment was low, per-capita income rose, spending on public needs such as education and social benefits increased, and progressive legislation was enacted: after the Civil War 1865–90s (civil rights amendments and laws); 1896–1914 industrial boom (Federal Reserve System and regulatory agencies created); post-World War II expansion 1946–73 (veterans' benefits, baby boom, the Interstate Highway System, civil rights laws, Medicare and Medicaid, President Johnson's "war on poverty," welfare expansion); second half of the 1990s (anti-immigrant sentiment waned, job growth extended even to young black men with a high school education).[44]

Conversely, Friedman identifies periods of economic stagnation in which both wages and social needs foundered: the 1880s and 1890s ("Jim Crow" legislation and *Plessy v. Ferguson* supported racial segregation); 1918–29 earnings stall (labor strikes, banks failed, aliens deported, immigration quotas, racial violence); and 1973–90s slowdown (limits placed on affirmative action and welfare and immigrants' benefits).[45]

Friedman says the Great Depression (1929–41), when one in three non-farm workers lost their jobs, was an exception to his rule, perversely fostering "a broader

Democracy itself hangs in the balance **55**

commitment to opportunity and mobility for all citizens." The difference, he asserts, was new federal leadership under President Franklin D. Roosevelt, inaugurated in 1933. At his behest, Congress passed the Civilian Conservation Corps, the Federal Emergency Relief Administration to support urban incomes, the Agricultural Adjustment Administration to support farm prices and give mortgage foreclosure relief, the Works Progress Administration to finance new public works, the Securities and Exchange Commission to police the stock market, the Tennessee Valley Authority to provide economical electricity to all or part of seven southeastern states, the Food and Drug Administration to oversee introduction of new drugs, the Glass–Steagall Act to separate investment and commercial banking, the Federal Deposit Insurance Corporation to insure bank accounts, and, notably, the Social Security Act.

Friedman's theory ends with his book in 2005, but subsequent years bear continuing witness to its validity. Wall Street's greedy infatuation with mortgage-backed securities of dubious validity and value led to the disastrous Great Recession of 2007–8, and the recovery from it—particularly static average wages (although unemployment dropped to near-record lows)—endured until the sudden pandemic recession of 2020, when unemployment soared to as high as 14 percent and thirty million lost their jobs. During this time, Congress did manage to narrowly pass one important social advance, President Barack Obama's Affordable Care Act, in 2010. But in late 2020, twenty million Americans were still out of work and dependent on state unemployment compensation, usually limited to thirty-nine weeks. Democracy made no other significant advance to improve American life during this time. As Harvard professors Steven Levitsky and Daniel Ziblatt note, "For many Americans, the economic changes of the last few decades have brought decreased job security, longer working hours, fewer prospects for upward mobility, and, consequently, a growth in social resentment."[46] It was this resentment that Donald Trump astutely recognized and capitalized on to win the presidential election of 2016.

Professor Friedman is hardly alone in linking the performance of democracy with wage growth. While his approach is economic, that of Robert Kuttner of Brandeis University is political. He declares: "Democracy is more fragile than we would like it to be. It is particularly vulnerable when the economy deserts the common people.... [D]emocratic government continues to lose broad legitimacy as it fails to solve pressing problems." In fact, Kuttner states that American democracy has been in decline for decades, and he fears ominous consequences if the decline continues.[47]

Democracy weakening, with weak wage growth

Let's consider from the workers' standpoint the decades-long flat personal income trend that underlies Kuttner's worry as well as Friedman's.

According to a 2014 report of the Economic Policy Institute, a Washington, D.C., think tank whose mission is "to defend and promote the interests of workers in economic policy debates," the median worker's wages and benefits grew just 7.9 percent between 1979 and 2013. This exceptionally slow pay growth is shocking considering that economic growth and productivity—up 64.9 percent in that same time period—were robust enough to support strong pay growth for all Americans. The break between productivity and pay means a disproportionate share of income growth is going to corporate profits, the returns to financial assets, and the pay of those at the upper end of the pay scale. In other words, economic growth is benefiting those at the top, not ordinary workers.

The average annual inflation-adjusted earnings of all workers increased by a very modest 0.9 percent, down from 2.1 percent between 1947 and 1979.[48]

In a more recent report, the EPI states, "In 2017, middle-wage workers earned just 16.8 percent more than their counterparts almost four decades earlier. This corresponds to an annualized inflation-adjusted growth rate over the 38-year period of just 0.4 percent per year." Furthermore, "For workers with less than a four-year college degree (over 60 percent of the workforce in 2017), real wages for the typical (median) worker were *lower* in 2017 than they had been in 1979."[49]

The EPI cites three factors behind these sobering figures:

> The first is the long-term decline in manufacturing employment, which has traditionally been the sector of the economy that pays relatively high wages to the non-college-educated workers who still make up a large majority of the U.S. workforce. The second countervailing force is the long-term decline in union membership, which has had a negative effect on the pay and benefits of both union and nonunion workers. The third factor is the persistent failure to run the economy at full employment, which has undermined the important leverage workers have in tight labor markets.[50]

In still another report, the EPI finds that 2019 compensation of chief executive officers rose 14 percent to an average 21.3 million dollars, 320 times the wages of a typical worker.

> Corporate boards running America's largest public firms are giving top executives outsize compensation packages that have grown much faster than the stock market and the pay of typical workers, college graduates, and even the top 0.1%. In 2019, a CEO at one of the top 350 firms in the U.S. was paid $21.3 million on average (using a "realized" measure of CEO pay that counts stock awards when vested and stock options when cashed in rather than when granted). This 14% increase from 2018 occurred because of rapid growth in vested stock awards and exercised stock options tied to stock market growth.[51]

Donald Trump capitalized on this unsettling disconnect particularly well in southern and rural states, where hourly wages were comparatively low. According to EPI, 2015–17 median hourly wages in a seven-state "manufacturing Southeast" region (excluding Florida) were only 16.20 dollars, and in a six-state, mostly rural "other Midwest" region 16.71 dollars, compared with the top 20.25 dollars in the "other Northeast" region (excluding New York), 19.00 dollars in the four-state "other Pacific" region ((excluding California) and 18.69 dollars in California.[52] Trump swept all fourteen states comprising the two lowest-wage regions, the "manufacturing Southeast" and "other Midwest." (Although Trump won only 46 percent of the popular vote in 2016, he carried thirty of the fifty states to win the electoral college vote, 305 to 227.)

Professor Kuttner declares:

> If the 2016 election of Donald Trump had aspects of an accident, it was an accident waiting to happen. Neither of the two parties was credibly addressing broad public anxiety; support for the premise that government could solve national problems was at an all-time low. Autocratic tactics such as suppressing the right to vote, hijacking courts, spreading systematic Big Lies, ridiculing the factual press, and steamrolling legislation with no role for the opposition were on the rise well before Trump.[53]

He adds:

> Recent events throughout the West have compelled us to revise our conception of democracy. Despite the popular impression, democracy entails a great deal more than majority rule. It also requires respect for political opposition, the rule of law, and the possibility of the opposition coming to power through free debate and fair elections. The neofascist parties in Europe have rejected these norms.

He points to Russia, Poland, Hungary and Turkey, averring, "[t]he slide to dictatorship in several nations abroad has been more abrupt. At home it has been slow and relentless, but potentially just as lethal."[54] Similarly, historian Jon Meacham warns: "Extremism, racism, nativism, and isolationism, driven by fear of the unknown, tend to spike in periods of economic and social stress—a period like our own."[55]

Like many American commentators, Professor Kuttner is particularly alarmed by the distorting influence of big money in the democratic process:

> When money crowds out civic participation, not only does the whole system tilt to the right but public confidence in democracy rightly suffers.... In the 2010 *Citizens United* case, the Supreme Court overturned all limits on corporate campaign donations ... The ruling inverted the usual meaning of the First Amendment, to give corporations the unlimited right to donate money to candidates, in the name of corporate personhood and free expression.[56]

His alarm is warranted. The Federal Election Commission reported in March 2017 that unprecedented, enormous sums engulfed the 2016 elections:

58 This is unacceptable

Presidential candidates raised and spent $1.5 billion during the 2015–2016 election cycle, according to campaign finance reports filed with the Federal Election Commission that cover activity from January 1, 2015 through December 31, 2016. Congressional candidates collected and disbursed $1.6 billion, political parties received and spent $1.6 billion, and political action committees (PACs) raised and spent $4 billion in the 24-month period. Disbursements for independent expenditures reported in this period totaled $1.6 billion.[57]

Candidates running for president in 2020, including primary election candidates, raised more than 3.7 billion dollars.

Concomitant news shrinkage

This undermining of the democratic process by big money is particularly distressing because at the same time newspapers, the most reliable purveyors of ethical local news, are in dire straits, steadily reducing their coverage—or vanishing altogether. As advertisers have migrated to the internet, newspaper finances generally are dire, and this is particularly evident at the community level. Most Americans—73 percent according to a Pew Research poll in 2018—"look to a local paper to provide information about the town council and the school board, among other events and happenings."[58] Yet, the loss of both display and classified advertising has doomed two thousand one hundred newspapers in recent years, according to a 2020 report by the School of Journalism and Media at the University of North Carolina. The report states that the losses comprised

70 dailies and more than 2,000 weeklies or nondailies. At the end of 2019, the United States had 6,700 newspapers, down from almost 9,000 in 2004. Today, more than 200 of the nation's 3,143 counties and equivalents have no newspaper and no alternative source of credible and comprehensive information on critical issues.

The report, UNC's fourth on the state of local news, warns:

In only a few months, the pandemic and the ensuing recession have greatly accelerated the loss of local news that has been occurring over the past two decades. Layoffs, pay cuts and furloughs have affected thousands of journalists in 2020. Dozens of newspapers have been closed, and there is the threat of dozens – even hundreds – more closures before year's end.[59]

"News deserts are ominous to democracy," declares the respected Poynter Institute, a media research organization. "Coverage of at least 900 communities across the nation has gone dry since 2004." Numerous studies have found that shrinking coverage diminishes interest and participation in local civic life. For instance, a 2019 article in *Urban Affairs Review* describes a twenty-year study of declining coverage of civic affairs by eleven California newspapers, which found that

> the loss of professional expertise in coverage of local government has negative consequences for the quality of city politics because citizens become less informed about local policies and elections....The data show that cities served by newspapers with relatively sharp declines in newsroom staffing had, on average, significantly reduced political competition in mayoral races. We also find suggestive evidence that lower staffing levels are associated with lower voter turnout.[60]

A 2018 study of municipal bond data by the Brookings Institution's Hutchins Center on Fiscal and Monetary Policy found that newspaper closures were costly to their communities. "The loss of government monitoring resulting from a closure," the report states,

> is associated with higher government wages and deficits, and increased likelihoods of costly advance refundings and negotiated sales. Overall, our results indicate that local newspapers hold their governments accountable, keeping municipal borrowing costs low and ultimately saving local taxpayers money.[61]

Can a weakened democracy still rise to the occasion?

The coronavirus pandemic posed an unprecedented challenge to governments of all stripes. The United States, the world's leading democracy, did not handle it well. The U.S. toll of coronavirus deaths, heading past three hundred thousand in the autumn of 2020, was by far the worst in the world. In other words, democracy as practiced in America failed to measure up to its most basic obligation: to meet the needs of society. The message of this book demands even more, calling on the ethical news media to create a public expectation that America's leaders will take effective action to ameliorate three ominous threats to American life—climate change, racial inequity and economic disparity. It remains to be seen whether twenty-first-century American democracy is up to the challenge, but we'll never know unless the news media make the case first. Current, ossified politics says it won't just happen spontaneously, that the free press is indeed an indispensable fourth leg on the three-legged stool of the democratic republic that the founders designed so presciently.

Notes

1 Margaret Sullivan, *Ghosting the News: Local Journalism and the Crisis of American Democracy*, New York: Columbia Global Reports, 2020, 15.
2 Andrew Marantz, "How to Stop a Power Grab," *New Yorker*, November 16, 2020, https://www.newyorker.com/magazine/2020/11/23/how-to-stop-a-power-grab

60 This is unacceptable

3 Jeffrey Goldberg, "Why Obama Fears For Our Democracy," *The Atlantic*, November 16, 2020, https://www.theatlantic.com/ideas/archive/2020/11/why-obama-fears-for-our-democracy/617087/

4 Chauncey Alcorn, "First-Time Buyers Fuel Pandemic-Related Surge in Gun Sales," CNN Business, October 24, 2020, https://www.cnn.com/2020/10/24/business/gun-sales-surge-black-americans-women/index.html

5 Phillip B. Levine and Robin McKnight, "Three Million More Guns: The Spring 2020 Spike in Firearms Sales," Brookings Institution, July 13, 2020, https://www.brookings.edu/blog/up-front/2020/07/13/three-million-more-guns-the-spring-2020-spike-in-firearm-sales/

6 Alexander Hamilton, "Federalist 71," *The Federalist Papers*, Clinton Rossiter, ed., New York and London: Penguin Books, 1961, 432.

7 James Madison, "Federalist 10," *The Federalist Papers*, op. cit., 79, 81, 82.

8 Jeffrey St. John, *Constitutional Journal: A Correspondent's Report from the Convention of 1787*, Ottawa, Ill.: Jameson Books, Inc., 1987, 48.

9 Arthur Herman, *How the Scots Invented the Modern World*, New York: Three Rivers Press, 2001, 15.

10 Ibid. 17, 18.

11 Ibid. 20, 21.

12 David Hume, *Hume: The Essential Philosophical Works*, Ware, Hertfordshire: Wordsworth Editions Limited, 2011, 360.

13 Ibid. 359.

14 Herman, op. cit. 255.

15 Ron Chernow, *Alexander Hamilton*, New York: Penguin Group (USA) Inc., 2004, 25.

16 Ibid. 33.

17 Ibid. 34.

18 Ibid. 35, 36, 37.

19 Ibid. 43, 44, 46.

20 bid. 52, 53.

21 Ibid. 51.

22 Ibid. 60.

23 Buchan, op. cit. 74.

24 Herman, op. cit. 258.

25 Quoted in Herman, op. cit. 259.

26 Madison, *Federalist 10*, 82, 83.

27 Mark D. Hall, "James Wilson: Presbyterian, Anglican, Thomist, or Deist? Does It Matter?," in Daniel L. Dreisbach, Mark D. Hall, Jeffry H. Morrison, eds., *The Founders on God and Government*, Lanham, Md.: Rowman & Littlefield, 2004, 192, 195. Mark D. Hall is a professor of political science at George Fox University in Oregon.

28 Ibid. 196.

29 Herman, op. cit. 264. Wilson subsequently was appointed by President George Washington as one of the original justices of the Supreme Court.

30 Quoted in St. John, op. cit. 144.

31 Ibid. 225.

32 Madison, op. cit. 77.

33 Alexis de Tocqueville, *Democracy in America, The Complete and Unabridged Volumes I and II*, New York: Bantam Dell, 2000 (first published 1835), 3.

34 Ibid. 294.

35 Ibid. 230-31.

36 Ibid. 241.

Democracy itself hangs in the balance **61**

37 Ibid. 293.

38 Ibid. 277.

39 Ibid. 278, 284, 285, 276.

40 Anne Case and Angus Deaton, *Deaths of Despair and the Future of Capitalism*, Princeton and Oxford: Princeton University Press, 2020, 13.

41 Benjamin M. Friedman, *The Moral Consequences of Economic Growth*, New York and Toronto: Alfred A. Knopf, 2005, 399.

42 Ibid. 79.

43 Ibid. 99.

44 Ibid. 212.

45 Ibid. 205.

46 Steven Levitsky and Daniel Ziblatt, *How Democracies Die*, New York: Broadway Books, 2018, 228.

47 Robert Kuttner, *Can Democracy Survive Global Capitalism?* New York and London: W. W. Norton & Company, 2018, 259, 273.

48 Economic Policy Institute, "Raising America's Pay," June 4, 2014, https://www.epi.org/publication/raising-americas-pay-summary-initiative/

49 Economic Policy Institute, "Raising America's Pay, Wage Data," June 4, 2014, italics added, https://www.epi.org/publication/raising-americas-pay-data/

50 Ibid.

51 Lawrence Mishel and Jori Kandra, "CEO Compensation Surged 14% in 2019 to $21.3 Million. CEOs Now Earn 320 Times as Much as a Typical Worker," EPI press release, August 18, 2020, https://www.epi.org/publication/ceo-compensation-surged-14-in-2019-to-21-3-million-ceos-now-earn-320-times-as-much-as-a-typical-worker/

52 EPI, op. cit. "Manufacturing South" is Alabama, Georgia, Kentucky, Mississippi, North Carolina, South Carolina, Tennessee." Other Midwest" is Iowa, Kansas, Missouri, Nebraska, North Dakota, South Dakota. "Other Northeast" is Connecticut, Delaware, District of Columbia, Maine, Maryland, Massachusetts, New Hampshire, New Jersey, Rhode Island, Vermont. "Other Pacific" is Alaska, Hawaii, Oregon, Washington.

53 Robert Kuttner, *The Stakes: 2020 and the Survival of American Democracy*, New York and London: W. W. Norton & Company, 2019, xv.

54 Ibid. xvi, xvii.

55 Jon Meacham, *The Soul of America: The Battle for Our Better Angels*, New York: Random House, 2018, 4.

56 Kuttner, op. cit. 34, 35. The case is *Citizens United v. Federal Election Commission*, 558 U.S. 310 (2010).

57 "Statistical Summary of 24-Month Campaign Activity of the 2015–2016 Election Cycle," Federal Election Commission, March 23, 2017, https://www.fec.gov/updates/statistical-summary-24-month-campaign-activity-2015-2016-election-cycle/

58 "For Local News, Americans Embrace Digital But Still Want Strong Community Connection," Pew Research Center on Journalism and Media, March 26, 2019, https://www.journalism.org/2019/03/26/for-local-news-americans-embrace-digital-but-still-want-strong-community-connection/

59 Penelope Muse Abernathy, "News Deserts and Ghost Newspapers: Will Local News Survive?," Hussman School of Journalism and Media, University of North Carolina, 2002, https://www.usnewsdeserts.com/reports/news-deserts-and-ghost-newspapers-will-local-news-survive/the-news-landscape-in-2020-transformed-and-diminished/vanishing-newspapers/

62 This is unacceptable

60 Meghan E. Rubado and Jay T. Jennings, "Political Consequences of the Endangered Local Watchdog: Newspaper Decline and Mayoral Elections in the United States," *Urban Affairs Review*, vol. 56:5, pp. 1327–1356, first published April 3, 2019.

61 Pengjie Gao, Chang Lee and Demot Murphy, Hutchins Center Working Paper #44, "Financing Dies in Darkness? The Impact of Newspaper Closures on Public Finance," Hutchins Center on Fiscal & Monetary Policy, Brookings Institution, September 2018, https://www.brookings.edu/wp-content/uploads/2018/09/WP44.pdf

6

POLITICIANS TODAY WON'T COMPROMISE, PRODUCING GOVERNMENT GRIDLOCK

With such appalling threats to American society and democracy so evident for so long, why haven't politicians dealt with them more effectively already? One reason is growing political polarity, seen as increasing ideological rigidity producing intransigence rather than compromise. The founders created checks and balances purposefully, to assure that no branch of government would predominate in the new democratic republic. In *Federalist 9*, Hamilton described "legislative checks and balances" as one of several "wholly new discoveries" and one of the "powerful means by which the excellencies of republican government may be retained and its imperfections lessened or avoided."[1] But that structure requires compromise, notably when the government is politically divided, for, as *Roll Call* noted in 2019, "Washington tends to work best when one party controls both Congress and the White House."[2]

In the forty-four years since the election of 1976, there have been far more years of divided government, thirty, than one-party control of both the executive and legislative branches, only fourteen. President Jimmy Carter, a Democrat, enjoyed all four years, 1977–81, with a Democratic Congress. Another Democrat, Bill Clinton, had a Democratic Congress in only two of his eight years, 1993–95. George W. Bush, a Republican, had Republican majorities in both houses of Congress for six of his eight years in the White House, 2001–7. Democrat Barack Obama enjoyed Democratic majorities in both houses of Congress for only two of his eight years, 2009–11. It's not to say that divided government necessarily means stasis, but it does require compromise that has become less and less popular in Washington, and in many politically significant "swing" states as well, as we shall see.

Scholars and journalists have long pondered times of federal gridlock, contrasting them with highly productive years. A paper published in 2000 by the Brookings Institution remarked that the

DOI: 10.4324/9781003140337-8

64 This is unacceptable

Great Society under Lyndon Johnson [Democrat, 1963–1969; Democrats also held both houses of Congress], for example, enacted landmark health care, environment, civil rights, transportation, and education statutes (to name a few). At other times, gridlock prevails, as when, in 1992 [President George H. W. Bush, Republican, and a Democratic Congress], congressional efforts to cut the capital gains tax and to reform lobbying, campaign finance, banking, parental leave, and voter registration laws (to name a few) ended in deadlock.

The paper observed that

[d]espite the first budget surplus in 30 years, Congress [Republican] and the president [Clinton, Democrat] remain deadlocked over numerous high-profile issues (including Social Security, Medicare, managed health care, and campaign finance reform), and they show few prospects of acting on these and other salient issues before the 2000 elections.[3]

Recent history demonstrates that even when the White House and both houses of Congress are controlled by one party, the federal government may still tie itself into knots. In January 2018, *The New York Times* reported that "Capitol Hill is absorbed with concern that Mr. Trump's presidency has pushed an already dysfunctional Congress [also Republican] into a near-permanent state of gridlock that threatens to diminish American democracy itself. The sense of gloom is bipartisan."[4]

In December 2018, during all-Republican control, Congress failed to appropriate funds even for operations of the federal government itself. So, as *Business Insider* reported it, the

federal government entered a partial shutdown as the House and Senate adjourned without a federal-spending deal on Friday, hours before a midnight EST deadline. President Donald Trump's demands for a wall along the US-Mexico border led to a standoff in the Senate. Trump's sudden turnaround after supporting a short-term funding extension left Congress with little time to find a compromise that would prevent a shutdown.

The story added that "Members of Congress still receive paychecks during a shutdown."[5]

It must be noted that a minority opinion maintains that gridlock isn't necessarily all bad. A USA TODAY opinion columnist, Glenn Harlan Reynolds, wrote after the Democrats won control of the House of Representatives in the 2018 election,

What does that mean? Gridlock. Is that good? It just might be. The idea that gridlock is good is based on the notion that most of what Congress does is probably bad, and that when Congress can't do much we're better off.[6]

As a result of a party difference in Congress, "[s]even months into a new era of divided government," *The New York Times* reported in August 2019, the Republican-led Senate limped out of Washington this week after the fewest legislative debates of any in recent memory, without floor votes on issues that both parties view as urgent: the high cost of prescription drugs, a broken immigration system and crumbling infrastructure. The number of Senate roll call votes on amendments — a key indicator of whether lawmakers are engaged in free and open debate — plummeted to only 18 this year, according to a review of congressional data. During the same time period in the 10 previous Congresses, senators took anywhere from 34 to 231 amendment votes.[7]

Recognizing the extreme dysfunction of the divided Congress, in 2019, *Politico Magazine* published a thoughtful series of articles by several "big thinkers" entitled "Everyone agrees something is broken. Can we make it better?" "Congress is a basket case," wrote Kevin Kosar of the R Street Institute, a nonpartisan research organization in Washington.

> Our national legislature has passed only a couple dozen laws this year, a count which includes legislation naming a post office and appointing former Senator Bob Dole a colonel. Committees, once congressional powerhouses, are moving little legislation and are conducting fewer oversight hearings than in past decades. Meanwhile, huge issues—like immigration and the ongoing military operations in Afghanistan and Syria—go unresolved. To citizens' disgust, legislators fritter away precious hours by holding made-for-television screamfest hearings, delivering stemwinder speeches to mostly empty chambers, and stirring up ruckuses on social media.

Kosar applauded a new bipartisan committee of the House that's studying reform ideas.[8]

Another contributor to the *Politico* series, Jennifer Lawless of the University of Virginia, called for ending "the permanent campaign." She lamented,

> The minute election results are in, federal candidates begin seeking reelection. But imagine an election reform bill that limits the length of federal campaigns and all campaign-related activities to 90 days or, what the heck, even six months. American politics would have no choice but to become a little less broken. After all, if campaigning took a back seat to governing, then politicians would have time to do their jobs, not just make a case to keep them.[9]

Still another contributor, Bob Woodson of the Woodson Institute, called for

> dramatically reducing the salaries and benefits of all elected officials, withholding their pay until the budget is balanced (forcing them to make tough decisions/trade-offs), and imposing term limits on all federal officeholders. Member of Congress should not retire from the job significantly richer than they were when they started, he asserted.[10]

66 This is unacceptable

Urban versus rural

Although Congressional deadlock is often seen as Republican versus Democrat, a cogent book-length analysis by the Brookings Institution sees it rather as urban versus rural. The authors, David F. Damore, Robert E. Lang and Karen A. Danielsen, declare that "just because the red state, blue state framework is ubiquitous does not mean it accurately captures the fissures defining contemporary American politics." They state further that the "urban/rural divide" infects state and local politics as well as the federal government, and they cite a recent tussle in Nevada over gun control as a prime illustration of how it plays out.

In 2013, the authors state, the Republican governor, Brian Sandoval, vetoed a bill "passed by the urban-dominated, Democratic-controlled legislature, requiring background checks for private gun purchases or transfers." A 2016 ballot initiative calling for the same background checks was approved on the strength of a heavy favorable vote in just one county, Clark County, home of the state's largest city, Las Vegas. But the Republican governor and attorney general "refused to implement the initiative over technical issues stemming from the initiative's language" and it "languished and remained unimplemented for more than two years." In 2017, after a shocking mass shooting that killed sixty and wounded eight hundred sixty-seven others in Las Vegas, the Democratic legislature and governor re-enacted the background check requirement, over a Republican protest that "most of our state is rural," a protest that ignored "the fact that a small percent of Nevadans reside in the state's rural ... counties. Rural sheriffs pledged not to enforce the law, and rural county commissioners passed resolutions declaring their counties as 'Second Amendment Sanctuary' zones." Similarly, in much of the country, the authors observe, "major metros often punch below their demographic and economic weight, allowing rural and exurban voters to impose policies potential adverse to the interests of blue metros."[11]

The Brookings authors, shifting their analysis to the federal level, note that Donald Trump won the presidency in 2016 "despite losing eighty-eight of the 100 most populated counties in America."[12] This divide was confirmed in the 2020 election, in which urban and suburban voters even in states that voted for Trump— such as Miami and Orlando, Florida; Charlotte, North Carolina; Indianapolis, Indiana; Dallas and Houston, Texas; Birmingham, Alabama; New Orleans, Louisiana; DesMoines, Iowa; Anchorage, Alaska; Cleveland, Ohio; St. Louis, Missouri— overwhelmingly preferred the Democrat, Joe Biden.

The federal gridlock was poignantly confirmed shortly before the 2020 election, when, despite rampant, lethal spreading of the Covid-19 pandemic and the exhaustion of federal relief for the unemployed and distressed businesses, Senate Republicans blocked additional relief legislation—even when both the House of Representatives and President Trump favored it. In fact, the Senate leadership refused to even participate in the negotiations—talks that apparently were progressing well—between the Speaker of the House, Nancy Pelosi, and the president's representative, Steven Mnuchin, the secretary of the Treasury. As *The New York Times* reported,

Senator Mitch McConnell, the majority leader, privately told Republican senators on Tuesday that he had warned the White House not to strike a pre-election deal with Speaker Nancy Pelosi on a new round of stimulus, moving to head off an agreement that President Trump has demanded but most in his party oppose. Mr. McConnell's remarks, confirmed by four Republicans familiar with them, threw cold water on Mr. Trump's increasingly urgent push to enact a new round of pandemic aid before Election Day.[13]

Unexpectedly, the Democrats won control of the White House and both houses of Congress in the November 2020 election, enabling President Biden to whisk through Congress, with no Republican votes, a monumental anti-Covid and health care relief bill, a huge 1.9-trillion-dollar package, in March 2021, an historical achievement that would have been impossible without such unified control of the government.[14]

Notes

1 Alexander Hamilton, Federalist 9, Clinton Rossiter, ed., *The Federalist Papers*, New York and London: Penguin Books, 1961, 72–73. The other "new discoveries": "distribution of power into distinct departments," courts with "judges holding their offices during good behavior," and "representation of the people in the legislature by deputies of their own election."

2 Shawn Zeller, "Divided government will pose an obstacle to lawmaking in 2019; Congress was most dysfunctional from 2011 to 2014 when control of House and Senate was split," *Roll Call*, January 3, 2019, https://www.rollcall.com/2019/01/03/divided-government-will-pose-an-obstacle-to-lawmaking-in-2019/

3 Sarah A. Binder, "Going Nowhere: A Gridlocked Congress," Brookings Institution, December 1, 2000, https://www.brookings.edu/articles/going-nowhere-a-gridlocked-congress/

4 Sheryl Gay Stolberg and Nicholas Fandos, "As Gridlock Deepens in Congress, Only Gloom Is Bipartisan," *The New York Times*, January 27, 2018, https://www.nytimes.com/2018/01/27/us/politics/congress-dysfunction-conspiracies-trump.html

5 Bob Bryan, "MERRY CHRISTMAS!: Government Enters Shutdown after Trump Border-Wall Demands Leave Congress in Gridlock," *Business Insider*, December 21, 2018, https://www.businessinsider.com/government-shutdown-trump-border-wall-demands-deadlocks-congress-2018-12

6 Glenn Harlan Reynolds, "Election Results 2018: Forget the Blue Wave and Behold the Purple Puddle; Democrats in the House and Republicans in the Senate Means Gridlock. That's a Good Thing, But It Is Only a Temporary Solution," *USA TODAY*, November 7, 2020, https://www.usatoday.com/story/opinion/2018/11/06/election-results-democrat-control-house-gridlock-republican-senate-congress-column/1906702002/

7 Sheryl Gay Stolberg, "McConnell Promised to End Senate Gridlock. Instead, Republicans Are Stuck in Neutral," *The New York Times*, August 3, 2019, https://www.nytimes.com/2019/08/03/us/politics/senate-votes-mcconnell.html

8 Kevin Kosar, "A Permanent Committee to Improve Congress," *Politico Magazine*, 2019, https://www.politico.com/interactives/2019/how-to-fix-politics-in-america/gridlock/

9 Jennifer Lawless, "End the Permanent Campaign," ibid.

10 Bob Woodson, "Cut Government Salaries," ibid.

68 This is unacceptable

11 David F. Damore, Robert E. Lang and Karen A. Danielsen, *Blue Metros, Red States: The Shifting Urban-Rural Divide in America's Swing States*, Washington: The Brookings Institution, 2021, 6, 3, 11.

12 Ibid. 6.

13 Emily Cochrane and Nicholas Fandos, "As McConnell Advises White House Against a Pre-Election Stimulus Deal, Pelosi Reports Progress in Talks," *The New York Times*, October 21, 2020, https://www.nytimes.com/2020/10/21/world/as-mcconnell-advises-white-house-against-a-pre-election-stimulus-deal-pelosi-reports-progress-in-talks.html?searchResultPosition=2

14 Emily Cochrane, "With House Passage, Congress Clears the Nearly $1.9 Trillion Stimulus Plan for President Biden's Signature," *The New York Times*, March 10, 2021, https://www.nytimes.com/2021/03/10/us/stimulus-vote.html?searchResultPosition=2

SECTION II

Discomfiting realities are also opportunities

7

THE ETHICS OF CARE NICELY COMPLEMENTS EXISTING CODES OF ETHICS

We sampled the ethics of care in the first chapter. Whence came it? What does it mean—for our view of our personal and professional relationships, for journalism, and, perhaps, for the world?

It's evident that moral philosophy moves slowly. We still read and admire long-ago philosophers, and we've seen here how readily we perceive bits and pieces of their writings reflected in today's high standards of fine, ethical journalism. Nevertheless, in the last decades of the twentieth century, as college-educated American women were emerging from the kitchen and the nursery into medicine, engineering, law, the ministry, architecture, journalism and corporate management, a few female academics, scholars of moral philosophy, began to formulate their own distinctive moral philosophy.

Their thinking, though they labeled it feminist, was more profound than the somewhat earlier advocacy of "women's rights," which seeks equality in employment, compensation, recognition and life status generally. The ethics of care, by contrast, envisions a distinct contribution to humanity. It's an elaborate moral philosophy although similar to women's rights in that it, too, is based in the distinct life experience of women.

The formulators of the ethics of care, as we have noted, took issue with the traditional reason-based moral philosophers, notably Immanuel Kant and his "categorical imperative" assertion of a duty to make personal decisions that could be fairly applied universally.

Instead, the care ethicists look to David Hume, the philosophical leader of the Scottish Enlightenment whom we've seen earlier as influencing the American founding fathers. Earlier, we quote him as asserting that "[r]eason is, and ought only to be the slave of the passions." He refers to the prevalent "supposed pre-eminence of reason above passion" in order to debunk that priority, averring that "reason alone can never produce any action, or give rise to volition." He allows, however,

DOI: 10.4324/9781003140337-10

72 Discomfiting realities are also opportunities

that appearances can be deceiving, that when "passions are calm, and cause no disorder in the soul, they are very readily taken for the determinations of reason, and are supposed to proceed from the same faculty, with that, which judges of truth and falsehood."[1] He scoffs in particular at one prong of rational moral philosophy, justice, declaring that "the sense of justice is not founded on reason," but derives from ownership of personal property: "if men were supplied with every thing in the same abundance, or if *every one* had the same affection and tender regard for *every one* as for himself; justice and injustice would be equally unknown among mankind."[2]

The practical Hume

There are at least three other aspects of Humean philosophy that are relevant for our purposes. One is his repeated insistence on including life experience in determining how people should live ethically. In fact, Hume suggests, incorporating experience into our judgments may be quite implicit, just second nature, "without the assistance of the memory." He posits that a traveler whose journey is interrupted by a river doesn't need to consciously reflect on the danger of drowning in order to decide not to enter the water.

> But as this transition proceeds from experience, and not from any primary connexion betwixt the ideas, we must necessarily acknowledge, that experience may produce a belief and a judgment of causes and effects by a secret operation, and without being once thought of. This removes all pretext, if there yet remains any, for asserting that the mind is convinced by reasoning of that principle, *that instances of which we have no experience, must necessarily resemble those, of which we have.* For we here find, that the understanding or imagination can draw inferences from past experience, without reflecting on it; much more without forming any principle concerning it, or reasoning upon that principle.[3]

A second pertinent factor in Hume's thinking is his admission that he could be wrong.

> When I reflect on the natural fallibility of my judgment, I have less confidence in my opinions, than when I only consider the objects concerning which I reason; and when I proceed still farther, to turn the scrutiny against every successive estimation I make of my faculties, all the rules of logic require a continual diminution, and at last a total extinction of belief and evidence.[4]

Furthermore, Hume allows room for discussion. "In every judgment, which we can form concerning probability, as well as concerning knowledge, we ought always to correct the first judgment, derived from the nature of the object, by another judgment, derived from the nature of the understanding." He goes on to observe that in any such discussion the person of greater experience is likely to have "a greater assurance in his opinions," but "this authority is never entire; since even such-a-one must be conscious of many errors in the past, and must still dread the like in the future."[5]

Looking to Hume, New Zealand native Annette C. Baier of the University of Pittsburgh was among the pioneers who first formulated the ethics of care. Baier notes that Hume observes that in any discussion he deems it natural to incline toward others' opposing views. Nevertheless, Baier declares,

> This psychological fact about us does not make conformism a virtue or independence of mind an impossibility. Hume himself clearly managed to follow his own reason and inclination in opposition to that of the majority of his Presbyterian friends and companions... . Hume also believed that every person needs the reaction of fellow persons in order to test and verify privately arrived at judgments and verdicts.

Moreover, Baier elaborates, when a person encounters widespread disagreement, "[t]he chances that one is right and everyone else wrong are about as great as that the one who testifies to having witnessed a miracle speaks the truth."[6] More on Baier later.

Other early philosophers of care also draw on Hume, if not quite as fervently as Baier. Virginia Held acknowledges that "[s]ome think the ethics of care is close to Hume's ethics," and she echoes his insistence on learning from experience: "The ethics of care builds on experience that all persons share, though they have often been unaware of its embedded values and implications." However, she draws a valid distinction between what she sees as virtues described by Aristotle and Hume "attaching to individual persons" and, on the other hand, the ethics of care being "more concerned with relations between persons."[7] Another contemporary philosopher, Michael Slote, declares that "the ethics of caring falls clearly within the Humean moral-sentimentalist tradition."[8]

What's important for us to note here is how both Hume and the care ethicists embrace what we can see today as the practical characteristics of ethical journalism: a continuing, relentless desire to learn, to absorb new knowledge, ideas and experience, to learn from others and to modify thinking and decisions as facts warrant. These characteristics might describe a fine journalist, or a fine newsroom. In fact, how could a vibrant, ethical newsroom operate otherwise?

Nel Noddings, a leader

Nel Noddings (1929–) of Stanford, not incidentally a former high school math teacher and the mother of ten, was among the first proponents of care ethics to gain prominence. In 1984, she published a groundbreaking tome: *Caring: A Feminist Approach to Ethics and Moral Education*. Her objective is goodness, not moral rectitude. She explains by contrasting principled, detached views of a father with the feminine view of a mother:

74 Discomfiting realities are also opportunities

> It is feminine in the deep classical sense—rooted in receptivity, relatedness, and responsiveness. It does not imply either that logic is to be discarded or that logic is alien to women. It represents an alternative to present views, one that begins with the moral attitude or longing for goodness and not with moral reasoning.[9]

In particular, Noddings throws down the gauntlet to Kant: "For Kant, acts done out of love or inclination earn no moral credit.... In care ethics ... we are not much interested in moral credit.... This is clearly a reversal of Kantian priorities."[10]

Noddings elaborates: "[A]n ethic of caring arises, I believe, out of our experience as women, just as the traditional logical approach to ethical problems arises more obviously from masculine experience."[11]

To make her point, Noddings critiques the Biblical challenge faced by Abraham as he prepares to sacrifice his son Isaac, an act commonly accepted by Christians as a demonstration of Abraham's trust in God:

> But for the mother, for us, this is horrendous. Our relation to our children is not governed first by the ethical but by natural caring We love not because we are required to love but because our natural relatedness gives natural birth to love. It is this love, the natural caring, that makes the ethical possible. For us, then, Abraham's decision is not only ethically unjustified but it is in base violation of the supra-ethical—of caring.[12]

Thus rejecting both Abraham and Kant, Noddings turns to David Hume, who "long ago contended that morality is founded upon and rooted in feeling."[13] In place of Kant's categorical imperative, Noddings posits a "moral imperative." She elaborates:

> Women, perhaps the majority of women, prefer to discuss moral problems in terms of concrete situations. They approach moral problems not as intellectual problems to be solved by abstract reasoning but as concrete human problems to be lived and to be solved in living.... . Moral decisions are, after all, made in situations; they are qualitatively different from the solution of geometry problems.[14]

Carol Gilligan

Another early theoretician of caring was Carol Gilligan (1936–), then an associate professor of education at Harvard, later at New York University. In 1982, she published an influential book called *In a Different Voice: Psychological Theory and Women's Development*.[15] She based it substantially on two interview studies, one of unexpectedly pregnant young women wrestling with the thought of abortion, the other of recent college graduates, men as well as women.

Existing codes of ethics **75**

The twenty-nine pregnant women (some hardly women) ranging in age from only fifteen to thirty-three, were of diverse ethnicity and social class, and were married and unmarried. Gilligan sets the stage this way:

> While society may affirm publicly the woman's right to choose for herself, the exercise of such choice brings her privately into conflict with the conventions of femininity, particularly the moral equation of goodness with self-sacrifice. Although independent assertion in judgment and action is considered to be the hallmark of adulthood, it is rather in their care and concern for others that women have both judged themselves and been judged.[16]

She describes Sarah, an unmarried twenty-five-year old, pregnant for the second time by a married man who refused again to marry her or to support their child, as having always had the notion of "a good person" defined by "her mother's example of hard work, patience, and self sacrifice." But that definition is changing now

> to include the value that she herself places on directness and honesty... . While accepting the necessity of abortion as a highly compromised resolution, Sarah turns her attention to the pregnancy itself, which to her denotes a failure of responsibility, a failure to care for and protect both other and self.

Gilligan quotes Sarah:

> I have this responsibility to myself, and you know, for once I am beginning to realize that that really matters to me. Instead of doing what I want for myself and feeling guilty over how selfish I am, you realize that is a very usual way for people to live—doing what you want to do because you feel that your wants and your needs are important, if to no one else, then to you, and that's reason enough to do something that you want to do.[17]

Another young woman interviewed was

> Janet, a twenty-four-year-old married Catholic, pregnant again two months following the birth of her first child... . The abortion decision is framed by Janet first in terms of her responsibilities to others, since having a second child at this time would be contrary to medical advice and would strain both the emotional and financial resources of the family.

Moreover, Janet says, there's "sort of an emotional reason. I don't know if it is selfish or not, but it would really be tying myself down, and right now I am am not ready to be tied down with two."

Gilligan notes:

> Against this combination of selfish and responsible reasons for abortion is her religious belief about abortion... . It is taking a life. Even though it is not

76 Discomfiting realities are also opportunities

> formed, it is the potential, and to me it is still taking a life But I have to think of mine, my son's and my husband's. And at first I thought it was for selfish reasons, but it is not. I believe that, too, some of it is selfish. I don't want another one right now; I am not ready for it.[18]

In the end, Gilligan reports, "[o]f the twenty-nine women, four decided to have the baby, two miscarried, twenty-one chose abortion, and two who were in doubt about the decision at the time of the interview could not be contacted."[19]

She sees a conflict between selfishness and responsibility: "The inflicting of hurt is considered selfish and immoral in its reflection of unconcern, while the expression of care is seen as the fulfillment of moral responsibility."[20]

Gilligan comes to a similar conclusion from a series of interviews with a very different group, women and men college graduates in the midst of the widespread assertion of women's rights.

> At age twenty-seven, the five women in the study all were actively pursuing careers—two in medicine, one in law, one in graduate study, and one as an organizer of labor unions. In the five years following their graduation from college, three had married and one had a child.

She asked them: "How would you describe yourself to yourself?"

Claire, one of the women, responds:

> This sounds sort of strange, but I think maternal, with all its connotations. I see myself in a nurturing role, maybe not right now, but whenever that might be, as a physician, as a mother … It's hard for me to think of myself without thinking about other people around me that I'm giving to.

Gilligan observes:

> In response to the question to describe themselves, all of the women describe a relationship, depicting their identity *in* the connection of future mother, present wife, adopted child, or past lover. Similarly, the standard of moral judgment that informs their assessment of self is a standard of relationship, an ethic of nurturance, responsibility, and care… . [T]hese highly successful and achieving women do not mention their academic and professional distinction in the context of describing themselves.[21]

This contrasts with the self-descriptions of the young men interviewed. Gilligan finds them focused on individual achievement justified by a traditional moral ethic of rights.[22] "While the ethic of rights," Gilligan declares, "is a manifestation of equal respect, balancing the claims of other and self, the [women's] ethic of responsibility rests on an understanding that gives rise to compassion and care."[23] Thus, "While an ethic of justice proceeds from the premise of equality—that everyone should be

Existing codes of ethics **77**

treated the same—an ethic of care rests on the premise of nonviolence—that no one should be hurt."[24]

Annette C. Baier

Back to Annette C. Baier (1929–2012) of the University of Pittsburgh. She brusquely dismisses "the great moral theorists in our tradition" as "mostly men who had minimal adult dealings with (and so were then minimally influenced by) women. With a few significant exceptions (Hume, Hegel, J. S. Mill, Sidgwick, maybe Bradley) they are a collection of clerics, misogynists, and puritan bachelors." As we noted above, Baier, like other early proponents of the ethics of care, greatly admires Hume, a prolific writer on many subjects whom she found "uncannily womanly in his moral wisdom."[25]

Baier tips her hat to Carol Gilligan, "whose book *In a Different Voice* caused a considerable stir both in the popular press and, more slowly, in the philosophical journals." The book, she says, stimulated discussion

> in an enlarged moral vocabulary, which draws on what Gilligan calls the ethics of *care* as well as that of *justice*. 'Care' is the new buzzword. It is not, as Shakespeare's Portia demanded, mercy that is to season justice, but a less authoritarian humanitarian supplement, a felt concern for the good of others and for community with them.

Opening the door to care by men, she adds,

> [t]he emphasis on care goes with a recognition of the often unchosen nature of responsibilities of those who give care, both of children who care for their aged or infirm parents and of parents who care for the children they in fact have.[26]

Baier takes repeated swipes at Immanuel Kant and his categorical imperative.[27] She complains that it does nothing for the unfortunate people who don't enjoy the benefits of the civil society willingly governed by the equitable rule Kant sought.

> They may well be lonely, driven to suicide, apathetic about their work and about participation in political processes, find their lives meaningless, and have no wish to leave offspring to face the same meaningless existence. Their rights, and respect for rights, are quite compatible with very great misery, and misery whose causes are not just individual misfortune and psychic sickness but social and moral impoverishment."[28]

She expands her criticism to encompass all of rational moral philosophy:

> For the moral tradition which developed the concept of rights, autonomy, and justice is the same tradition that provided 'justifications' of the oppression of

78 Discomfiting realities are also opportunities

those whom the primary rights-holders depended on to do the sort of work they themselves preferred not to do."[29]

In contrast, Baier sees in Hume a "sympathy and concern for others," a "downplaying of the role of reason and a playing up of the role of feeling in moral judgment," all grounded ultimately in the relationship of parents and children.

> At the very heart of Hume's moral theory lies his celebration of family life and of parental love. Justice, the chief artificial virtue, is the offspring of family cooperativeness and inventive self-interested reason which sees how such a mutually beneficial cooperative scheme might be extended.[30]

Accordingly, Baier declares,

> Hume in the end transforms the concept of reason. From being a quasi-divine faculty, something we share with God, reason becomes a natural capacity and one that is essentially shared with those who learn from experience in the way we do, sharing expressive body language, sharing or able to share a language, sharing or able to share our sentiments, sharing or able to share intellectual, moral and aesthetic standards, and sharing or aspiring to share in the setting of those standards.[31]

In a more personal observation, Baier welcomes and celebrates the emergence of other feminist moral philosophers, but warns that as they expose the "sexist bias of our society, our academic establishment," their academic advancement will at the same time depend on senior professors, all men.

> These women are bold; they may be rash. How many tenured women philosophers who write in provocatively feminist ways wrote this way, or wrote mainly this way, before they had tenure? Maybe I stand out as conspicuously cowardly, but I certainly did not.[32]

Virginia Held

One of the next generation of feminist philosophers identified by Baier was Virginia Held (1929–) of the City University of New York. In 2006, a dozen years after Baier's book, Held put *The Ethics of Care* on the cover of her own.[33] She differentiates the ethics of care from the traditional values cited by journalism ethicists:

> Care ethics emerged as the gender bias of such dominant moral theories as Kantian ethics and utilitarianism came under attack … . In contrast with the dominant views that give primacy to such values as autonomy, independence, noninterference, fairness, and rights, the ethics of care values the interdependence and caring relations that connect persons to one another… .

Existing codes of ethics **79**

Rather than rejecting the emotions as threats to the rationality and impartiality seen as the foundations of morality, the ethics of care attends to and values such moral emotions as empathy and shared concern... . The ethics of care ... is more suitable than traditional moral theories for dealing with many of the concerns of civil society.[34]

It's fair to ask whether Held is merely advocating charity, a virtue preached by major religions. But no. She declares that

> care is not the same as charity—when we take care of our children we are not being charitable—and being caring is not the same as being charitable. Valuing care is entirely independent of any religious foundation and is the stronger for this, since those not sharing a given religious tradition have few reasons to attend to arguments that appeal to that tradition. Understanding the value of care can be based on a universal experience of having been cared for and being able to engage in caring.[35]

Asserting that the ethics of care "should be seen as applicable to political and social life," Held posits:

> I now think that caring relations should form the wider moral framework into which justice should be fitted. Care seems the most basic moral value. As a practice, we know that without care we cannot have anything else, since life requires it. All human beings require a great deal of care in their early years, and most of us need and want caring relationships throughout our lives... . When in society individuals treat each other with only the respect that justice requires but no further consideration, the social fabric of trust and concern can be missing or disappearing... . Without some level of caring concern for other human beings, we cannot have any morality.[36]

For instance, she cites health care, asserting that it "ought to provide what members of a political community need when they are medically vulnerable."[37] Furthermore, "Environmental concerns would be accorded the importance they deserve."[38] Maybe even street crime? "Practices of care may need to include the use of coercion to restrain a person who is or is threatening to become violent, but the objective is to do so without damaging the person physically or psychologically."[39]

To Held, the ethics of care is no mere aspiration. It's a must: "An aim of the ethics of care is to promote the responsible autonomy of the cared-for where this is appropriate... . The ethics of care requires us to pay attention to, rather than ignore, the material psychological and social prerequisites for autonomy. Persons without adequate resources cannot adequately exercise autonomous choices... . Without care there is no society, there are no people. Why should we even look for a basis for morality that disregards care? ... Possibly the ethics of care might provide a new and stronger basis than previous moralities on which to recognize the responsibilities of society to respond to the needs of the vulnerable."[40] This is truly a breathtaking vision of a public commitment, at least in the United States.

Explicitly included in Held's vision are the news media.

> Citizens should be informed and news should be produced primarily for the sake of democratic political values and true understanding, not principally for commercial gain as at present... . [I] have written about how a culture, including its news media, that is subordinated to the demands of the market cannot perform the function that culture *needs to perform* to keep society healthy, the function of critical evaluation, of imagining alternatives not within the market, of providing citizens the information and evaluations they need to act effectively as citizens.[41]

Michael Slote

More recently, some male philosophers, too, contribute to the ethics of care. Michael Slote of the University of Miami expresses an overarching vision much like Held's. To him the ethics of care is

> nothing less than a total or systematic *human* morality, one that may be able to give us a better understanding of the whole range of moral issues that concern both men and women than anything to be found in traditional ethical theories.[42]

Why? Because "empathy is crucial to moral motivation," and it is "reasonable to think that we can justify moral claims by reference to empathy."[43]

Slote declares that "morality—both in the form of moral virtue and in the form of moral obligation or duty—centers around the empathically caring concern to promote the welfare of other individuals or groups of individuals... . [E]ven if morality isn't based on reason, there is no reason to suppose that moral individuals, as conceived by care ethics, have no need for their rational, or reasoning, powers." In fact, he goes on, "[a]nyone who thinks and makes claims about the ethics of care has to place a value on theoretical reason and reasoning."[44]

Slote even goes so far as to suggest that the ethics of care might serve to support a new form of Kant's categorical imperative, the idea that a "maxim" guiding a person's ethical decision must be equally appropriate as a general rule for all:

> What we need to be able to say is that moral claims are *categorical*, are categorical imperatives in Kant's sense; and if care ethicists can say such a thing, I think they will have subscribed to an appropriate level or sense of normativity. But can they?

So Slote pulls back a bit from such an aggressive assertion, but goes on to state, "there is no reason why a care ethicist should deny or want to deny that the moral judgments s/he subscribes to are categorical in Kant's sense."[45]

Notably (or perhaps not), eminent thinkers in quite different disciplines come to caring conclusions quite similar to those of the ethicists of care. Cognitive neuroscientist Michael S. Gazzaniga believes that

> we should look for not a universal ethics comprising hard-and-fast rules, but for the universal ethics that arises from being human, which is clearly contextual, emotion-influenced, and designed to increase our survival.... This is the mandate for neuroethics: to use our understanding that the brain reacts to things on the basis of its hard-wiring to contextualize and debate the gut instincts that serve the greatest good—or the most logical solutions—given specific contexts.[46]

Similarly, and even more explicitly, Old Testament scholar Walter Brueggeman declares that the Covid-19 pandemic calls for acts "performed by neighborly gesture in time of fear, by neighborly generosity and hospitality in a time of self-preoccupation, and by neighborly policies in the face of predatory greed."[47]

Caring journalism?

Some writers propose applying the ethics of care to journalism, at least in a limited way. Bastiaan Vanacker of Loyola University Chicago and John Breslin, a freelance journalist, state:

> In providing specific guidelines for the coverage of crime stories and crime victims, we suggest that a care-based approach can enrich and diversify media ethics, both from a theoretical and practical perspective. For example, the more vulnerable a crime victim is as the unexpected subject of a news story, the more the values of compassion and dignity from a care-based approach should trump traditional journalistic values, such as objectivity and truth telling. Care-based ethics can help journalists assess the vulnerability of these involuntary news subjects in balancing the potential cathartic and traumatic effects of media coverage on crime victims, while not surrendering journalistic integrity or autonomy.[48]

Mohammed Delwar Hossain and James Aucoin of the University of South Alabama also call for applying the ethics of care to journalism. They sharply criticize coverage of the recent migrant crisis in the Mediterranean area, asserting that the media failed, unethically, to appreciate and report sufficiently the poignant stories of desperate people:

> We believe that much of the problem with the sensationalism, grandstanding, and jingoism found in the media reports of the migrant crisis occurred because of a lack of ethical behavior by the media. And, further, we argue that caring, as shown in the articles and Internet posts by the world's media after

82 Discomfiting realities are also opportunities

the photograph of the drowned young migrant boy appeared in the news media, can be seen as evidence of the type of reporting that can occur when journalists adopt a universal ethical standard of care… . Indeed, care ethics, if applied globally by journalists, can lead to more humane reporting about many stories, from global warming to local effects from international wars.[49]

The authors assert that the ethics of care

can specifically contribute to ethical decision making by teaching journalists to incorporate more sustained and focused attention to the suffering and discrimination of vulnerable groups in society such as women, children, and refugees… . Scholars have referred to how important it is to understand the situation of others by putting oneself into their positions. The concept of putting oneself in another's position also is applicable to ensure gender and racial equality in society. For example, even when one might support gender and racial equality, one may not completely understand the situation of others. If one puts oneself into their situations through empathy, then one gains a better understanding.[50]

These philosophical aspirations for the ethics of care in journalism are not dissimilar to media scholar Jay Rosen's averring that journalists should reach beyond the purely rational, to

set mind and soul in balance for a craft that draws on both… . The press needs to watch for places where we lose touch with the public world by letting our attention lapse, our indifference grow. It should keep itself alert to the points of contact between our felt troubles and larger issues that rise on the public screen.[51]

The Hutchins Commission

Especially significantly, applying the ethics of care to journalism squares remarkably well with the imperatives demanded by arguably the most prominent and trenchant appraisal of the American press in the twentieth century: the 1946 report of the Hutchins Commission, more properly The Commission on Freedom of the Press, chaired by Robert M. Hutchins, chancellor of the University of Chicago. The vice chairman of the privately financed commission was noted legal scholar Zechariah Chafee, Jr. of Harvard Law School, and it included ten other prestigious academicians, plus the influential chairman of the Federal Reserve Bank of New York, Beardsley Ruml—but no journalists.[52] They were "a group of intellectual superstars," in the words of Stephen Bates of the University of Nevada, Las Vegas, who just recently wrote the story of the extraordinary commission. "Many of its concerns remain timely," he writes.[53]

Existing codes of ethics **83**

Although preceding universal television and the internet, the Commission conveyed a forceful message that still rings true today, perhaps even more so with the multiplication of media. The Commission's report speaks in almost apocalyptic terms of the press's *mandatory duties and responsibilities* in the emerging post-war atomic world:

> With the means of self-destruction that are now at their disposal, men must live, if they are to live at all, by self-restraint, moderation, and mutual understanding. They get their picture of one another through the press. The press can be inflammatory, sensational, and irresponsible. If it is, it and its freedom will go down in the universal catastrophe. On the other hand, the press can do its duty by the new world that is struggling to be born. It can help create a world community by giving men everywhere knowledge of the world and of one another, by promoting comprehension and appreciation of the goals of a free society that shall embrace all men... . The Commission believes in realistic reporting of the events and forces that militate against the attainment of social goals as well as those which work for them. We must recognize, however, that the agencies of mass communication are an educational instrument, perhaps the most powerful there is, and they must assume a responsibility like that of educators in stating and clarifying the ideals toward which the community should strive.[54]

To be clear, the Commission was not at all pleased with contemporary post-war journalism:

> The news is twisted by the emphasis on firstness; on the novel and sensational; by the personal interests of owners; and by pressure groups. Too much of the regular output of the press consists of a miscellaneous succession of stories and images which have no relation to the typical lives of real people anywhere. Too often the result is meaninglessness, flatness, distortion, and the perpetuation of misunderstanding among widely scattered groups whose only contact is through these media.[55]

The Commission celebrated freedom of the press, but impatiently floated the threat of government regulation to get it right:

> the important thing is that the press accept the public standard and try for it. The legal right will stand if the moral right is realized or tolerably approximated. There is a point beyond which failure to realize the moral right will entail encroachment by the state upon the existing legal right.[56]

To avoid such state "encroachment," the Commission advised:

> We suggest that the press look upon itself as performing a public service of a professional kind... . An over-all social responsibility for the quality of press

84 Discomfiting realities are also opportunities

> service to the citizen cannot be escaped … This means that *the press must now take on the community's press objectives as its own objectives.*[57]

This implied some responsibility on the part of the community, but even this was put up to the press. As historian Bates puts it, "the commission contended that reinvigorating the democratic system was a job for journalists. A more responsible press would help to produce more responsible citizens."[58]

The commission's stirring call to arms, never realized but still worth considering today, cannot be accomplished by the press's being merely factual, accurate, truthful, honest and fair, as vital as those qualities are, especially in the debilitating age of "fake news" fostered by the forty-fifth president, Donald Trump.

So, imagine that the news media actually embrace the ethics of care. What kind of journalism would result? What would "social responsibility" demand? How would the "moral right" be realized?

As contemporary Australian philosopher and columnist Peter Singer views the world, ethical living is not simply a matter of obeying the ordinary rules of "you must not":

> It fails to consider the good we can do to others less fortunate than ourselves, not only in our own community, but anywhere within the reach of our help. We ought also to extend our concern to future generations …[59]

In the most concise of its many imperative admonitions, the Hutchins Commission declared tartly that the press "must supply the public need" as well as realize its "moral right."[60]

How might journalists size up these obligations today? While keeping the ethics of care in mind, let's look first at journalism's current working guidelines as expressed in professional codes of ethics.

Notes

1 Hume, op. cit. 360, 362.
2 Ibid. 431, 430.
3 Ibid. 96, 97. Italics in the original.
4 Ibid. 163.
5 Ibid. 162.
6 Baier, op. cit. 89.
7 Held, op. cit. 21, 52.
8 Slote, op. cit. 17.
9 Nel Noddings, *Caring: A Feminist Approach to Ethics and Moral Education*, Berkeley and Los Angeles: University of California Press, 1984, 1.
10 Nel Noddings, Ibid., Preface to the 2013 Edition, renamed *Caring: A Relational Approach to Ethics and Moral Education.*
11 Ibid. 8, 31.
12 Ibid. 43.
13 Ibid. 79.

Existing codes of ethics **85**

14 Ibid. 96.
15 Carol Gilligan, *In a Different Voice: Psychological Theory and Women's Development*, Cambridge and London: Harvard University Press, 1982.
16 Ibid. 70.
17 Ibid. 93, 94.
18 Ibid. 83.
19 Ibid. 72.
20 Ibid. 73, 74.
21 Ibid. 158, 159.
22 Ibid. 163.
23 Ibid. 164–65.
24 Ibid. 173, 174.
25 Annette C. Baier, *Moral Prejudices: Essays on Ethics*, Cambridge and London: Harvard University Press, 1994, 62.
26 Ibid. 18–19, 30.
27 "Act only on that maxim whereby thou canst at the same time will that it should become a universal law."
28 Baier, op. cit. 23.
29 Ibid. 25.
30 Ibid. 56, 57–58.
31 Ibid. 94.
32 Ibid. 297.
33 Virginia Held, *The Ethics of Care: Personal, Political, and Global*, Oxford and New York: Oxford University Press, 2006.
34 Ibid. 129, 131.
35 Ibid. 44.
36 Ibid. 71, 73.
37 Ibid. 83.
38 Ibid. 159.
39 Ibid. 139.
40 Ibid. 84, 85. Italics mine.
41 Ibid. 122, 123. Italics mine.
42 Michael Slote. *The Ethics of Care and Empathy*, London and New York: Routledge, 2007, 3.
43 Ibid. 125, 128.
44 Ibid. 118, 120
45 Ibid. 107.
46 Michael S. Gazzaniga, *The Ethical Brain*, New York and Washington: Dana Press, 2005, 177. Italics added.
47 Walter Brueggemann, *Virus as a Summons to Faith: Biblical Reflections in a Time of Loss, Grief, and Anxiety*, Eugene, Oregon: Cascade Books, 2020, 32.
48 Bastiaan Vanacker and John Breslin, "Ethics of Care: More Than Just Another Tool to Bash the Media?", *Journal of Mass Media Ethics*, 21:2–3, 2006, 196–214, DOI: 10.1080/08900523.2006.9679733, https://doi.org/10.1080/08900523.2006.9679733
49 Mohammad Delwar Hossain and James Aucoin (2018), "The Ethics of Care as a Universal Framework for Global Journalism," *Journal of Media Ethics*, 33:4, pp. 198–211, published online Nov. 1, 2018, https://www.tandfonline.com/doi/abs/10.1080/23736992.2018.1509713
50 Ibid.
51 Jay Rosen, *What are Journalists For?* New Haven and London: Yale University Press, 1999, 297–98.

52 The Commission on Freedom of the Press, *A Free and Responsible Press: A General Report on Mass Communication: Newspapers, Radio, Motion Pictures, Magazines, and Books*, originally published in Chicago: The University of Chicago Press, 1946, reproduced by Andesite Press, an imprint of Creative Media Partners. The back cover declares immodestly: "This work has been selected by scholars as being culturally important, and is part of the knowledge base of civilization as we know it." The other members of the Commission: John M. Clark, economics, Columbia University; John Dickinson, law, University of Pennsylvania; William F. Hocking, philosophy, Harvard; Harold D. Lasswell, law, Yale; Archibald D. MacLeish, Pulitzer Prize-winning poet, former Librarian of Congress, former assistant secretary of state (and later professor of rhetoric and oratory at Harvard); Charles E. Merriam, political science, University of Chicago; Reinhold Niebuhr, ethics and philosophy of religion, Union Theological Seminary; Robert Redfield, anthropology, University of Chicago; Arthur M. Schlesinger, history, Harvard; and George N. Shuster, president, Hunter College.

53 Stephen Bates, *An Aristocracy of Critics: Luce, Hutchins, Niebuhr, and The Committee That Redefined Freedom of the Press*, New Haven and London: Yale University Press, 2020, 2, 7.

54 Ibid. 4, 27–8.

55 Ibid. 68.

56 Ibid. 131.

57 Ibid. 92, 126. Italics in the original.

58 Stephen Bates, op. cit. 219.

59 Peter Singer, *Ethics in the Real World: 82 Brief Essays on Things That Matter*, Princeton: Princeton University Press, 2016, ix.

60 Hutchins Commission, op. cit. 131.

8

CURRENT CODES OF ETHICS RENDER HIGH PROFESSIONAL STANDARDS THAT ENDURE, AND SHOULD

We observed in Chapter 1 that the ethics of care, while challenging the reasoned morality seen by journalism ethicists as the intellectual foundation of today's journalism codes of ethics, does not take issue with the codes themselves. In fact, care philosophers don't address journalism ethics at all, with the exception of Virginia Held's brief admonition noted in the previous chapter.

So let's examine what the relationship is, or, more accurately, might be.

Most major news organizations have an admirable code of ethics or a code of standards, and it's published.[1] They have great similarities. They agree that journalists should do the following:

- Pursue truth.
- Be courageous.
- Be accurate.
- Be honest.
- Be fair.
- Be transparent.
- Verify.
- Act independently.
- Identify yourself as a journalist.
- Get a response from anyone criticized in your story.
- Attribute your information; name sources.
- Use anonymous sources only when you can't get the story any other way.
- Never plagiarize; respect copyright.
- Avoid conflicts of interest, for example, investing in an industry you cover.
- Do not participate in partisan political activity.
- Do not accept gifts or special treatment from sources.
- Do not favor advertisers or sponsors; label sponsored content.

DOI: 10.4324/9781003140337-11

88 Discomfiting realities are also opportunities

- Do not name children or the victims of sex crimes.
- Be considerate of the impact on sources and subjects of your story.
- Distinguish news from commentary.
- Admit mistakes and correct them.

Conflicts of interest

In addition to these common and admirable expectations, the ethics codes of numerous major news organizations (some listed in the Appendix) lay down many additional markers, sometimes at great length. In particular, they stress the need to avoid conflicts of interest, variously described. It's at the top of a very long list at business-news specialist Bloomberg News, whose parent company, Bloomberg LP, makes its money by renting proprietary data terminals to securities firms and other financial businesses. Bloomberg's two thousand three-hundred reporters and editors are counseled:

> We are in the often-difficult position of reporting on our customers. Altering a story because it embarrasses a company or individual would create the perception that we shade our news judgment under pressure, and that would cost us our integrity. When exposing the wrongdoing of others, we should be above reproach. The greater the story's impact, the greater our obligation to withstand the most exacting scrutiny.

Conflict of interest is also the first ethics concern of *The New York Times*:

> Conflicts of interest, real or apparent, may come up in many areas. They may involve the relationships of staff members with readers, news sources, advocacy groups, advertisers, or competitors; with one another, or with the newspaper or its parent company. And at a time when two-career families are the norm, the civic and professional activities of spouses, family and companions can create conflicts or the appearance of conflicts.... In some cases, disclosure is enough. But if The Times considers the problem serious, the staff member may have to withdraw from certain coverage. Sometimes an assignment may have to be modified or a beat changed. In a few instances, a staff member may have to move to a different department — from business and financial news, say, to the culture desk — to avoid the appearance of conflict.

The Times also sees a different kind of conflict of interest: "Clearly, romantic involvement with a news source would foster an appearance of partiality." In 2018, *The Times* abruptly moved one young reporter, Ali Watkins, from Washington to New York, after it learned that many of her scoops on national intelligence came from a romantic partner thirty years her senior, a married man who was a long-time employee of the Senate Intelligence Committee.[2] *The Times* itself recounted that their three-year affair "is now part of a federal investigation that has rattled the world of Washington journalists and the sources they rely on." The story quoted one of Watkins's former editors. "People all across Washington are in all sorts of various relationships," Ryan Grim, Watkins's one-time editor at The Huffington Post, said in an interview. "You manage it, you put up walls, but you can't pretend that you're not human. Ali is a great reporter and I trust her judgment."[3]

The Associated Press, like other news organizations greatly concerned about conflicts, is comparatively concise: "We avoid behavior or activities that create a conflict of interest that compromises our ability to report the news fairly and accurately, uninfluenced by any person or action."

The Texas Tribune, an online nonprofit that subsists mainly on donations, subscriptions and sponsorships, declares:

> Those who contribute to the Tribune do so with the understanding that we are only beholden to great journalism. Our fundraisers inform all potential donors —individuals, foundations, corporate sponsors, underwriters — that their contributions to the Tribune do not entitle them to preferential treatment or to relationships with newsroom staff, and in no way protect them from investigations or scrutiny.

Similarly, another nonprofit, the Center for Public Integrity, states that it "will not hesitate to report on its donors when events warrant."

The *Los Angeles Times* addresses a concern peculiar to coverage of the entertainment industry, admonishing its employees to

> take special care not to create the appearance of conflicts should they seek work in that industry … . No Times journalist who covers the entertainment industry should ever propose a script or movie idea — or any other entertainment product — to anyone working in that industry.

Possible conflicts of interest involving personal investments are accorded, not surprisingly, great emphasis by Dow Jones & Co., publisher of *The Wall Street Journal* and *Barron's* financial weekly. In 1984, *The Journal* fired a stock market writer, G. Foster Winans, for relaying to a broker friend stock information to be printed in the next day's paper, enabling the broker to profit handsomely and share the proceeds with Winans and his roommate. At Winans' subsequent trial for insider trading and fraud, his lawyer admitted that Winans knew he was violating the corporate policy of *The Journal's* parent, Dow Jones & Co., requiring confidentiality of information learned at work.[4] Dow Jones subsequently tightened its code of ethics so that it now states: "Any and all information and other material obtained by a Dow Jones employee in connection with his or her employment is strictly the property of Dow Jones." The Code then specifically prohibits trading securities on inside information obtained at work, any "speculation or the appearance of speculation," short-term trading, short-selling [betting that a security will decline], investing in options or futures, and investing in any industry the reporter covers. Dow Jones also imposes this unusual requirement: "all Dow Jones employees shall be required each year to

90 Discomfiting realities are also opportunities

provide a written attestation that they have read and abided by this code during the previous calendar year."

Other news organizations covering business and finance, such as the Associated Press, giant nonprofit ProPublica, and *The New York Times*, also lay down rigid investment prohibitions. *The Times* elaborates: "A book editor, for example, may not invest in a publishing house, a health writer in a pharmaceutical company or a Pentagon reporter in a mutual fund specializing in defense stocks.... Because of the sensitivity of their assignments, some business financial staff members may not own stock in any company (other than the New York Times Company). These include the Market Place writer, other market columnists, the regular writer of the daily stock market column, reporters regularly assigned to mergers and acquisitions, the daily markets editor, the Sunday investing editor, the Sunday Business editor, the business and financial editor and his or her deputies."

Another particular kind of conflict of interest, accepting gifts or favors from news sources, is universally prohibited, but still is subject to considerable elaboration in many journalism codes of ethics. The *Washington Post* is typically blunt:

> We pay our own way. We accept no gifts from news sources. We accept no free trips. We neither seek nor accept preferential treatment that might be rendered because of the positions we hold. Exceptions to the no-gift rule are few and obvious — invitations to meals, for example, may be accepted when they are occasional and innocent but not when they are repeated and their purpose is deliberately calculating.

TEGNA, operator of more than four dozen television stations, instructs its employees to refuse gifts from any entity that just *might* be covered by *any* of them: "personnel in news operations may not accept gifts, meals or entertainment from any individuals or organizations that are covered by (or likely to be covered by) a TEGNA news organization." The *Los Angeles Times*, acknowledging receipt of much unsolicited merchandise for review, says a reporter may keep books, CDs and the like, but "Items of significant value — such as electronic equipment, rare books and premium wine — must be returned." Similarly, the *Chicago Tribune* states: "Unsolicited merchandise whose value exceeds that of a key chain will be donated to charity by the newspaper."

Another universally prohibited conflict of interest, political activity, also commands considerable attention in journalism codes. Make no mistake about it. At Dow Jones, "Partisan political activity includes passing out buttons, posting partisan comments on social-networking sites, blogging, soliciting campaign contributions, hosting a fundraiser for a partisan candidate, as well as making a financial contribution to a candidate's campaign." *New York Times* employees are admonished to "recognize that a bumper sticker on the family car or a campaign sign on the lawn may be misread as theirs," and to "be sensitive that perfectly proper political activity by their spouses, family or companions may nevertheless create conflicts of interest or the appearance of conflict." AP employees "may not run for political office or accept political appointment; nor may they perform public relations work for politicians or their groups."

Concerned about partisan fund-raising, National Public Radio (NPR) recently extended its code of ethics to cover programs not produced by NPR but acquired and broadcast by it. As reported by NPR itself:

> The changes follow the debate sparked when *The Washington Post* reported that Diane Rehm, the host of the NPR-distributed *The Diane Rehm Show*, was taking part in fundraising dinners for Compassion & Choices. That non-profit organization's activities include lobbying for states to permit medically-assisted death. Rehm's appearances were in violation of the code of ethics covering NPR journalists. [The code states that "we should not sign petitions or otherwise contribute support or money to political causes or public campaigns."[5]] But ... Her show is produced by WAMU-FM, the Washington, D.C. public radio station.... NPR journalists are expected to follow the code, obviously, but the new wording says it also applies to "those who work for shows, podcasts and programming that are not part of the News division."[6]

Fairness

Always a standard in journalism ethics codes, fairness is accorded substantial emphasis in many, in particular to require a response from anyone depicted unfavorably in a story. The Associated Press insists: "We must be fair. Whenever we portray someone in a negative light, we must make a real effort to obtain a response from that person." That "real effort," news organizations agree, must be more than perfunctory. The *Los Angeles Times* declares,

> In covering contentious matters — strikes, abortion, gun control and the like — we seek out intelligent, articulate views from all perspectives. Reporters should try genuinely to understand all points of view, rather than simply grab quick quotations to create a semblance of balance.

In an extensive elaboration on fairness, Bloomberg says, "If the subjects of a story are surprised by what we publish, we have failed at making a good-faith effort." The concern extends to securities: "When an analyst or investor pans a stock or bond, we should ask company officers whether they consider the assessment valid." ProPublica indicates that publication may have to be delayed to get the necessary response: "We should give them a reasonable amount of time to get back to us before we publish."

Company reputation

Some news organizations admonish their employees to live up to the company's good name and reputation. Dow Jones puts it this way:

92 Discomfiting realities are also opportunities

All companies profess business integrity. But the impact of our work on the work of others, and on their lives and fortunes, places special responsibilities upon all Dow Jones employees. The clear implication of these beliefs is that the responsibility for safeguarding and growing a company that lives up to this code lies with each and every one of us. Every Dow Jones employee holds a position of trust.

Bloomberg says simply: "Our name is Bloomberg. It is a good name and must never be tarnished by anything we say or do."

The National Public Radio Code of Ethics states, in italics:

> *Because our words and actions can damage the public's opinion of NPR, we comport ourselves in ways that honor our professional impartiality. We have opinions, like all people. But the public deserves factual reporting and informed analysis without our opinions influencing what they hear or see. So we strive to report and produce stories that transcend our biases and treat all views fairly. We aggressively challenge our own perspectives and pursue a diverse range of others, aiming always to present the truth as completely as we can tell it.*[7]

In 2010, NPR abruptly fired commentator Juan Williams for voicing a hostile opinion about Muslims, saying it violated the ethics code. On Fox News, where he was also a paid commentator, Williams had expressed agreement with host Bill O'Reilly's explaining why he blamed Muslims for the September 2001 attacks on New York and Washington:

> I mean, look, Bill, I'm not a bigot. You know the kind of books I've written about the civil rights movement in this country. But when I get on a plane, I got to tell you, if I see people who are in Muslim garb, and I think, you know, they are identifying themselves first and foremost as Muslims, I get worried. I get nervous.

Dismissing Williams, NPR's chief executive officer, Vivian Schiller, declared: "Our reporters, our hosts and our new analysts should not be injecting their own views about a controversial issue as part of their story. They should be reporting the story."[8]

A journalist's personal connections may create story opportunities, but may also raise ethical questions. In 2019, *The Tampa Bay Times* reported that a TEGNA, Inc. television station, WTSP in Tampa-St. Petersburg, Florida, had dismissed a long-time anchor, Reginald Roundtree, without public explanation. According to *The Times*,

> Roundtree's lawyer said TEGNA told them they let the anchor go because of questions raised in a recent *Times* article about the news anchor's professional ethics in using his close personal friendship with a local criminal defense attorney to land an interview with his client in a high-profile shooting case.[9]

The exclusive interview, with a white man accused of manslaughter in the death of a black man during an altercation about a handicap parking space, had taken place in the county jail.

Although TEGNA didn't elaborate publicly, the first sentences of its Principles of Ethical Journalism state:

> TEGNA is committed to the highest ethical standards and dedicated to the principles of truth, independence, public interest, fair play and integrity. These principles apply to everything we do, from gathering information to reporting and producing content.

The Times later reported that Roundtree, age sixty, had sued the station, alleging retaliation for raising a complaint about age discrimination, noting that his lawsuit substantially reiterated claims already deemed inconclusive by the federal Equal Employment Opportunity Commission.[10]

Corrections

Commonly mentioned in most ethics codes, corrections are given elaborate, almost contrite, attention by many major news organizations. The nonprofit Marshall Project, which focuses on criminal justice, after declaring that truth and accuracy come first, adds this: "Because journalism is produced by human beings, we will sometimes get things wrong. So our second rule is, when we fall short of our expectations, we will promptly and prominently acknowledge our mistakes and correct them." The Associated Press makes its point with italics:

> When we're wrong, we must say so as soon as possible. *When we make a correction, we point it out both to subscriber editors (e.g. in Editor's notes, metadata, advisories to TV newsrooms) and in ways that news consumers can see it (bottom-of-story corrections, correction notes on graphics, photo captions, etc.)* ... A correction must always be labeled a correction. We do not use euphemisms such as "recasts," "fixes," "clarifies," "minor edits" or "changes" when correcting a factual error.

The *Los Angeles Times* declares, "Readers and staff members who bring mistakes to our attention deserve our gratitude. A staff member who receives a complaint about the accuracy of our work should inform an editor." In the same vein, Bloomberg states:

> People complaining about a story should always be treated with courtesy. Ask them to identify any error. In cases where the fairness of the story is questioned, be prepared to listen and provide supervisors a summary of the complaints. Deference is sensible and honorable.

If a mistake is serious, the *Washington Post* emphasizes:

94 Discomfiting realities are also opportunities

> A correction that calls into question the entire substance of an article, raises a significant ethical matter or addresses whether an article did not meet our standards, may require an Editor's Note and be followed by an explanation of what is at issue.

Baring all, the Texas Tribune, after correcting errors, actually maintains a public running list of its corrections.

Anonymous sources

All journalism ethics codes frown on using anonymous sources, but everyone does it anyway. The *Washington Post* explains the apparent contradiction this way:

> We recognize that there are situations in which we can give our readers better, fuller information by allowing sources to remain unnamed than if we insist on naming them. We realize that in many circumstances, sources will be unwilling to reveal to us information about corruption in their own organizations, or high-level policy disagreements, for example, if disclosing their identities could cost them their jobs or expose them to harm. Nevertheless, granting anonymity to a source should not be done casually or automatically.

The *Post* adds: "We must strive to tell our readers as much as we can about why our unnamed sources deserve our confidence. Our <u>obligation</u> is to serve readers, not sources."

The *Post's* code then goes on to explain, as much for the benefit of readers as its own staff, the code words of attribution especially common in reporting on government and politics that reporters and sources understand to justify using anonymous sources.

"**On background**, or **not for attribution**: These both mean the same thing: information that can be attributed to 'a police department official' or 'a player on the team' who is not named."

"**Deep background**: This is a tricky category, to be avoided if possible. Information accepted on 'deep background' can be included in the story, but not attributed."

> **Off the record**: This is the trickiest of all, because so many people misuse the term. By the traditional definition, off-the-record information cannot be used for publication or in further reporting... . If they really mean off the record as the term is traditionally defined, then in most circumstances, we should avoid listening to such information at all. We do not want to be hamstrung by a source who tells us something that becomes unusable because it is provided on an off-the-record basis.

Tricky indeed.

The Associated Press sets forth similar definitions, and adds: "We must explain in the story why the source requested anonymity. And, when it's relevant, we must describe the source's motive for disclosing the information." Bloomberg is similarly cautious:

> People who routinely tell reporters something only when their names and positions are withheld may have something to conceal—a situation that should make any reporter or editor suspicious, if not skittish, about justifying the concession to anonymity. We want to be the agent of the reader, not of our sources.

Another take on fairness regards coverage of criminal suspects. The *Los Angeles Times* lays down a general rule that it "does not identify suspects of criminal investigations who have not been charged or arrested." But, if

> the prominence of the suspect, the importance of the case or the public statements of law enforcement … warrant an exception… . we must take great care that our sourcing is reliable and that law enforcement officials have a reasonable basis for considering the individual a suspect.

Furthermore, if the identified suspect "ultimately is not charged, we should make that known in follow-up coverage. The follow-up should be played comparably to the original reporting if possible."

Plagiarism

In journalism, as Bloomberg puts it, plagiarism "is a capital crime … a theft. Be prepared to lose your job if you plagiarize. Always credit original reporting to those who did the legwork, and never reproduce quotes made to others as if we heard them ourselves." Similarly, the Associated Press emphasizes, in italics: "*When we match a report that a news outlet was first with due to significant reporting effort, we should mention that the other outlet first reported it.*" At *The New York Times*, "Staff members who plagiarize or who knowingly or recklessly provide false information for publication betray our fundamental pact with our readers. We will not tolerate such behavior." Bloomberg notes that plagiarism may entail a violation of law as well as ethics: "While facts are in the public domain, the selection and arrangement of those facts may constitute creative expression, which can be protected by *copyright*."

Social media

NPR is particularly concerned about the language employed by its journalists when they take to social media. It insists, "We shouldn't take the bait from trolls and sink to their level. We don't use foul language." However, the NPR code goes on,

96 Discomfiting realities are also opportunities

> There is room to be a little looser with our language on social media. There are words and phrases that, if written with the right tone, are OK. Take 'badass,' for example. Used as a compliment, it's a wonderful word.

As a general rule,

> We challenge those putting information on social media to provide evidence. We raise doubts and ask questions when we have concerns — sometimes 'knocking down' rumors is of enormous value to our readers.

NPR journalists who receive social media criticisms of their work are advised,

> If the message is unpleasant but not threatening and is about work you've done, try responding with something along these lines – "I appreciate constructive feedback. Can you tell me more about what concerned you?" If the person responds constructively, you've got a conversation going.

The Center for Public Integrity also endeavors to make constructive use of social media,

> using social networking platforms to distribute its work and build an engaged audience. Staff members are mindful that their actions online may be seen as a representation of the Center. They are therefore expected to be polite and avoid any impression of partisanship.

Less prescriptive, the *Washington Post* simply reminds its staff,

> Even as we express ourselves in more personal and informal ways to forge better connections with our readers, we must be ever mindful of preserving the reputation of The Washington Post for journalistic excellence, fairness and independence. Every comment or link we share should be considered public information, regardless of privacy settings.

Libel and other legal concerns

Unusual among major new organizations, Bloomberg's ethics statement also gives attention to considerations of law, especially libel. "Telling the truth is the surest way to avoid libel," the company says, while advising its journalists to "be humble," "be specific," "weigh your words" and "never let down your libel guard." This caution is motivated in part by the company's vast international operations carried on by more than one hundred foreign bureaus. Thus, "In many nations, truth is not an absolute defense;" "in many countries, an organization that publishes a libelous statement made in another publication adopts it as its own—and can be held just as liable;" and other nations "may hold a reporter in contempt for publishing court papers" that would be considered public documents in the United States. If Bloomberg publishes a summary of another organization's story that "accuses or implies wrong-doing or incompetence, try to obtain comment or denial from the person, company or organization whose reputation is at stake."

Bloomberg also touches on other legal concerns. It notes that "privacy claims cover the sense of intrusion arising from publishing true, but private, facts about people," so "be wary about publishing medical facts, names and photos of juveniles, or financial data that isn't public and directly related to the thrust of a story." Bloomberg lists thirty-eight states in which a reporter may legally record a phone call, cautioning that "All other states require the consent of all parties to a phone call before recording." And,

> Reporters who interview people with firsthand knowledge or evidence of wrongdoing may become targets of law-enforcement agencies wanting to search those notes for evidence. A court sympathetic to law enforcement will require the reporter to disclose the notes or face a contempt charge.

Helpfully, the statement notes that "Bloomberg News always has a lawyer available, including a network of media lawyers around the world who can be called for assistance."

Nevertheless, fabrications happen

In the face of these thoughtful and thorough codes of ethics, American journalism from time to time has experienced humiliating instances of flagrant violations of the profession's first principle: truth.

In 2003, a young reporter for *The Times*, Jayson Blair, resigned when he was found to have written a number of prominent but bogus stories. As *The Times* itself reported subsequently, in embarrassment:

> A staff reporter for The New York Times committed frequent acts of journalistic fraud while covering significant news events in recent months, an investigation by Times journalists has found. The widespread fabrication and plagiarism represent a profound betrayal of trust and a low point in the 152-year history of the newspaper. The reporter, Jayson Blair, 27, misled readers and Times colleagues with dispatches that purported to be from Maryland, Texas and other states, when often he was far away, in New York. He fabricated comments. He concocted scenes. He lifted material from other newspapers and wire services. He selected details from photographs to create the impression he had been somewhere or seen someone, when he had not.
>
> And he used these techniques to write falsely about emotionally charged moments in recent history, from the deadly sniper attacks in suburban Washington to the anguish of families grieving for loved ones killed in Iraq.[11]

98 Discomfiting realities are also opportunities

The fraud was so egregious that *Times* Executive Editor Howell Raines and Managing Editor Gerald Boyd also were forced out.

In 1980, another young reporter, Janet Cooke of the *Washington Post*, wrote an arresting story about a third-generation heroin addict, an eight-year-old named Jimmy, in a low-income Washington neighborhood. Her story won a Pulitzer Prize. But suspicions promptly arose about Cooke's claimed educational and personal background, then the focus shifted to the validity of her story, and under intense questioning by her editors she finally admitted immediately after her Pulitzer was announced that there was no Jimmy, he was a composite. The *Post*, deeply embarrassed, fired Cooke and returned the Pulitzer Prize.[12]

At Gannett's USA TODAY, the Principles of Ethical Conduct for Newsrooms are clear: "WE ARE COMMITTED TO:

I. Seeking and reporting the truth in a truthful way
    - We will be honest in the way we gather, report and present news - with relevancy, persistence, context, thoroughness, balance, and fairness in mind."

But a scandal that erupted in 2004 showed how difficult it may be to ensure the veracity of foreign correspondents' work, for they commonly operate independently. An internal investigation of stories by a long-time star foreign correspondent, Jack Kelley, led to his resignation. The Associated Press reported that the newspaper found many falsehoods:

> For one of the stories that helped make him a Pulitzer Prize finalist in 2001, Kelley wrote that he was an eyewitness to a suicide bombing in Jerusalem and described the carnage in graphic detail. But the investigation showed that the man Kelley described as the bomber could not have been the culprit, and his description of three decapitated victims was contradicted by police.
>
> The newspaper also said "the evidence strongly contradicted" other published accounts by Kelley: that he spent the night with Egyptian terrorists in 1997; met a vigilante Jewish settler named Avi Shapiro in 2001; watched a Pakistani student unfold a picture of the Sears Tower and say, "This one is mine," in 2001; interviewed the daughter of an Iraqi general in 2003; or went on a high-speed hunt for Osama bin Laden in 2003.

"Hotel, phone or other records contradicted Kelley's explanations of how he reported stories from Egypt, Russia, Chechnya, Kosovo, Yugoslavia, Cuba and Pakistan, the newspaper said."[13]

The New Republic was embarrassed twice in the 1990s, by Stephen Glass, who admitted fabricating all or part of twenty-seven stories,[14] and by Ruth Shalit, who admitted plagiarizing in three stories.[15] Respected NBC anchor Brian Williams, rated number one in television evening news, was suspended and dethroned in 2015 for embellishing his role and the dangers he encountered in a military helicopter flight in Iraq.[16]

These glaring, sad yarns stand as continuing reminders of how heavily all ethical news organizations rely on the faithful professional conduct of their individual journalists—notwithstanding the organizations' thoughtful, admirable codes of ethics.

Back to the ethics of care

What's called for at this point in our analysis is to consider whether today's ethical journalism standards are compatible with the ethics of care. In this, we simply set aside the rational moral philosophies seen by journalism ethicists as the intellectual foundations of journalism codes of ethics—duty, utility and rights or justice—recognizing that they are entirely incompatible with the empathy-based ethics of care. We can do this because the journalism codes of ethics, while certainly moral, are not dependent on the rational moral philosophies; they stand well by themselves.

As the previous chapter states, the ethics of care calls on people to reach out purposefully, helpfully, at least to family and friends to neighbors, perhaps even to strangers in need. The moral measure is not just the effort, it's the results. The help must be effective, productive, beneficial. It must make a difference in people's lives.

So, before we proceed, we need to consider whether there's a way to reconcile the rational moral philosophies reflected in journalism's contemporary codes of ethics with the empathy-based ethics of care, so emphatically contrary to Kant especially, as well as to other esteemed rationalists Jeremy Bentham, John Stuart Mill, John Locke and John Rawls. It seems dubious. Michael Slote tackles this head-on: "care ethics and traditional approaches like Kantian ethics or liberalism are actually inconsistent with one another and cannot, therefore, be harmonized or integrated." However, in Slote's view, that incompatibility doesn't rule out morality. He finds it "reasonable to think that we can justify moral claims by reference to empathy."[17]

That, indeed, must be our resolution. Surely journalism's codes of ethics can be, perhaps must be, understood to have a moral as well as ethical purpose. After all, ethics is "the discipline dealing with what is good and bad or right and wrong or with moral duty and obligation."[18] That definition suits ethical journalism just fine. It means that we can proceed to adopt the ethics of care without rejecting current journalism ethics on the grounds that they align with the traditional rational moral philosophies rejected by the ethics of care. Both the rational philosophies and journalism ethics have served the profession well through the twentieth century and a bit beyond. Put simply, they are still valid, as far as they go, but they're insufficient for the pressing societal needs of the twenty-first century. We will consider how the ethics of care not only co-exists comfortably with the journalism codes, but in fact supports a more ambitious role of ethical journalism necessary for this new century. Taken together they lay the groundwork for authoritative, powerful journalism, solid stories that go beyond facts and events but aren't simply opinion or commentary. Thus, the author of an empathy-based story about racial inequity or economic disparity or climate change necessarily incorporates the authority and

100 Discomfiting realities are also opportunities

credibility afforded by truth, accuracy, fairness, facts, honesty, sensitivity, transparency and the rest.

This is not a new notion. It simply needs to bulk up.

Here's an example combing the best of care ethics and codes of ethics, the top of a fine enterprise story from *The New York Times* of July 5, 2020, reporting on abundant data obtained by a Freedom of Information Act request to the Centers for Disease Control and Prevention:

Coronavirus cases per ten thousand people:

White	23
All	38
Black	62
Latino	73

The Fullest Look Yet at the Racial Inequity of Coronavirus, by Richard A. Oppel Jr., Robert Gebeloff, K. K. Rebecca Lai, Will Wright and Mitch Smith, July 5, 2020.

Teresa and Marvin Bradley can't say for sure how they got the coronavirus. Maybe Ms. Bradley, a Michigan nurse, brought it from her hospital. Maybe it came from a visiting relative. Maybe it was something else entirely.

What is certain—according to new federal data that provides the most comprehensive look to date on nearly 1.5 million coronavirus patients in America—is that the Bradleys are not outliers.

Racial disparities in who contracts the virus have played out in big cities like Milwaukee and New York, but also in smaller metropolitan areas like Grand Rapids, Michigan, where the Bradleys live. Those inequities became painfully apparent when Ms. Bradley, who is black, was wheeled through the emergency room.

"Everybody in there was African-American," she said. "Everybody was."

Early numbers had shown that black and Latino people were being harmed by the virus at higher rates. But the new federal data—made available after *The New York Times* sued the Centers for Disease Control and Prevention—reveals a clearer and more complete picture: Black and Latino people have been disproportionately affected by the coronavirus in a widespread manner that spans the country, throughout hundreds of counties in urban, suburban and rural areas, and across all age groups.

[The story goes on at length to delineate and plot on three large maps the race or ethnicity with the highest coronavirus rate in each county of the entire country, and to detail with still more data, interviews and photographs the extent and disparities of the infection nationwide. Significantly, at the end of story, in the interest of transparency, the paper published several paragraphs explaining its methodology, including this:

> The data was acquired after The Times filed a Freedom of Information Act suit. The C.D.C. provided data on 1.45 million cases reported to the agency by states through the end of May. Many of the records were missing critical information The Times requested, like the race and home county of an

infected person, so the analysis was based on the nearly 640,000 cases for which the race, ethnicity and home county of a patient was known.][19]

This is superb journalism, entirely consistent with both existing standards of ethical journalism and the ethics of care. More is needed. American society, and democracy, are threatened.

At the same time, it must be noted that the high-minded company ethics codes, while necessary and important, are in the main defensive, designed to produce unassailably ethical, truthful journalism, avoiding errors and any concomitant legal consequences. So the journalism codes are fully coincident with the empathetic aspirations of the ethics of care—the affirmative intention, even obligation, to reach out to persons in need and bring about discernible amelioration of their condition.

Still, there's a hint of the more ambitious ethics of care in some aspirational wording of the codes of ethics of two leading journalism professional associations. The Society of Professional Journalists code proclaims, "Boldly tell the story of the diversity and magnitude of the human experience. Seek sources whose voices we seldom hear." Similarly, the Radio Television Digital News Directors code declares: "Journalism empowers viewers, listeners and readers to make more informed decisions for themselves; it does not tell people what to believe or how to feel… . Journalism challenges assumptions, rejects stereotypes and illuminates – even where it cannot eliminate – ignorance."

The tone of these association statements is quite consistent with the ethics of care, and, as we've noted earlier, also with the imperative admonition of the 1946 Hutchins Commission: the press "must supply the public need" and realize its "moral right."[20]

Most journalists want to do the right thing, ideally, try to make a difference. So it's quite understandable that even those who subscribe, perhaps quietly, to the humanitarian aspirations of the ethics of care, would at the same time quite naturally hold to truth, accuracy, fairness, sensitivity, transparency and all the other fine standards of their organization's codes of ethics.

One may wonder, though, whether ethical journalism actually prevails, in this time of declining newspaper finances and innumerable, unbridled voices—the vast international cacophony on the internet.

We will explore that.

Notes

1 Fox News does not, according to *The Washington Post's* media columnist Margaret Sullivan in 2018: "When Fox News Staffers Break Ethics Rules, Discipline Follows — or Does It?" *The Washington Post*, November 29, 2018. https://www.washingtonpost.com/lifestyle/style/when-fox-news-staffers-break-ethics-rules-discipline-follows--or-does-it/2018/11/28/02a11b98-f32a-11e8-80d0-f7e1948d55f4_story.html

2 Michael M. Grynbaum, "New York Times Reassigns Reporter in Leak Case," *The New York Times*, July 3, 2018, https://www.nytimes.com/2018/07/03/business/media/ali-watkins-times-reporter-memo.html

102 Discomfiting realities are also opportunities

3 Michael M. Grynbaum, Scott Shane and Emily Flitter, "How an Affair Between a Reporter and a Security Aide Has Rattled Washington Media," *The New York Times*, June 24, 2018, https://www.nytimes.com/2018/06/24/business/media/james-wolfe-ali-watkins-leaks-reporter.html
4 Tamar Lewin, "Reporter's Trial Begins; Insider Issue Is Argued," *The New York Times*, January 22, 1985, https://www.nytimes.com/1985/01/22/business/reporter-s-trial-begins-insider-issue-is-argued.html. Winans was convicted. Eleanor Randolph, "Ex-Reporter Convicted of Fraud," *Washington Post*, June 25, 1985, https://www.washingtonpost.com/archive/politics/1985/06/25/ex-reporter-convicted-of-fraud/5061efec-cc1a-4e49-b6e3-e045f5c6b64a/
5 "Impartiality as Citizens and Public Figures," NPR Code of Ethics, https://www.npr.org/about-npr/688413430/impartiality
6 Elizabeth Jensen, "NPR Updates Ethics Code to Cover Acquired Programming," March 26, 2015, https://www.npr.org/sections/publiceditor/2015/03/26/395535110/npr-updates-ethics-code-to-cover-acquired-programming
7 "Impartiality," NPR Code of Ethics, https://www.npr.org/about-npr/688413430/impartiality
8 David Folkenflik, "NPR Dismisses News Analyst Juan Williams,'"All Things Considered," National Public Radio, October 21, 2010, https://www.npr.org/templates/story/story.php?storyId=130732174
9 Kathryn Varn, "Channel 10 Anchor Reginald Roundtree Fired after Two Decades," *The Tampa Bay Times*, https://www.tampabay.com/news/publicsafety/anchor-reginald-roundtree-at-channel-10-news-more-than-20-years-fired-after-internal-review-20190208/
10 Kathryn Varn, "Ousted Channel 10 Anchor Reginald Roundtree Sues Former Employer," *The Tampa Bay Times*, October 22, 2019, https://www.tampabay.com/news/business/2019/10/22/ousted-channel-10-anchor-reginald-roundtree-sues-former-employer/
11 Dan Barry, David Barstow, Jonathan D. Glater, Adam Liptak and Jacques Steinberg, "CORRECTING THE RECORD; Times Reporter Who Resigned Leaves Long Trail of Deception," *The New York Times*, May 11, 2003, https://www.nytimes.com/2003/05/11/us/correcting-the-record-times-reporter-who-resigned-leaves-long-trail-of-deception.html
12 Matt Schudel and Emily Langer, "Bill Green, Post Ombudsman Who Investigated Fabricated Janet Cooke Story, Dies at 91," *Washington Post*, March 30, 2016, https://www.washingtonpost.com/national/bill-green-post-ombudsman-who-investigated-fabricated-janet-cooke-story-dies-at-91/2016/03/30/bf494b66-f6ad-11e5-8b23-538270a1ca31_story.html
13 "Principles of Ethical Conduct for Newsrooms," *USA Today*, https://cm.usatoday.com/ethical-conduct/"USA Today Says Reporter Falsified Major Stories," Associated Press, March 19, 2004, http://www.nbcnews.com/id/4562064/ns/us_news/t/usa-today-says-reporter-falsified-major-stories/#.XvDVLi2ZOu4
14 Robin Pogrebin, "Rechecking a Writer's Facts, A Magazine Uncovers Fiction," *The New York Times*, June 12, 1998, https://www.nytimes.com/1998/06/12/us/rechecking-a-writer-s-facts-a-magazine-uncovers-fiction.html
15 Alicia C. Shepard, "Too Much Too Soon?" *American Journalism Review*, December 1995, https://ajrarchive.org/article.asp?id=1622
16 Emily Steel and Ravi Somaiya, "Brian Williams Suspended From NBC for 6 Months without Pay," *The New York Times*, February 20, 2015, https://www.nytimes.com/2015/02/11/business/media/brian-williams-suspended-by-nbc-news-for-six-months.html

17 Michael Slote, *The Ethics of Care and Empathy*, Abingdon, OX: Routledge, 2007, 129, 128.
18 Webster's Third New International Dictionary.
19 Richard A. Oppel Jr., et al, "The Fullest Look Yet at the Racial Inequity of Coronavirus," *The New York Times*, July 5, 2020, https://www.nytimes.com/interactive/2020/07/05/us/coronavirus-latinos-african-americans-cdc-data.html?campaign_id=56&emc=edit_cn_20200707&instance_id=20074&nl=on-politics-with-lisa-lerer&regi_id=12942352&segment_id=32789&te=1&user_id=7d0e5105b76418ac21466ea00fa29497
20 Hutchins Commission, op. cit. 131.

9

THE BRIGHT SIDE OF THE FINANCIAL PRESSURE ON THE MEDIA

Consider the costs. American news media have been under financial pressure for years, as advertising moves to the internet, and there's no end in sight. As of mid-2020, this abysmal trend had pulverized one thousand eight hundred newspapers, one thousand seven hundred of them dailies, according to a running count kept by Penny Abernathy of the University of North Carolina. "Print readers are disappearing even faster than print newspapers, and the pace appears to be accelerating," she reports.

> Over the past 15 years, total weekday circulation - which includes both dailies and weeklies – declined from 122 million to 73 million... . This decrease in print readers raises serious questions about the long-term financial sustainability of both small community and large metro newspapers.

She finds multiple damage being done to community and civic life:

> By devoting a team of investigative reporters to the task of sifting through government records, analyzing data and then translating what they had found into lucid prose and compelling articles that consumed tons of newsprint, these large papers were able to set the agenda for debate of important policy issues that ultimately affected all residents in the state and region... . Even if the metro paper transitions to online delivery – as the Seattle Post-Intelligencer did in 2009 – research suggests there is still a diminishment in both the quantity and quality of government news stories in the online versions. As a result, residents in a community are likely to be less aware of the issues and less likely to vote in local elections.[1]

DOI: 10.4324/9781003140337-12

The coronavirus pandemic appeared to quicken the pace of newspaper closures to ninety in just six months, according to the research Poynter Institute.[2]

On top of the closures, many remaining newspapers owned by chains have been eviscerated, now called "zombies" because they've been pared down to one or two local reporters, dependent for existence on press releases, unpaid contributions, wire services and stories produced elsewhere by the corporate owner for a number of its papers.

Counter-punchers

To be sure, there are exceptions, notably *The New York Times* and *The Wall Street Journal*, both national newspapers printed in several cities. While *The Times* print circulation has declined to eight hundred thousand, ballooning digital subscriptions, counting special subscriptions to its food section and its crossword puzzles, have carried total subscriptions past 6.5 million, a prodigious achievement for a daily newspaper. The paper states that it's "on a course to achieve its stated goal of 10 million subscriptions by 2025." Despite widespread business contraction caused by the Covid-19 pandemic, for the second quarter of 2020, *The New York Times* Company reported that for the first time its revenues from digital subscriptions and advertising exceeded its revenues from print.[3] *The Wall Street Journal's* total circulation soared to "approximately" three million in mid-2020, including 2.2 million digital-only, up 20 percent in the previous twelve months.[4]

However, not all the leading newspapers are making up their print losses with digital subscriptions. At last report, *The Washington Post* and *Los Angeles Times*, in particular, were lagging *The Times* and *The Journal*. Gannett Corporation, publisher of USA TODAY and two hundred sixty other daily papers, reported that in its second quarter 2020 circulation revenue declined 14 percent from a year earlier, although paid digital subscriptions rose 31 percent, and the net result for the quarter was a loss. The company acknowledged that "online subscriptions are viewed as critical to the success of media companies in the digital age as newspaper dollars decline."[5]

To be sure, this is a fast-moving picture, particularly in light of wrenching business uncertainties including widespread bankruptcies during the Covid-19 pandemic. The certain truth is that printing and distributing newspapers remains a costly business, so, as print circulations decline, papers must vigorously boost their digital subscriptions to stay afloat. Is there some sort of maximum potential in this endeavor? At least *The New York Times*, as we've seen, doesn't seem to think so.

Silver linings

Could there be a silver lining around these dark clouds? Yes. In fact, several.

First, the sheer scope and immediacy of the financial threat is triggering some creative thinking about the journalism of the future. One experiment: realistic about its sagging profit potential, in 2019, the owner of the *Salt Lake Tribune* converted his

106 Discomfiting realities are also opportunities

paper to a not-for-profit. Moreover, as we'll see in Chapter 10, the not-for-profit realm is strong and getting stronger. The difference here is that nearly all the non-profits were established in that form, i.e., without printing and distribution costs; the Salt Lake conversion is the first of a major daily. (There were a few conversions years earlier, the largest being the transfer of the ownership of the St. *Petersburg Times*, now the *Tampa Bay Times*, to the newly formed nonprofit Poynter Institute for journalism research.) So the Salt Lake City conversion remains a test case, closely watched in the industry.

Another novel transition was wrought by the *Arkansas Democrat-Gazette* in Little Rock. Pressed financially, the paper ceased print publication six days a week (all but Sunday) and instead loaned twenty-seven thousand iPads to its subscribers, producing a print-like replica for them. "You know what's going to happen if it doesn't work? We're going to eventually go out of business," publisher Walter E. Hussman, Jr. told a Northwestern University journalism project. "Newspapers are not going to make it. In fact, you're going to start seeing a lot of newspapers probably become weeklies and some of them just going out of business." In 2020, he reported an encouraging subscriber retention rate of 78 percent. "Hussman said while there have been exceptions, most of his feedback suggests that the iPad experience has been a pleasant surprise."[6]

Advertiser influence

Still another silver lining: relief from advertiser influence, real or imagined. Most American journalism is a for-profit business (although quality not-for-profit journalism is now on the rise, as Chapter 10 relates). Owners seek profits, and advertisers want readers or eyeballs. Do these necessities influence newsroom judgments about what stories to cover and what prominence to give them? One scholar and former reporter, John H. McManus of Santa Clara University, after reviewing conflicting arguments concludes that "[o]f the four trading partners—consumers, advertisers, sources, and investors—only the last is also a boss." But McManus goes on to point out that

> because advertisers seek public attention rather than public education, news programmers and newspapers are not competing in a *news market*, but in a *public attention market*. Such a market may contain many persons with little interest in understanding the significant events and issue of the day.

So, he declares, "news departments should avoid turning up negative information about advertisers and ignore or downplay reporting of such information made public by others," though he doesn't cite any illustrations of such a non-event.[7]

Another scholar, Victor Pickard of the Annenberg School for Communication at the University of Pennsylvania, paints with even broader strokes. "The market has been an unreliable provider for the public service journalism that democracy requires," he asserts. "[F]or more than a century the US press system has been inordinately dependent on advertising revenue… . Advertisers were never especially concerned about whether their revenues supported foreign bureaus or good local news: they were chasing consumers." Therefore, Pickard concludes, "[m] arket failure is a central cause of the lack of quality journalism and the ongoing disinvestment in news production," and "Donald Trump's election was a symptom, not a cause, of a deeper institutional rot within the United States' core systems, especially its media system."[8]

With an encouraging nod to not-for-profit journalism, Pickard goes on to advocate a combination of government regulation of news media that resembles an echo of the Hutchins Commission's threat, to include "ascertainment of society's information needs," and concurrently government-funded "public media institutions" that "will require tens of billions of dollars" financed in part by a new "public media tax" on Facebook and Google. Thus, Pickard envisions what he terms a "public value journalism" fostered by the government:

> Removing commercial values (an emphasis on sensational, conflict-driven trivial news that attracts attention to advertising) and adding public values (an emphasis on high-quality information, diverse voices and views, and reporting that confronts concentrated power and social problems) could foster a journalism that is universally accessible but attentive to diverse cultures and social contexts… . The US media system is riven with stark inequalities—it reflects class and racial divides, just as it perpetuates them. But given the right structural conditions, journalism can instead be a force for social justice and radical change.[9]

Pickard salutes the United Kingdom, Canada, Sweden and other European countries that subsidize journalism, both broadcast and print.[10]

Needless to say, the United States has never considered robust government-financed and government-run news media. It's simply not on the agenda. Even relatively modest appropriations for the Public Broadcasting Service (public TV) and National Public Radio are contentious.

However, the assessments of commercial influence set forth by John McManus, Victor Pickard and others merit consideration in this very different context here. As advertising support for quality journalism declines, does commercial influence necessarily decline, too?

There's no definitive answer. But logic dictates that, since the influence of advertisers is largely presumed (from lack of investigations of advertisers, for instance), we can fairly presume further that the decline of advertising equates to a decline of influence. Media companies might prefer to have the income of old, but this is the new reality, and, if a publisher or broadcaster can survive by creating online subscriptions, memberships, sponsorships, paid events or other new sources of revenue, commercial influence is likely diminished. Newspapers clearly are less beholden to important industries, thus will be less constrained, for instance, to devote resources to special sections on autos or luxury vacations or residential real estate.

108 Discomfiting realities are also opportunities

The salubrious affect of declining advertising may be most clearly witnessed in not-for-profit journalism that never was heavily dependent on advertising. For instance, ProPublica, from its outset the beneficiary of formidable and growing contributions that, in 2019, exceeded thirty-seven million dollars, seeks to dispel any notion of undue influence by publishing a list of "some of our larger donors," thirty-five of them in 2020, mostly foundations.[11] One would wish that the list be more inclusive than that, and that the amount of each contribution (or the minimum to make the list) be specified, but at least it indicates that ProPublica is sensitive to the notion that contributors might be favored in its news judgment and coverage. Be that as it may, ProPublica continues to vigorously expand its reach and content, illustrated by the establishment of its first regional bureau, in Chicago, staffed by ten experienced reporters, and planned regional bureaus in Atlanta and Phoenix.

By contrast, perhaps just a straw in the wind: for-profit, advertising-based Vox Media, Inc., another vigorous, relative newcomer prominent in the news business (as well as entertainment), was forced by the business contraction of 2020 to cut seventy people, about 6 percent of its staff.[12]

Not new: newsletters

Another promising innovation—or perhaps a throwback—is subscription newsletters. Substack, a new website, plays host to two dozen or more established journalists and academics who have left advertising-dependent publications to write a wide variety of newsletters sold to subscribers. Co-founder Hamish McKenzie writes in a newsletter, "If you don't rely on ads for your revenue, you don't have to be a pawn in the attention economy … you can stop chasing clicks and instead focus on quality." And the money is attractive, he asserts: a "couple thousand" subscriptions at five dollars a month yields one hundred thousand dollars. He says former *New Republic* writer Emily Atkin makes "comfortably in six figures" from her climate change newsletter and quotes her, "I make more money now than I had at any salaried journalism job." Among a number of other converts to Substack identified by McKenzie are Matt Taibbi, formerly of *Rolling Stone*, who writes about corruption in politics, Polina Marinova, late of *Fortune*, who writes "deep-dives on fascinating people," and Tony Mecia, who left *The Weekly Standard* to produce a newsletter on business.[13] A gushing *New York Times* story about Substack in 2020 named newsletter writers Heather Cox Richardson, a Boston College historian and prominent commentator, and essayist Andrew Sullivan, formerly of *New York* magazine. *The Times* also quoted Steve Hayes, a former editor in chief of *The Weekly Standard*, as saying that his conservative newsletter founded with two collaborators has "more than a dozen employees" and "almost 18,000 paid" subscribers producing nearly two million dollars in its first year.[14]

One news industry expert, Tim Franklin of Northwestern University's Medill School of Journalism, Media, Integrated Marketing Communications, is quoted as saying,

> An email newsletter is like a friend who checks in every day like clockwork. You don't have to seek it out… . It makes you smarter. It gives you something

The bright side of the financial pressure **109**

to talk about. And for a news organization, it's relatively inexpensive to produce, it connects you directly with your readers, it builds brand loyalty and it's a pathway to a subscription or membership. What could be better?[15]

For-profit Axios Media, founded in 2017 with a commitment to keep its stories short, publishes subscription newsletters with advertising, boasting that they feature "news, scoops & expert analysis by award-winning Axios journalists."[16] The company's daily newsletters include Axios AM and Axios PM.

Other innovative online publishers offer to pay freelance journalists to publish their work, and they're beginning to raise money to do it. Strangely named Unicorn Riot, a not-for-profit founded in 2015, secured contributions and grants totaling one hundred thirty-seven thousand dollars in 2019.[17] Similarly, an Oakland, California-based nonprofit, Independent Institute, which raised three million dollars in its fiscal 2018, sponsors The Beacon, a website that publishes the stories of more than a dozen "featured authors."[18]

To be sure, not all such novel ventures have succeeded. WikiTribune, created in 2017 by Wikipedia co-founder Jimmy Wales and financed by crowdfunding, employed established journalists whose work, like Wikipedia encyclopedia entries, could be edited or corrected by the public. It fizzled in a year.[19]

Billionaires aren't all bad

It's also worth noting that several important newspapers are now owned—and perhaps subsidized by—billionaires. Amazon.com, Inc. founder Jeff Bezos purchased *The Washington Post* in 2013 for two-hundred-fifty million dollars and has pumped significant resources into its digital operations. In 2018, finance billionaire and Boston Red Sox owner John Henry acquired New England's leading newspaper, *The Boston Globe*, for seventy million dollars. Also in 2018, Abraxane inventor Patrick Soon-Shiong purchased for five-hundred-ninety million dollars *The San Diego Union-Tribune* and the *Los Angeles Times*, which boasts the nation's third-largest print circulation.

If we may assume that these wealthy new owners have a benevolent interest in maintaining these papers, we must also note that the *Las Vegas Review-Journal*, Nevada's largest daily, was surreptitiously purchased in 2015 for one-hundred-forty million dollars by casino magnate (and prodigious Republican donor) Sheldon Adelson. When he was unmasked, his intentions were questioned, but in 2020, the *Review-Journal* was singled out by the Nevada Press Association for "general excellence in the urban category." And several of the paper's journalists won individual awards.[20]

Advertising loss still predominates

Helpful and hopeful though current journalism initiatives may be (and that includes the vigorous expansion of not-for-profit online news media described in Chapter 10), they offset only some of the pain and loss caused by the glacial drift of advertising

110 Discomfiting realities are also opportunities

to the internet. They cannot overcome it. More newspapers will fail, and more journalists will lose their jobs, through no fault of their own. More communities, especially smaller ones, will become news deserts, leaving more local governments and officials unwatched, undermining civic spirit and participation. But the bright side is the imagination of journalists and news organizations already displayed to push back against the *force majeure* of advertising movement. To what extent can subscriptions and contributions to nonprofits slake the inherent democratic thirst for news? Even more journalistic innovation is required.

Notes

1 Penny Abernathy, "The Loss of Newspapers and Readers," The Expanding News Desert, Hussman School of Journalism and Media, University of North Carolina, https://www.usnewsdeserts.com/reports/expanding-news-desert/loss-of-local-news/loss-newspapers-readers/

2 Kristen Hare, "The Coronavirus Has Closed More Than 50 Local Newsrooms across America. And Counting," Poynter Institute, September 9, 2020, https://www.poynter.org/locally/2020/the-coronavirus-has-closed-more-than-25-local-newsrooms-across-america-and-counting/

3 Marc Tracy, "Digital Revenue Exceeds Print for 1st Time for New York Times Company," *The New York Times*, August 5, 2020, https://www.nytimes.com/2020/08/05/business/media/nyt-earnings-q2.html?searchResultPosition=1

4 "News Corp. Announces New Performance Records at Dow Jones, *The Wall Street Journal*, Amid Increased Demand for Trusted News, Data And Analysis," News Corp. press release, May 7, 2020, https://newscorp.com/2020/05/07/news-corp-announces-new-performance-records-at-dow-jones-the-wall-street-journal-amid-increased-demand-for-trusted-news-data-and-analysis/

5 Nathan Bomey, "Gannett Posts Decline in Second-Quarter Revenue, Expenses as COVID-19 Takes Toll," USA TODAY, August 6, 2020, https://www.usatoday.com/story/money/2020/08/06/gannett-second-quarter-earnings-2020/3298459001/

6 Mark Jacob, "The Arkansas Gamble: Can a Tablet and a Print Replica Rescue Local News?" Local News Initiative, Medill School of Journalism, Media, Integrated Marketing Communications, Northwestern University, January 13, 2020, https://localnewsinitiative.northwestern.edu/posts/2020/01/13/arkansas-democrat-gazette-tablet/

7 John H. McManus, *Market-Driven Journalism: Let the Citizen Beware?* Thousand Oaks, Calif. and London: Sage Publications, Inc., 1994, 32, 78.

8 Victor Pickard, *Democracy Without Journalism? confronting the misinformation society*, New York: Oxford University Press, 2020, 38, 43, 66, 166.

9 Ibid. 168, 169, 171, 174.

10 Ibid. 151–54.

11 ProPublica, https://www.propublica.org/reports/

12 Lukas I. Alpert, "Vox Media Lays Off 6% of Workforce," *The New York Times*, July 16, 2020, https://www.wsj.com/articles/vox-media-lays-off-6-of-workforce-11594913365?mod=searchresults&page=1&pos=7. Privately-held Vox Media's several websites include The Verge and SB Nation, and it recently acquired the publisher of *New York* magazine. Vox's coverage of the 2020 presidential election was saluted by *New York Times* opinion columnist David Leonhart: "In Praise of Vox," June 26, 2019, https://www.nytimes.com/2019/06/26/opinion/2020-democrats-vox.html

The bright side of the financial pressure **111**

13 Hamish McKenzie, "What's Next for Journalists?" Substack newsletter, May 18, 2020, https://on.substack.com/p/whats-next-for-journalists

14 Marc Tracy, "Journalists Are Leaving the Noisy Internet for Your Email In-Box," *The New York Times*, September 23, 2020, https://www.nytimes.com/2020/09/23/business/media/substack-newsletters-journalists.html?searchResultPosition=751

15 Quoted by Mark Jacob, "8 Reasons Why Email Newsletters Are a Game-Changer for Local News," Local News Initiative, Medill School of Journalism, Media, Integrated Marketing Communications, Northwestern University, November 9, 2020, https://localnewsinitiative.northwestern.edu/posts/2020/11/09/newsletters-eight-reasons-why/index.html

16 Axios website, https://www.axios.com/newsletters/

17 Unicorn Riot, I.R.S. Form 990, 2019. https://unicornriot.ninja/about-unicorn-riot/

18 Independent Institute, I.R.S. Form 990, FY 2018. https://blog.independent.org

19 "WikiTribune," Wikipedia entry, https://en.wikipedia.org/wiki/WikiTribune

20 Associated Press, "Las Vegas Review-Journal Wins NPA's General Excellence Award," *Las Vegas Sun*, September 24, 2020, https://lasvegassun.com/news/2020/sep/24/las-vegas-review-journal-wins-npas-general-excelle/

10

NOT-FOR-PROFIT JOURNALISM MAKES SENSE (IF NOT MONEY)

In 2019, the *Chicago Tribune* told a damning story on its front page: an investigation of one hundred Illinois school districts found twenty thousand incidents of children being locked up in small "quiet rooms" or "calming rooms," sometimes for hours.

> Children as young as 5 wail for their parents, scream in anger and beg to be let out. The students, most of them with disabilities, scratch the windows or tear at the padded walls. They throw their bodies against locked doors. They wet their pants. Some children spend hours inside these rooms, missing class time… . Children were sent to isolation after refusing to do classwork, for swearing, for spilling milk, for throwing Legos. School employees use isolated timeout for convenience, out of frustration or as punishment, sometimes referring to it as 'serving time.'[1]

The *Tribune*, like most American newspapers hampered by declining revenues and a shrinking staff, had a powerful ally in this shocking investigation: an assertive not-for-profit called Pro Publica, Inc. Founded in New York just a decade earlier, ProPublica is in the vanguard of a vibrant not-for-profit journalism movement that has sprung up across the country as newspapers have faded away. A trade association, the Institute for Nonprofit News, lists a constantly growing roll of some one hundred fifty news organizations, most of them focused on a single city or state. Some are as small as two or three reporters, but all are online, avoiding printing expense, and they find ways to generate life-sustaining revenue, usually including subscriptions and tax-deductible donations, so they're not dependent on the advertising revenue that used to sustain the papers.

Before its collaboration with the *Chicago Tribune*, ProPublica had already won dozens of prestigious journalism awards, prizes and other enviable recognition, notably for investigations outing official misconduct and other nefarious

DOI: 10.4324/9781003140337-13

Not-for-profit journalism makes sense   **113**

dealings from Washington, D.C. to cities and states across the nation. Among ProPublica's awards were five Pulitzer Prizes, the gold standard of the American journalism profession.

We'll return to ProPublica's distinguished record presently, but first we need to emphasize that ProPublica is just the tip of an iceberg. Not-for-profit journalism, which actually has a long history in American publications and broadcasting, is gathering steam. That's reflected in the burgeoning membership of the Institute for Nonprofit News. It was born in 2009 as the Investigative News Network, but quickly attracted so many nonprofits that weren't exclusively investigative that it changed its name—and grew even faster. In mid-2020, it counted no fewer than two hundred forty members, mostly state and local nonprofits. For instance, a good example at the local end of the pack is BlockClub Chicago. It dispatches its several reporters every day to gather news of stores, restaurants, parks, problems and people in city neighborhoods forsaken by the daily newspapers. After street demonstrations protesting the police murder of George Floyd in Minneapolis in June 2020 erupted into widespread violence around the country, including in Chicago, BlockClub Chicago covered the wrecking and looting of neighborhood stores, but soon also reported, happily, that a GoFund Me campaign raised seventy-five thousand dollars to help the owner of two badly damaged stores in black neighborhoods rebuild.[2]

Journalism not-for-profits, some of them decades-old, are gaining strength—professionally and financially—in audience support, philanthropy and extensive coverage of state, local and national affairs. While daily and weekly newspapers face an unending struggle for survival, the online nonprofits are geared for the future, freed from advertising dependence and the expense of printing and distributing their product, energetically roaming their territories, digging up fresh stories to inform the public and, not incidentally, to improve American life. So it's no wonder that the Federal Communications Commission, in a comprehensive report detailing the decline of local news organizations in all media published in 2011, declared that "the nonprofit sector will, in many cases, need to play a greater role in filling remaining media gaps."[3]

Money, of course, is critical to continuing operation of any news organization, no matter how fine its product. In fact, failure to mount concerted fund-raising efforts has led to surprising and embarrassing failures of well-staffed nonprof-its. The Chicago News Cooperative launched auspiciously in 2009 under James O'Shea, formerly the editor of the *Los Angeles Times* and managing editor of the *Chicago Tribune*, with generous startup financing from the Chicago-based John D. and Catherine T. MacArthur Foundation. Helping his launch, O'Shea obtained a prized contract to provide two pages of Chicago news twice a week to a regional edition of *The New York Times*. He recruited top Chicago reporters, mostly from the *Tribune*, who produced insightful, original stories not seen in the Chicago papers. But in the midst of all that apparent success, as O'Shea himself later admitted rue-fully, he neglected to mount a sufficient fund-raising effort to replace the short-term MacArthur grant. When it ran out, the once-promising venture collapsed.

114 Discomfiting realities are also opportunities

Another well-staffed local startup was even less mindful of the need for revenue. When Denver's *Rocky Mountain News*, a fine tabloid with a daily circulation of two-hundred-fifty thousand and seven-hundred thousand on Sunday, folded in 2009, several of its prominent reporters announced that they would continue covering Denver news in a new website they dubbed "I Want My Rocky." Readers were invited to send money. They didn't.

Another casualty was the St. Louis Beacon, an online not-for-profit with a commitment to civil rights news in particular. Struggling financially, in 2013, it merged into St. Louis Public Radio, which operates under the auspices of the University of Missouri-St. Louis.

Fortunately, however, many journalism not-for-profits have recognized the need for fund-raising sufficient to sustain their mission. But first, what is a not-for-profit organization? The website of the Internal Revenue Service states that it

> must be organized and operated exclusively for exempt purposes set forth in section 501(c)(3) [of the Internal Revenue Code], and none of its earnings may inure to any private shareholder or individual. In addition, it may not be an action organization, i.e., it may not attempt to influence legislation as a substantial part of its activities and it may not participate in any campaign activity for or against political candidates.[4]

Examples of "exempt purposes" include religion, education, science, neighborhood improvement, human rights and civil rights.

Not-for-profit news organizations may qualify as charitable, presumably under several of the listed categories. For an organization approved by the Internal Revenue Service as "charitable," there are two important benefits: it is exempt from paying federal income tax, and donations to it may be deducted from the donor's taxable income. Although a nonprofit news organization may still sell advertising and earn other commercial revenues, provided they are used in the operation of the organization, it's obvious that the financial model is distinct from the "market-driven" model of a conventional, taxable, for-profit business. Viability is not dependent on advertising. A different revenue stream is available: philanthropic grants and individuals' contributions, increasingly bolstered in recent years by subscriptions or "memberships," attendance at live events, and some commercial services. If the organization proves adept at fund-raising as well as producing trustworthy journalism, it can find firm financial footing. Many have.

An especially imaginative pursuit of financial support was launched by one ambitious not-for-profit newcomer when it was created in 2009. Texas Tribune, based in Austin, is not a newspaper at all, but a lively website and Texas government database that generates a diverse stream of revenues now exceeding ten million dollars annually. It was founded, admittedly amid considerable uncertainty at first, by a team of two journalists—*Texas Monthly* editor-in-chief Evan Smith and politics newsletter editor and TV host Ross Ramsey—and a generous venture capitalist, John Thornton of Austin, a news junkie who helped provide initial seed capital of four million dollars.

The Tribune successfully solicits major support from several local foundations as well as the Bill and Melinda Gates Foundation and the John S. and James L. Knight Foundation. It charges thirty-five dollars for a monthly membership. Other income comes from rentals of its events space and subscriptions to a daily politics newsletter. Its Texas Tribune Festival, an "ideas weekend," in 2019, welcomed nearly nine thousand registrants and generated 2.3 million dollars in receipts. The Tribune also sponsors each year dozens of free "town-hall style conversations and symposia" around the state in which Texans have "the rare opportunity to see, hear and directly question their elected officials, community leaders and policymakers." Most of these events are live-streamed; the Tribune provides the same coverage of the Texas legislature. It gathers and maintains publicly accessible databases of the salaries of public employees, U.S. Senate fundraising, state demographics and the capacity of shelters for migrant children.

Texas Tribune's prodigious fund-raising supports a staff of eighty-five, and its journalism is as potent as its solicitation. It claims to operate the largest statehouse bureau in the country. In one recent story the Tribune teamed with Grist, a Seattle-based nonprofit "independent, irreverent news outlet," to show that Texas regulators enabled "cash-strapped coal companies" to skirt legal requirements with just bare-minimum restoration of despoiled land. Another Texas Tribune investigation, part of a national project, reported that law enforcement officials in four Texas counties, despite their representations that civil asset forfeitures were a powerful weapon against big criminal organizations, instead often seized small amounts of cash or property from regular people—typically as a result of traffic stops—without any subsequent prosecution or conviction.

By contrast with Texas Tribune, one of the nation's older nonprofits, *Mother Jones* magazine (founded in 1976), which boasts of "smart, fearless journalism," emphasizes solicitation of subscriptions and donations. They provide two-thirds of the magazine's annual budget of sixteen million dollars. Its website declares proudly, "We're fortunate to be supported by one of the largest networks of reader supporters outside public broadcasting—46,000 individual donors and a paid magazine circulation to more than 190,000 subscribers."[5] Named for charismatic pioneer union organizer and progressive rabble-rouser Mary Jones, the magazine sent its reporter Shane Bauer, who had once been imprisoned for two years in Iran, undercover for four months in 2014 as a nine-dollars-an-hour Louisiana prison guard for an inside look at America's private, for-profit prison system. Bauer's story, described by his editor as "revealing as hell," chronicled systemic mismanagement, mistreatment of prisoners and grossly inadequate mental health care to cope with rife psychiatric debilities.[6] The for-profit, publicly held prison operator, Corrections Corporation of America, subsequently surrendered its contract for that prison. (It subsequently changed its name to CoreCivic.)

However, when it comes to journalism not-for-profit financial prowess, as *Mother Jones* indicates on its website, the clear leader is public broadcasting: the Public Broadcasting Service (public television; formed in 1969) and its three hundred local member stations, and National Public Radio (1970) and its thousand-plus local stations.

116 Discomfiting realities are also opportunities

The eight-hundred-pound gorilla in public television is WGBH Boston, which produces popular and widely used science ("NOVA"), history ("American Experience"), arts ("Masterpiece") and education ("Learning Media") programming as well as news. In 2019, WGBH booked revenues of a stunning two-hundred-thirty million dollars. This included one-hundred-thirty-four million dollars of "program support from corporations, foundations, campaign gifts and others," forty-one million dollars in "general support from members, patrons and other individuals," plus nearly nine million dollars from the government-financed Corporation for Public Broadcasting.

Another giant, KQED San Francisco, which operates both public television and radio stations, reported 2019 income of eighty-five million dollars, forty-nine million of it from contributions and membership fees, plus twenty million from underwriting (commercial sponsorships) and grants.

The richest public radio station, WNYC New York, reported total operating support and revenue in 2019 of eighty-seven million dollars, including seventy-eight million from contributions, and "production and other income" of five million, partly from nationally syndicated programs such as "On the Media" and "New Yorker Radio Hour."

Another strong local National Public Radio station, WBEZ Chicago, boasts more than seventy thousand members and reported 2018 revenues of thirty-three million dollars, retaining most of the prior year's five-million pop in contributions and grants enjoyed after Donald Trump's election. WBEZ produces network broadcasts "Wait, Wait … Don't Tell Me" and "This American Life." In 2020, the staff of "This American Life" shared a Pulitzer Prize with the *Los Angeles Times* and a Vice News freelancer, Emily Green, for a story illuminating the personal impact of the Trump Administration's "Remain in Mexico" policy.

Other long-standing journalism not-for-profits are the Associated Press (founded in 1846), a storied membership news service; respected magazines *Consumer Reports* (founded in 1936), *The Nation* (1865) and *National Geographic* (1888); and the *Christian Science Monitor*, a thoughtful daily newspaper founded in 1908 that thrived for several decades until changing economics forced it to become solely a website and monthly magazine.

Contrasted with the financial prowess of the public broadcasters, many internet not-for-profits carry on still notable journalism with relatively modest support. The California-based Center for Investigative Reporting, which bills itself as the nation's oldest investigative journalism organization (founded in 1977), reported 2018 revenues, mostly contributions, of 8.7 million dollars—after enjoying a temporary surge to 13.5 million in 2017, following Donald Trump's election. The CIR maintains a hefty reporting staff of fifty plus a dozen administrators and fundraisers, and in recent years has shrewdly plunged into radio podcasting. These productions effectively re-imagine the same reporting CIR does for print stories. Under the name "Reveal," the podcasts are featured on National Public Radio and other outlets. One podcast won broadcasting's top prize, a Peabody, in 2013. Another was runner-up for a Pulitzer Prize, in 2020. The CIR has won several awards from

Investigative Reporters and Editors, a prestigious professional organization, and has been a finalist for the Pulitzer Prize, most recently in 2018 for an expose of drug rehabilitation facilities in Oklahoma, and in 2019, for a story on discriminatory "redlining" practices in the home mortgage business.

Also demonstrating durability, the Washington, D.C.-based Center for Public Integrity, founded in 1989, a winner of Pulitzer and other prizes, had 2018 revenues, mostly grants and contributions, of a comparatively modest 4.2 million dollars, down from twice that in the Trump bulge of 2017.

Single-purpose nonprofits

Now supported by contributions and other revenues of about eight million dollars annually, The Marshall Project went live in 2014 under the auspicious editorship of former *New York Times* executive editor Bill Keller, a Pulitzer Prize winner himself. Named for former Supreme Court Justice Thurgood Marshall and focused solely on criminal justice, The Marshall Project almost immediately shared a Pulitzer Prize in 2016, teaming with ProPublica for "An Unbelievable Story of Rape," about a young woman in Washington State who reported being raped but was disbelieved and eventually, under pressure, said her story was false, leading to a humiliating plea bargain in court. But her story, it turned out, was true, when her assailant was subsequently convicted of other attacks. The story became a Netflix series.

In 2018, The Marshall Project reported that between 2006 and 2016, tens of thousands of children were placed into foster care solely because a parent was incarcerated. For about five thousand of these children, according to the story, their parents' rights were eventually terminated, often without testimony from the parent. Mothers and fathers who have a child placed in foster care because they are incarcerated—despite not having been accused of child abuse, neglect, endangerment, or even drug or alcohol use—are more likely to have their parental rights terminated than those who physically or sexually assault their kids, according to the Marshall Project's analysis of approximately three million child-welfare cases nationally.

Another Marshall Project story, "Old, Sick and Dying in Shackles," revealed that the federal Bureau of Prisons barely used its "compassionate release" program—intended to allow extremely sick or elderly inmates to get out on parole—approving just 6 percent of applications over five years. The story ran on the front page of *The New York Times*, and was cited by voices who successfully supported enactment of the federal First Step Act—so prisoners can now appeal the Bureau of Prisons' denial or neglect of a request for compassionate release. It's notable that in 2019, five of this criminal justice-reform organization's contributing writers were then incarcerated.

Another single-subject nonprofit, Chalkbeat, covers elementary and secondary education. Founded in 2016, Chalkbeat raised 6.7 million dollars in its fiscal 2018. It boasts an editorial staff of forty scattered over the East and Midwest, plus Colorado, supported by an administrative and fund-raising staff of twenty-four. A newcomer called Open Campus was established recently by two former editors of *The Chronicle of Higher Education*, declaring that "We believe more thoughtful, aggressive coverage

118 Discomfiting realities are also opportunities

of all parts of the American higher education system can help decrease public cynicism."[7] The Bill and Melinda Gates Foundation provided initial funding.

Tiny by any measure, Brooklyn-based Inside Climate News punches above its weight. It was launched in 2007 with a grant of one-hundred-fifty thousand dollars from the Rockefeller Brothers Fund, and in 2018, reported revenues of just two million dollars, still primarily from foundations along with other large and small donors. Nevertheless, Inside Climate News carried on a seven-month investigation into a million-gallon spill of Canadian tar sands oil from an Enbridge, Inc. pipeline into the Kalamazoo River, which empties into Lake Michigan. The story broadened into a critique of national pipeline safety regulation, deeming it flawed and inadequate. The stories won a Pulitzer Prize in 2013. Another InsideClimate News investigation, which won numerous other prestigious awards and was a finalist for the Pulitzer Prize, disclosed that, beginning in the 1970s, oil behemoth Exxon had actually been a covert pioneer in the emerging science of climate change but hid its own findings to lead the propaganda of climate-change denial for many years.

Although its finances are not public, any account of vigorous American not-for-profit journalism must include the presumably very solvent Kaiser Health News, a project of the Henry J. Kaiser Family Foundation, which reports assets of nearly seven hundred million dollars. The news service employs three dozen reporters and editors. It revealed in 2019 that the Food and Drug Administration since 2016 had permitted medical device manufacturers to use a "hidden pathway" to quietly inform the agency of 1.1 million injuries and malfunctions involving such devices as surgical staplers and balloon pumps used in the vessels of heart-surgery patients. The FDA commissioner promptly announced that all such data would be made available to the public. Another Kaiser investigation, with *Fortune* magazine, revealed that reports of thousands of injuries, deaths or near misses tied to software defects, user errors and related problems had accumulated in various government-sponsored and private repositories. The report stated that such software glitches could confuse patients, prevent doctors from accessing files quickly, or send vital test results to the wrong file, contributing to serious injuries or even deaths.

Geographic focus

Many nonprofit news organizations cover just a single state or city. CalMatters, founded in 2014, reported a one-year 70 percent jump in revenue to 3.7 million dollars in 2018. Its website stated proudly in 2020:

> Today, with a staff of 31 in Sacramento and Los Angeles, it produces hundreds of stories each year that reach tens of millions of people through CalMatters. org and more than 188 news organizations including all of California's major newspapers and public radio stations.

Burrowing into California's epic homelessness affliction, CalMatters reported in 2019 that "across the state, the U.S. Census shows about 6.5% of Californians

Not-for-profit journalism makes sense **119**

identify as black or African American, but they account for nearly 40% of the state's homeless, according to a Department of Housing and Urban Development report to Congress."[8]

Star sponsorship may help. In 2007, after eleven years Minneapolis-based MinnPost raised in its most recent fiscal year a relatively modest 1.6 million dollars—from three foundations donating at least fifty thousand dollars each and four-thousand three-hundred contributing members. But MinnPost employs more than a dozen editors and reporters. The unlikely founders were Joel Kramer, retired publisher and chief executive of the *Minneapolis Star Tribune*, and his wife Laurie; they and three other couples generously funded the startup with eight hundred fifty thousand dollars.

The New Haven (Connecticut) Independent, founded in 2006, is even smaller, indeed much smaller. In 2018, it booked total revenues, mostly contributions, of just four hundred fifty thousand dollars, and its founder and editor, Paul Bass, took home only sixty-six thousand dollars. Despite its penury, the Independent was the focus of a 2013 book that saluted it as "one of the brightest stars of local online journalism." A book excerpt in a Harvard publication stated that the Independent gained prominence in reporting on the grisly murder of a twenty-four-year-old Yale graduate student, whose body was discovered hidden in a Yale Medical School laboratory wall on the day she was to be married.

> Among other developments, the Independent broke the news that the police had identified a possible suspect. And it was the first to report on what the suspect's fiancée and a former girlfriend who claimed that he had sexually assaulted her had written about him on social-networking sites.[9]

The fiancée was subsequently identified as the murderer.

Also miniscule but durable is the San Francisco Public Press, launched in 2009 by a determined college journalism teacher and researcher named Michael Stoll. In 2017, it received contributions of just two-hundred-forty-nine thousand dollars affording Stoll a paltry salary of only fifty-one thousand dollars. The Public Press, which also produces a radio service, focuses on poverty, homelessness and education. Its 2018 disclosure of abundant hotel room vacancies, Stoll claims, eventually led to housing some of the city's huge homeless population in hotels during the Covid-19 pandemic.[10] The Public Press has won two awards from the Society of Professional Journalists.

Newspapers in nonprofit garb

Operating under the radar as subsidiaries of not-for-profit corporations are a handful of daily newspapers whose family owners have over the years donated their stock to those corporations, most of them formed for this purpose. For instance, Nelson Poynter, owner of the *St. Petersburg Times* (now the *Tampa Bay Times*), in 1978 willed his stock to a nonprofit journalism school and research organization he created, the

120 Discomfiting realities are also opportunities

Poynter Institute for Media Studies. Originally the newspaper's profits were available to support the research and training of the Institute, but in recent times its outside contributions and grants received are by far its principal support, as investment income is relatively insignificant.

In another novel conversion, the Ayers family owners of the *Anniston Star* and other Alabama community newspapers are very gradually, though their wills, donating their stock to a new nonprofit, the Ayers Family Foundation. "The idea is to keep the paper as a community institution, a paper that won't be bought by a chain," said publisher Josephine Ayers.[11]

In the first conversion of a major metropolitan daily, Paul Huntsman, despairing of the profit prospects for the newspaper business, in 2019, surrendered his ownership of *The Salt Lake Tribune* to make it a nonprofit. Worth watching.

The Pulitzer Prizes

In this surge of nonprofit journalism ProPublica stands out both financially and journalistically, the winner, as noted above, of several coveted Pulitzer Prizes. What are "the Pulitzers" anyway? And why are they so significant?

The Pulitzer Prizes were established by the 1904 will of one Joseph Pulitzer, an immigrant from Hungary who became publisher of *The St. Louis Post-Dispatch* and the *New York World*. Among other distinctions, Pulitzer was the first prominent American newspaperman to advocate university training in journalism for future reporters, and he endowed the Graduate School of Journalism at Columbia University, one of the country's most prestigious journalism schools. The Pulitzer Prizes are awarded by the president of Columbia University upon recommendations by committees of respected journalists. Joseph Pulitzer specified awards for "the most disinterested and meritorious public service rendered by any American newspaper during the preceding year," including one for "the best example of a reporter's work during the year, the test being strict accuracy, terseness, the accomplishment of some public good." Several other awards have been added since. Any winner of a Pulitzer is inevitably known for the rest of his career, indeed the rest of his life, as "a winner of the Pulitzer Prize."

So it was noteworthy that in 2020, ProPublica won two more Pulitzer Prizes, its sixth and seventh (in just thirteen years), as well as other top prizes in criminal justice, business, investigation, education and local accountability reporting, and more awards for magazine reporting and podcasting.

How could this be, at a time when journalism is widely seen as in decline, or, as Donald Trump characterized it, "the enemy of democracy" publishing "fake news"?

ProPublica remains in many respects unique in American journalism. But, as we have seen, it is not alone as a reliable and respected not-for-profit news organization, nor is it a pioneer of the form.

Still, it's worth examining this remarkable story. To start, ProPublica was born to ermine. Herbert and Marion Sandler, who had made a fortune in the California

Not-for-profit journalism makes sense **121**

savings and loan business, committed an astounding thirty million dollars, in three annual installments of ten million each, to create this new not-for-profit. But the money didn't guarantee success, as was demonstrated a few years later when another lavishly financed nonprofit startup, the Bay Citizen in San Francisco, abruptly collapsed. It had been blessed at birth in 2010 with a multi-million-dollar pledge from philanthropist Warren Hellman. Less than two years later, it was gone, merging quietly into the Center for Investigative Reporting. One post-mortem called it "the disappointing failure of a once promising media entity... . Instead of providing an alternative that would attract the younger, more racially diverse demographic that has abandoned the *Chronicle*, the Bay Citizen largely echoed that declining publication."[12]

The Sandlers made no such mistake. They entrusted ProPublica to a distinguished journalist named Paul Steiger, then the managing editor of *The Wall Street Journal*. It proved to be a shrewd match. Offering princely salaries, some exceeding two-hundred thousand dollars, Steiger assembled an impressive cast of two dozen experienced investigative reporters who promptly set to work at a craft they knew well: exposing misconduct in high places.

For instance, scrutinizing the wake of a devastating 2005 tropical storm called Hurricane Katrina, ProPublica teamed up with the *New Orleans Times-Picayune* and public television's Frontline to expose incidents of police violence in New Orleans. Their stories led to federal grand jury indictments of police officers, three of whom soon pleaded guilty. Separately, another ProPublica reporter spotlighted questionable "deadly choices" at a New Orleans hospital, a story that triggered a libel suit (which a federal trial court dismissed) and brought a Pulitzer Prize to reporter Sheri Fink.

In another ProPublica investigation, nearly two years of reporting yielded more than seventy-five stories that disclosed how hydraulic-fracturing drillers had averted New York State approval for wells near some of the state's reservoirs. Later, ProPublica was gratified to observe that these stories about fracking's danger to water supplies "heightened awareness around the country."

In 2019, ProPublica reported "callous behavior" by certain U.S. Border Patrol agents at the Mexican border, and revealed a secret Facebook group

> for present and former Border Patrol agents where they posted racist, sexist and misogynistic comments about immigrants and certain members of Congress. The Border Patrol promptly launched an investigation and sent "cease and desist" orders to a number of agents.

In 2020, ProPublica listed several of its most popular stories in its eleven-year history, including "How the Red Cross Raised Half a Billion Dollars for Haiti and Built Six Homes," and "Never-Before-Seen Trump Tax Documents Show Major Inconsistencies." Another top story showed great disparities in state workers' compensation valuations of a lost limb.

122 Discomfiting realities are also opportunities

The Sandlers' generosity yielded still another early benefit to ProPublica. Because their enormous pledge was for just three years, Editor Steiger was constrained to commence immediately an ambitious fund-raising effort to replace that grant. Wisely, not relying solely on the high quality of ProPublica's journalism to spontaneously attract new sources of revenue, Steiger recruited a full-time development staff that promptly began to solicit support from other wealthy individuals and foundations, as well as the general public. This undertaking, as much as its investigative prowess, became ProPublica's hallmark in not-for-profit journalism.

Other foundations came on board: the John D. and Catherine T. MacArthur Foundation, the John S. and James L. Knight Foundation (a three-year grant), The Eli and Edythe Broad Foundation, The William and Flora Hewlett Foundation, and the Woodtiger Fund. Smaller, online gifts from five to five hundred dollars jumped quickly, with the number of donors nearly tripling in the first four months of 2010 over those in the first eight months of fund-raising in 2009. By 2019, more than thirty-two thousand donors large and small were providing thirty-three million dollars in total revenues, three times the original annual Sandler pledge, enabling ProPublica to expand its robust reporting staff to more than one hundred, including ten in its first regional bureau, in Chicago.

With the combined strength of for-profit and not-for-profit organizations—in print, on the air, on cable and on the internet—how can American journalism ensure that America's pressing needs, the needs of the society and of the democracy, are adequately addressed to ensure tangible progress? It's a challenge, to be sure. But let's tackle it.

Notes

1 Jennifer Smith Richards, Jodi S. Cohen and Lakeidra Chavis, photography by Zbigniew Bzdak, "The Quiet Rooms," *Chicago Tribune*, November 19, 2019, p. 1.
2 Alexandra Chaidez, "An Immigrant Lost His Businesses to Looting, But Donors Give $75,000 to Help Them Pick Up the Pieces," BlockClub Chicago, June 9, 2020. https://blockclubchicago.org/2020/06/09/an-immigrant-lost-his-businesses-to-looting-but-donors-give-75000-to-help-them-pick-up-the-pieces/?mc_cid=e4c24039ca&mc_eid=50e880ab47
3 Steven Waldman and the Working Group on the Information Needs of Communities, *The Information Needs of Communities: The Changing Media Landscape in a Broadband Age* (Washington: Federal Communications Commission, 2011), 346.
4 "Charitable Organizations," Internal Revenue Service website, https://www.irs.gov/charities-non-profits/charitable-organizations/exempt-purposes-internal-revenue-code-section-501c3
5 "Financials," motherjones.com, https://www.motherjones.com/about/financials/
6 Shane Bauer, "My Four Months as a Private Prison Guard," *Mother Jones*, July/August 2016, https://www.motherjones.com/politics/2016/06/cca-private-prisons-corrections-corporation-inmates-investigation-bauer/

Not-for-profit journalism makes sense **123**

7 opencampusmedia.org, https://www.opencampusmedia.org/about-open-campus/
8 Kate Cimini, "Black People Disproportionately Homeless in California," CalMatters, October 5, 2019. https://calmatters.org/california-divide/2019/10/black-people-disproportionately-homeless-in-california/
9 Dan Kennedy, "A Murder, a Media Frenzy, and the Rise of a New Form of Local News," NiemanLab, published by the Nieman Foundation at Harvard, June 5, 2013, excerpted from Kennedy's book, *The Wired City: Reimagining Journalism and Civic Life in the Post-Newspaper Age*, University of Massachusetts Press, 2013.
10 Michael Stoll, interview with the author, July 20, 2020.
11 Josephine Ayers, interview with the author, December 14, 2020.
12 Randy Shaw, "Why the Bay Citizen Failed," *Beyond Chron*, February 6, 2012, https://beyondchron.org/why-the-bay-citizen-failed/

SECTION III

The road to success redefined

11

ETHICAL MEDIA CONTINUE TO DRIVE PUBLIC DISCOURSE

American newspapers are older than the country. The very first, in 1690, lasted only one issue, but the second, in 1704, was a Boston weekly that endured. Others followed, in Philadelphia and New York. The founders were printers or postmasters. In some cities second and third newspapers emerged. James Franklin, a young printer, established the *New-England Courant* in Boston in 1721; it was the city's third paper and. Princeton sociologist Paul Starr writes, it "introduced controversy to the colonial press. The triggering issue was Cotton Mather's proposal in June 1721 to use inoculation to fight smallpox, an idea that the *Courant's* writers relentlessly mocked."[1] Franklin's younger brother, Benjamin, later removed to Philadelphia and in 1729 bought a newly established newspaper, *The Pennsylvania Gazette*, which he published for many years.

During those early days, an important criminal case tested the royal governors' ability to control the press, as the Crown did in England. The governor of New York, William Cosby, charged an immigrant printer, John Peter Zenger, with seditious libel for printing in his *New York Weekly Journal* accusations that Cosby had exceeded his authority. The actual authors of the accusations, who were not charged, engaged a prominent Philadelphia lawyer named Andrew Hamilton, a friend of Benjamin Franklin's, to defend Zenger. Under existing English law, the prosecution needed to prove only that a criticism seen as damaging a person's reputation was published; truth was not a defense. However, pointedly disregarding instructions from the trial judge, Hamilton argued that the criticisms were in fact true and therefore the jury should acquit Zenger, which it did. Though the case had no formal precedential value, the verdict was historic and highly influential. According to Starr, "while royal officials still had authority to suppress seditious libel, they virtually gave up trying to do so ... and the risk of being tried for seditious libel by British colonial authorities effectively disappeared."[2]

DOI: 10.4324/9781003140337-15

128 The road to success redefined

Instruments of opposition

The role and influence of the press continued to increase. When Parliament in 1765 imposed a stamp tax on the colonists' newspapers, almanacs and other publications, some printers held to their customary neutrality, but

> others put their newspapers at the service of the resistance by reporting protests, championing the cause, and perhaps most important, providing a forum for discussion and helping to turn what could have been mere disorder into a more coherent opposition movement,

in Starr's telling.[3] Continuing his trail-breaking role in the creation of the American press, Benjamin Franklin, as the appointed deputy postmaster general for North America, in 1753 permitted newspapers to exchange copies by mail at no charge, fostering what historian Starr calls "a proto-national public sphere."[4] He adds: "Later on, during the Revolution and in the early republic, the majority of newspapers would take on a partisan identity."[5]

In the meantime, most of the rebellious colonies adopted, before or during the War of Independence, constitutional provisions guaranteeing freedom of the press, unprecedented in human history. Virginia's Declaration of Rights was first, in 1765. Drafted by an unlikely author, a planter of modest formal education named George Mason, it stated that "the Freedom of the Press is one of the great Bulwarks of Liberty, and can never be restrained but by despotic Government." After Independence and adoption of the United States Constitution in 1787, Congress promptly passed ten constitutional amendments known as the Bill of Rights that included federal guarantees of freedom of speech and freedom of the press. The amendments were ratified by the states and became effective in 1791.

Personalized agenda-setting

Thus, by precedent and now by law, the stage was set for newspapers to guide public discourse in America. Government officials were so well aware of this truth that some of them instigated creation of their own papers to make sure they could get their public messages out. For instance, Alexander Hamilton's biographer Ron Chernow states that Hamilton probably provided one thousand dollars of the startup ten thousand needed to launch, with several colleagues, a new Federalist newspaper, the *New-York Evening Post*, after Hamilton's rival Thomas Jefferson was elected president in 1800. The paper is a little-noticed aspect of Hamilton's considerable legacy; as Chernow notes, it is "now the oldest continuously active paper in America." Hamilton's vision for the paper was personal and ambitious, not limited to politics.

> For chief editor, Hamilton plucked one of his most colorful disciples, thirty-five-year-old William Coleman, an engaging man with a broad, florid face and a nimble wit... . When the newspaper's first issue appeared on

November 16, 1801, it sounded a patrician note, promising 'to diffuse among the people correct information on all interesting subjects, to inculcate just principles in religion, morals, and politics, and to cultivate a taste for sound literature.'[6]

In the nineteenth century, American newspapers progressed from the archly political papers like Hamilton's *Evening Post* through "penny papers" circulation wars beginning in the 1830s to the emergence of a new breed of better-educated, more professional reporters in the last two decades of the century. Journalism sociologist Michael Schudson describes the "new reporter" as "younger, more naive, more energetic and ambitious, college-educated, and usually sober."[7]

Crusaders

Enter the crusading journalist. One of the first was most unlikely: a young black woman born a slave in Mississippi. Her name was Ida B. Wells, and her first "newspaper" was a black church weekly in Memphis. In 1884, while working as a teacher, Wells began writing about the indignities and inequities of black life. After a few years, she became the co-owner and editor of a real newspaper called *The Free Speech and Headlight*. In the 1890s, she wrote a pamphlet, *Southern Horrors: Lynch Law in all its Phases*, castigating lynching as a barbaric practice employed systematically to punish and intimidate southern blacks. Her exposé was carried in a number of black newspapers. It so angered local whites that a mob destroyed her office and her press. Fortunately, she was out of town, so never returned. She relocated to Chicago, where she married, raised six children, continued to teach and write, advocated for women's suffrage, and co-founded the National Association for the Advancement of Colored People.[8]

At about the same time, in 1887, another unlikely journalist, a young woman using the nom de plume of Nellie Bly, persuaded Joseph Pulitzer of the *New York World* to pay her to feign insanity in order to write about oppressive conditions in a New York mental asylum for the poor. She behaved strangely enough to warrant being committed to the Women's Lunatic Asylum on Blackwell's Island and spent ten dismal days there, until she was released upon the *World's* intervention. Paul Starr calls Bly's two-part series published in October 1887 "one of journalism's great exposés."[9] It was later published in book form, *Ten Days in a Mad-House*.

Buoyed by her new fame, Bly sold the *World* on still another audacious undertaking: travel around the world alone by conventional transport in an effort to beat the mark of the recently published, fictional *Around the World in Eighty Days*. She departed from New York by steamer on November 18, 1889, and, as the *World* conducted a contest to guess her exact return time, offering a prize of a free trip to Europe, Bly traveled by ship and rail through England, France, Italy, the Suez Canal, Ceylon, Singapore, Hong Kong and Japan to San Francisco, where Pulitzer hired a special train that wafted her to a triumphant return to New York—in seventy-two days. Journalism? Of a sort. But was it based on facts? Yes indeed. And did it command attention? Oh, yes.

130 The road to success redefined

Another memorable reporting success of that time was achieved by a young, ardent socialist named Upton Sinclair. With an advance from *Appeal to Reason*, a socialist weekly, Sinclair took a job in a Chicago meat-packing plant to observe unsanitary and unsafe conditions there. His stories and, more significantly, a novel, *The Jungle*, published in 1906, were powerful. They portrayed a dangerous, marginal struggle of immigrant workers, and unsavory products such as "Durham canned goods," a waste product that the workers were routinely expected to process for sale to an unsuspecting public. It's worth quoting Sinclair at length:

> And then there was 'potted game' and 'potted grouse,' 'potted ham,' and 'devilled ham' … made out of the waste ends of smoked beef that were too small to be sliced by the machines and also tripe, dyed with chemicals so that it would not show white and trimmings of hams and corned beef: and potatoes, skins and all; and finally the hard cartilaginous gullets of beef, after the tongues had been cut out. All this ingenious mixture was ground up and flavored with spices to make it taste like something.

Sinclair also told of painful, disabling injuries and diseases contracted by workers in various dangerous jobs.

> There were those who worked in the chilling-rooms, and whose special disease was rheumatism; the time-limit that a man could work in the chilling-rooms was said to be five years. There were the wool-pluckers, whose hands went to pieces even sooner than the hands of the pickle-men; for the pelts of the sheep had to be painted with acid to loosen the wool, and then the pluckers had to pull out this wool with their bare hands, till the acid had eaten their fingers off…. Some worked at the stamping-machines, and it was very seldom that one could work long there at the pace that was set, and not give out and forget himself, and have a part of his hand chopped off…. Worst of any, however, were the fertilizer-men, and those who worked in the cooking-rooms…. tank-rooms full of steam, and in some of which there were open vats near the level of the floor, their peculiar trouble was that they fell into the vats, and when they were fished out, there was never enough of them left to be worth exhibiting, sometimes they would be overlooked for days, till all but the bones of them had gone out to the world as Durham's Pure Leaf Lard![10]

The Jungle alarmed the public and Congress, too, which promptly enacted strong regulatory legislation signed by President Theodore Roosevelt: the Pure Food and Drug Act of 1906 and the Federal Meat Inspection Act of 1906, which makes it illegal to adulterate or misbrand meat and meat products sold as food, and requires that meat and meat products be slaughtered and processed under strictly regulated sanitary conditions.[11]

Twentieth-century discourse

The powerful exposés of Nellie Bly, Ida B. Wells and Upton Sinclair established a high bar for the press—especially investigative journalism—in the twentieth century. Despite a hiccup in World War I, when the government artfully manipulated coverage, newspapers acquired a new public role and responsibility that endures to this day. "Journalism's first loyalty is to citizens," declare Bill Kovach and Tom Rosenstiel in the third edition of their seminal work, *The Elements of Journalism*. This commitment, they write, is "more than professional egotism. It is the implied covenant between someone producing a work of journalism and the public that consumes it that the work is honest." To what end? "Civilization has produced one idea more powerful than any other: the notion that people can govern themselves. And it has created a largely unarticulated theory of information to sustain that idea, called journalism."[12]

This overarching responsibility is executed every day by editors and reporters who exercise a judgment somewhat comparable to that of prosecuting attorneys: what (or whom) we'll pursue today. Those decisions determine not only what stories to cover, but, necessarily, what the public discourse will be, thus what responsible public officials will address. To illustrate, the agenda-setting influence of the news media was affirmed by a study of the coverage in North Carolina of the three-way 1968 presidential campaign among Republican Richard Nixon, Democrat Hubert Humphrey and George Wallace, a segregationist southern Democrat running as the candidate of the American Independent Party. "The data suggest," Maxwell E. McCombs and Donald L. Shaw write,

> a very strong relationship between the emphasis placed on different campaign issues by the media (reflecting to a considerable degree the emphasis by candidates) and the judgments of voters as to the salience and importance of various campaign topics. But while the three presidential candidates placed widely different emphasis upon different issues, the judgments of the voters seem to reflect the *composite* of the mass media coverage. This suggests that voters pay some attention to all the political news *regardless* of whether it is from, or about, any particular favored candidate... . [T]he evidence in this study that voters tend to share the media's *composite* definition of what is important strongly suggests an agenda-setting function of the mass media.[13]

As McCombs and Shaw note, editors have great discretion in choosing what to cover each day; "a newspaper, for instance, uses only about 15 percent of the material available on any given day."[14] It follows that each decision to cover a story means that other possible stories will not be covered, at least not that day. This is a huge responsibility, and it's a vital aspect of what makes journalism influential—and satisfying to its practitioners. What's important? What's wrong? What's exemplary in our circulation area?

132 The road to success redefined

Making good decisions attracts readers or viewers. Joseph Pulitzer's *New York World* "combined sensationalism and storytelling with a crusading liberal reformism," notes Paul Starr, "and built circulation not just with stunts but with investigations of tenement housing, adulterated food, official misconduct (including police brutality), and corporate malfeasance."[15]

There were other measures of success as well. Early in the new century the *Chicago Tribune* launched "Friend of the People," an ombudsman column intended to hold public officials accountable, and an Anti-Loan Shark Bureau. "[S]oon the *Tribune* was drawing 3,500 letters a week from readers seeking help or information," according to the biographer of longtime publisher Robert R. McCormick.[16]

Golden age of newspapers

Newspapers thrived through most of the twentieth century. For many years in mid-century, there were more than one thousand seven hundred dailies. New York had seven, Chicago four. Then the three broadcast television networks—ABC, CBS and NBC—and local stations determinedly entered the news business, taking audience from the afternoon dailies, and eventually causing them to fail, or, in a few cases, convert to morning publication. Both newspapers and broadcasters adopted codes of ethics mandating truth, facts, accuracy, fairness, named sources, transparency and sensitivity to the privacy of crime victims and other people not used to dealing with journalists.

Newspapers continued to lead in investigative journalism, though undercover reporting, ruled out by most ethics codes, weren't respectable to some eyes. For instance, one of the best investigations ever published exploded on the front pages of the *Chicago Sun-Times* in 1977. The newspaper's editors, despairing of finding small business owners who would speak on the record about city inspectors holding their hands out, collaborated with the Better Government Association, a civic organization, to buy and begin to operate a seedy downtown tavern that they named appropriately The Mirage. As reporters and investigators pretending to be owners and employees busied themselves with cosmetic cleaning and painting, a stream of city inspectors dropped in to look for any violations of various city codes. "We had lots of violations," one of the BGA investigators, Mindy Trossman, recalled years later.

> Exposed wiring, peeling paint, a leaky basement, doors that swung in rather than out. The inspectors came from the fire department, the building department, the health department, the liquor commission, the electrical inspector, even a signage inspector. But instead of demanding corrections, all the inspectors were looking for bribes to overlook those violations. Not a single inspector fulfilled his obligation to protect the health and safety of the public and the employees.[17]

So the investigators, previously schooled by an Illinois law enforcement official to avoid breaking laws such as prohibitions against offering a bribe and clandestine

Ethical media continue to drive public discourse **133**

recording of a conversation, responded to hints by the inspectors that they could be persuaded to overlook the violations, slipping each one a modest cash bribe, perhaps twenty-five or fifty dollars. Although the investigators couldn't legally record their conversations, photographs and TV film from a concealed booth over the bar—quite legal—clearly identified each inspector and his transaction. After a few weeks of preparations and a brief opening for business, the Mirage abruptly closed.

The resulting stories enthralled the public—and stunned City Hall. For nearly three weeks, the *Sun-Times* ran a new Mirage exposé on the front page each day, describing the sting and identifying each unscrupulous inspector. It was, as one headline read, "A Report on the 'fix' in Chicago." One of the hidden TV cameras had come from New York: CBS, Mike Wallace and "60 Minutes," which ran its report strategically on the eve of the newspaper's first eye-popping story. City department heads, seeing denials impossible, responded by disciplining and firing inspectors, usually claiming that they were outliers, not representative of city enforcement operations. The *Sun-Times* series became a finalist for a Pulitzer Prize, but in the end it was denied because the reporters and investigators had gone undercover, not honestly identifying themselves as ethics codes required—and still do. As the Associated Press code puts it, "we don't misidentify or misrepresent ourselves to get a story."[18] However, some codes create an exception that would allow what the *Sun-Times* did. The Society of Professional Journalists states: "Avoid undercover or other surreptitious methods of gathering information unless traditional, open methods will not yield information vital to the public."[19]

Fortunately, though, undercover journalism continues today, often with admirable results. Remember *Mother Jones* magazine's revealing exposé of stabbings, an escape, poor medical and mental healthcare for prisoners, mismanagement and lack of training for the staff in a Louisiana prison?—all witnessed by reporter-cum-guard Shane Bauer targeting private, for-profit prison operator Corrections Corporation of America. Under public pressure, the company subsequently surrendered its contract for that prison, and later, amid a public and Congressional furor over private prison operations generally, changed its name to CoreCivic, Inc.[20]

As media ethicist Stephen J. A. Ward puts it, "Journalists not only have freedom to publish; they have duties to use their freedom to foster reasonable political discourse."[21]

This is not to say that twentieth-century newspapers were always successful in persuading the public. Colonel Robert R. McCormick, the imperious and conservative publisher of the *Chicago Tribune*, who dominated every aspect of the paper for decades in the first half of the century, was singularly determined in 1927 to defeat the corrupt but colorful Mayor William "Big Bill" Thompson. Aligned with top gangster Al Capone, Thompson cheerfully and openly defied the prohibition of alcoholic drinks mandated by the Eighteenth Amendment to the Constitution, to the *Tribune's* dismay—but nevertheless handily won re-election.

134 The road to success redefined

What do the news media do?

What, indeed, was expected of the press in the twentieth century—above and beyond the stated ethical standards of truth, facts, accuracy, fairness, transparency and sensitivity? Shortly after the end of the century, scholar Michael Schudson, never a journalist but a perceptive observer of the profession over several decades, nicely articulated: "I see six primary functions that news has served or can serve in a democracy":

1. "fair and full information so citizens can make sound political choices"
2. "investigate concentrated sources of power, particularly governmental power"
3. "provide coherent frameworks of interpretation to help citizens comprehend a complex world"
4. "tell people about others in their society and their world so that they can come to appreciate the viewpoints and lives of other people, especially those less advantaged than themselves"
5. "provide a forum for dialogue among citizens and serve as a common carrier of the perspectives of varied groups in society"
6. "serve as advocates for particular political programs and perspectives and mobilize people to act in support of these programs"[22]

This remains a good statement of the role of the ethical news media, but Schudson's last point, though admirable, isn't as easily affirmed as the previous five. Do journalists really strive to "advocate for particular political programs" and "mobilize people to act"? Generally not. However, this aspirational statement calls to mind the ringing admonitions of the blue-ribbon 1946 Hutchins Commission, which rendered the most salient critique of American journalism in the twentieth century, and is worth reviewing here. Seeing the post-war world as presenting new challenges for both democracy and the press, the Commission challenged journalism to

> do its duty by the new world that is struggling to be born.... help create a world community by giving men everywhere knowledge of the world and one another, by promoting comprehension and appreciation of the goals of a free society that shall embrace all men.

As to reporting domestic affairs, the Commission was ahead of its time in perceiving the challenge presented by racial differences. It recognized that "the country has many groups which are partially insulated from one another," and warned presciently that

> factually correct but substantially untrue accounts of the behavior of members of one of these social islands can intensify the antagonisms of others toward them. A single incident will be accepted as a sample of group action unless the press has given a flow of information and interpretation concerning

the relations between two racial groups such as to enable the reader to set a single event in its proper perspective.

And what was the Commission's remedy for simplistic though accurate reporting? The press "must assume a responsibility like that of educators in stating and clarifying the ideals toward which the community should strive... . We suggest that the press look upon itself as performing a public service of a professional kind."[23] The Commission did not have a high regard for the contemporary press: "The news is twisted by the emphasis on firstness, on the novel and sensational; by the personal interests of owners; and by pressure groups." The press "is not meeting the needs of our society."[24] In fact, the Commission intoned, in italics: "*the press must now take on the community's press objectives as its own objectives.*" This imperative was defined as a *duty* of the press, so that the consumer's interest in the news "acquires the stature of a *right*."[25] To enforce this obligation, the Commission clearly threatened government regulation: "the press dare no longer indulge in fallibility—it must supply the public need... . There is a point beyond which failure to realize the moral right will entail encroachment by the state upon the existing legal right," the freedom of the press.[26]

Adopting the humanistic ethics of care would bring ethical journalism closer to realizing the aggressive charge of the Hutchins Commission than it has ever been, taking the initiative to actually meet the needs of society—mobilizing public opinion and elected leaders to achieve results—rather than simply chronicling events and problems.

Of course, there's no need to resort to public polling or focus groups to determine that there are three persistent, overriding and disrupting threats to society: climate change, racial inequity and economic disparity. These represent *needs* in the Hutchins lexicon.

Inside climate news focuses

Nor did the ethical news media ignore these threats in 2020 despite the insufficient attention given them by the candidates in the pervasive political campaign. Inside Climate News, the small but assertive Pulitzer Prize-winning online news organization devoted entirely to coverage of the environment, wrote tartly at the end of the Republican convention that re-nominated President Donald Trump:

> As a cascade of extreme weather disasters upended life across the nation this week, there was no mention of climate change during the four days of the Republican National Convention. The only party leader to refer to 'climate' was President Donald Trump, who boasted about withdrawing from the Paris climate accord. Amid devastating California wildfires, one of the most powerful hurricanes to hit the Gulf Coast in fifty years and the fallout from an unprecedented 'derecho' storm system in Iowa—all exacerbated by climate change—Republican leaders were silent about the science linking the increased frequency and intensity of such calamities to a warming planet.[27]

136 The road to success redefined

A few days later Inside Climate News headlined that "President Donald Trump's Climate Change Record Has Been a Boon for Oil Companies, and a Threat to the Planet." The story went on to declare that Trump's revocation of President Obama's restriction on methane leaks culminated

> a busy four years, and a breakneck 2020, as Trump and the former industry executives and lobbyists he'd placed in control of the Environmental Protection Agency and the Department of the Interior raced to rollback auto emissions standards, weaken the nation's most important environmental law, open the Arctic National Wildlife Refuge to drilling and reject stronger air pollution standards, even as research showed a link between those pollutants and an increased risk of death from Covid-19.[28]

Problems of race and poverty, also understated by most politicians in 2020, were amplified by the raging Covid-19 pandemic, and the press seized on this painful collateral damage. *The New York Times* reported in August 2020 on the expiration of emergency unemployment benefits:

> Now, with the $600 payments expired as of the end of July and with congressional leaders and the White House debating whether to extend them, Black workers stand to be hurt the most if they fail to reach a deal. This is in large part because Black workers disproportionately live in states with the lowest benefit levels and the highest barriers to receiving them. Without the $600 federal payments, the most an unemployed worker in Florida or Alabama can receive is $275 a week.[29]

Although they didn't get the attention they merited, the issues of climate change, racial inequity and economic disparity remained alive and in the public mind despite the demanding, competitive news of the pandemic, a painful recession and the 2020 election. Thanks to the ethical news media.

The Trumpers

But were the ethical media alone in feeding the public appetite for news? No, as in Fox News, which for two decades before the pandemic had been taking an increasingly partisan and truculent stance that made it the top-rated cable news channel, catering especially to an older, male, white clientele. As Brian Stelter of CNN tells it in his book about the close collaboration between Fox and Donald Trump,

> Trump's entanglement with Fox has no historical precedent. Never before has a TV network effectively produced the president's intelligence briefing and staffed the federal bureaucracy. Never before has a president promoted a single TV channel, asked the hosts for advice behind closed doors, and demanded for them to be fired when they step out of line… . Trump props up the network and the network props up Trump.[30]

Stelter says ferociously pro-Trump commentators Sean Hannity and Tucker Carlson were paid thirty million dollars and ten million dollars, respectively, as a reward for their huge ratings, with reporter Bret Baier making twelve million dollars and commentator Laura Ingraham, ten million dollars. Whatever President Trump said or did, Fox News and its well-paid personalities invariably took his side—at least until election day November 3 when Fox called the Arizona vote for Democratic candidate Joe Biden much earlier than other news organizations.[31] Throughout his campaign and presidency Fox gave Trump substantial personal exposure through exclusive on-air interviews and frequent telephone call-ins.

Breitbart News, too, reliably got the Trump message out. When candidate Joe Biden said in September that climate change aggravated wildfires raging in California and other western states, Breitbart gave prominent space to a blogger named Steve Milloy and his JunkScience.com:

> @JoeBiden doesn't mention or even refer to forest management for wildfires. California will burn to a crisp under Democrat rule. Steve Milloy said in a statement moments after Biden's environmental speech that it was 'filled with one falsehood after another, falsehoods that guarantee wildfires will burn much more of the American West.'[32]

As most news organizations were fixated on the wildfires raging in the West during September, and Trump's denial that climate change was exacerbating them, another determinedly conservative newspaper, *The Epoch Times*, chose to feature an off-beat Trump-friendly story, an admission by the FBI that the independent Robert Mueller investigators did in fact have a cell phone belonging to dismissed agent Lisa Page, contradicting their earlier statement that they didn't have it.[33]

Although any president of the United States will have no difficulty getting his message out, the pro-Trump news organizations made sure that his words and actions always received favorable play and ample support, while the more dispassionate media—what Trump derisively called the "mainstream media" or the "lamestream media"—were more likely to squint with a critical eye. That may have been in part because, as of July 13, 2020, The *Washington Post's* fact-checkers had counted more than twenty thousand Trump falsehoods uttered during his presidency, the pace increasing as he proceeded along.[34]

The point is that while Trump's word—and his side of any controversial story—was always transmitted to a waiting world by his supportive media, what assured a robust, fact-based public discourse during the Trump presidency was what the more independent, more ethical media reported. Do not believe the rumors that journalism is dying. One reason is that this vital profession continues to attract bright, capable, ambitious young people, as we'll see in the next chapter.

Notes

1 Paul Starr, *The Creation of the Media: Political Origins of Modern Communications*, New York: Basic Books, 2004, 57.

2 Ibid. 59.

138 The road to success redefined

3 Ibid. 65.

4 Ibid. 66.

5 Ibid. 60.

6 Ron Chernow, *Alexander Hamilton*, New York: The Penguin Press, 2004, 649, 650.

7 Michael Schudson, *Discovering the News: A Social History of American Newspapers*, New York: Basic Books, 1978, 69.

8 In 2020, Ida B. Wells received much-belated posthumous recognition: a Pulitzer Prize special citation for "outstanding and courageous reporting on the horrific and vicious violence against African Americans during the era of lynching," and an important Chicago street renamed for her.

9 Paul Starr, op. cit. 256.

10 Upton Sinclair, *The Jungle*, New York: Modern Library, 2002, 105–06, 107–08.

11 In a long career, Sinclair wrote nearly hundred books and other works, several of them about working conditions in other industries. He won the Pulitzer Prize for fiction in 1943. He ran unsuccessfully for Congress and California governor as a candidate of the Socialist Party.

12 Bill Kovach and Tom Rosenstiel, *The Elements of Journalism: What Newspeople Should Know and the Public Should Expect*, New York: Three Rivers Press, 2014, 72, 299.

13 Maxwell E. McCombs and Donald L. Shaw, "The Agenda-Setting Function of Mass Media," *The Public Opinion Quarterly*, Vol. 36, No. 2 (Summer, 1972), 181, 184.

14 Ibid. 184.

15 Paul Starr, op. cit. 256.

16 Richard Norton Smith, *The Colonel: The Life and Legend of Robert R. McCormick*, New York: Houghton Mifflin, 1997, 139.

17 Mindy Trossman, speaking to a graduate class at Northwestern University's School of Journalism, Media, Integrated Marketing Communications, May 5, 2020.

18 Associated Press News Values and Principles, https://www.ap.org/about/news-values-and-principles/introduction

19 Society of Professional Journalists Code of Ethics, https://www.spj.org/pdf/spj-code-of-ethics-poster.pdf

20 Shane Bauer, "My Four Months as a Prison Guard," *Mother Jones*, July/August 2016, https://www.motherjones.com/politics/2016/06/cca-private-prisons-corrections-corporation-inmates-investigation-bauer/

21 Stephen J. A. Ward, *Ethics and the Media: An Introduction*, Cambridge and New York: Cambridge University Press, 2011, 115.

22 Michael Schudson, *Why Democracies Need an Unlovable Press*, Cambridge and New York: Polity Press, 2008, 12.

23 The Commission on Freedom of the Press, *A Free and Responsible Press: A General Report on Mass Communication: Newspapers, Radio, Motion Pictures, Magazines, and Books*, Chicago: University of Chicago Press, 1946, 4, 23, 28.

24 Ibid. 68.

25 Ibid. 126, 125.

26 Ibid. 131.

27 Marianne Lavelle, "With Wild and Dangerous Weather All Around, Republicans Stay Silent on Climate Change," Inside Climate News, August 28, 2020, https://insideclimatenews.org/news/28082020/republican-national-convention-trump-climate-change

28 Vernon Loeb, Marianne Lavelle and Stacy Feldman, "President Donald Trump's Climate Change Record Has Been a Boon for Oil Companies, and a Threat to the Planet," Inside Climate News, September 1, 2020, https://insideclimatenews.org/news/31082020/candidate-profile-donald-trump-climate-change-election-2020

29 Emily Badger, Alicia Parlapiano and Quoctrung Bui, "Why Black Workers Will Hurt the Most if Congress Doesn't Extend Jobless Benefits," *The New York Times*, August 7, 2020, https://www.nytimes.com/2020/08/07/upshot/unemployment-benefits-racial-disparity.html?searchResultPosition=1

30 Brian Stelter, *Hoax: Donald Trump, Fox News, and the Dangerous Distortion of Truth*, New York: One Signal Publishers Atria, 2020, 22, 23.

31 Annie Karni and Maggie Haberman, "Fox's Arizona Call for Biden Flipped the Mood at Trump Headquarters," *The New York Times*, November 4, 2020, https://www.nytimes.com/2020/11/04/us/politics/trump-fox-news-arizona.html

32 Dr. Susan Berry, "Junk Science Founder: Biden Climate Speech 'One Falsehood After Another'," *Breitbart News*, September 14, 2020, https://www.breitbart.com/politics/2020/09/14/junk-science-founder-biden-climate-speech-one-falsehood-after-another/

33 Ivan Pentchoukov, "Mueller Team Had Lisa Page's Phone It Claimed Was Lost, Email Shows," *The Epoch Times*, September 15, 2020. The story went on to state that the Justice Department's inspector general had looked into controversial anti-Trump emails exchanged by Page and agent Peter Strzok, concluding that "their bias cast a cloud over the email probe but didn't ultimately influence the outcome of the investigation." https://www.theepochtimes.com/mueller-team-had-lisa-pages-phone-it-claimed-was-lost-email-shows_3501024.html?ref=brief_News&utm_source=morningbriefnoe&utm_medium=email&utm_campaign=mb

34 Glenn Kessler. Salvador Rizzo and Meg Kelly, "President Trump Has Made More Than 20,000 False or Misleading Claims," *The Washington Post*, July 13, 2020, https://www.washingtonpost.com/politics/2020/07/13/president-trump-has-made-more-than-20000-false-or-misleading-claims/

12

COVERAGE OF CONSCIENCE COINCIDES WITH JOURNALISTS' MOTIVATIONS

Why do some college graduates choose journalism despite its longstanding reputation for low pay? And how do their motivations square with the ethics of care?

Most young journalists know better than their contemporaries who opt for business or engineering or law (but not medicine) why they want to ply their chosen profession. Many are drawn to reporting as youngsters, finding school newspapers exciting and gratifying. A first-grader named Dan Rather even *started* a school newspaper—launching him toward stardom at CBS. Having failed at sports, future Washington columnist Robert D. Novak fell back on sports reporting in high school and college—until he discovered politics, and changed his byline from Bob to Robert D. A shy youngster, Jonathan Eig, now a best-selling author, found that as a school newspaper reporter he could talk to anybody—even girls. To Chinese environmental engineering student Ren Gufeng, his university paper's newsroom was more alluring than the laboratories he was tethered to; as Henry Ren, he's now reporting for Bloomberg News in New York. *The New York Times* globe-trotting reporter, Washington bureau chief and gourmet R. W. ("Johnny") Apple, Jr., although he grew up in Akron, Ohio, was an early reader of *The Times* and admired "wonderful, romantic" bylines of foreign correspondents. "It seeped into my consciousness that these people were actually being paid to do this," he said.[1] A black youngster growing up on Chicago's South Side read the newspapers, too, but found them lacking rather than inspiring. "The South Side [that] reporters described wasn't *my* South Side," WBEZ Chicago reporter Natalie Moore wrote in her memoir. "The limited coverage prioritized crime." She loved reading and writing, so "journalism seemed like a good path to pursue," not "to be an apologist only creating 'positive' stories about black people but to show the breadth of our communities."[2]

For some young people, an early exposure to journalism—or even just the idea—is simply a good fit with their self-assessment of personal skills and interests.

DOI: 10.4324/9781003140337-16

Coverage of conscience coincides with journalists' motivations   **141**

For Chicago ABC anchor Tanja Babich, it was "an aha moment" in Toronto, her home town. After a city official complimented her about how well she emceed a community event and suggested she might do well in broadcasting, she decided to study journalism in graduate school. There she "recognized almost immediately that this industry had the potential to connect my strengths (performing, critical thinking) and interests (storytelling, meeting new people, learning about their lives) with meaningful work."[3] Similarly, television reporter Bre'onna Richardson of 13WMAZ in Macon, Georgia, went to high school in Detroit, where she first thought of TV journalism when she saw herself in video replays of local school board meetings she was assigned to cover for news of her high school. "Mm, maybe I should get a career in broadcast?" she thought.[4]

Another early starter, Brian Stelter of CNN, was more entrepreneurial than most. "My first stabs at journalism," he writes in his book on the relationship between Fox News and Donald Trump, "were homemade websites about Goosebumps books and Nintendo video games. From my basement in Maryland, I would tie up the home phone line calling companies for video game gossip." In college

> I created a website dedicated to cable news … . in the name CableNewser because I figured nobody would take me seriously if they knew I was an eighteen-year-old college freshman at Towson University in Maryland! The blog took off.

Soon Stelter revealed himself and changed the name of his blog to TVNewser; just three years after he launched it, he was hired by *The New York Times* to cover the news media.[5]

Often there's a streak of idealism, of high purpose, that attracts students to journalism. "Every journalist," state Bill Kovach and Tom Rosenstiel, "must have a personal sense of ethics and responsibility—a moral compass…. Ethics are woven into every element of journalism and every critical decision that journalists make."[6] According to his biographer, legendary CBS anchorman Walter Cronkite was entranced in high school by the teachings of a former Houston reporter named Fred Birney:

> "Cronkite said of Birney, 'I had a sense, whenever I was in his presence that he was ordering me to don my armor and buckle on my sword to ride forth in a never-ending crusade for the truth…. He was so in love with his work that he passed it on to all of us.'"[7]

Early on Jonathan Eig sensed a desire to "comfort the afflicted and afflict the comfortable."

Hannah Farrow also felt a purpose. In her senior year at the University of Tampa, she took an internship at the *Tampa Bay Times*.

> I wrote a story about a 53-year-old man who was adopted at birth, and his reunion with his birth family. It was such an emotional piece—I spoke with

142 The road to success redefined

his wife, his biological siblings. When the piece was published, the man called me, crying, thanking me for writing about such a meaningful event in his life.

Farrow then spent two years as an advertising copywriter. "However, during those years, I kept revisiting that phone call from the adopted 53-year-old. Journalism gave my writing *meaning*, and I felt like I was helping, which is something I never felt in advertising." She went back to school for a master's degree in journalism, "and I never plan on leaving this field again."[8] She now reports for Politico.

When a Kansas law student named Bill Kurtis took a part-time television job to pay his way through school, it led to a life-changing experience. As he delivered the news one evening, a tornado suddenly approached and he blurted out, "For God's sake, take cover." His viewers fortunately heeded his words just before the twister demolished much of the town. It persuaded him that "this business can affect lives … I've taken it *very* seriously after that," abandoning the idea of law practice to spend the next several decades as a reporter, anchorman, documentarian and producer, a recipient of many awards.[9]

The journalism life

As Kurtis's experience shows, these early motivations, rational or merely emotional, can last a lifetime. "For those who practice it," the craft has a moral aspect, Bill Kovach and Tom Rosenstiel tell us.[10] Johnny Apple of *The Times* once told an interviewer, "Newspaper people love impossible dreams. I suppose we're reckless sentimentalists. If we didn't love impossible dreams, we would not still be working in an industry whose basic technology was developed in the 16th and 17th centuries."[11] Jimmy Breslin, the irascible but witty and very popular New York columnist for fifty years, was quoted as saying, "Rage is the only quality which has kept me, or anybody I have ever studied, writing columns for newspapers." At his death in 2017, Breslin was lauded by a *New York Times* obituary as being "unmatched in his attention to the poor and disenfranchised. If there is one hero in the Breslin canon, it is the single black mother, far removed from power, trying to make it through the week."[12]

After nearly two decades in television news, Tanja Babich of ABC is grateful:

> I have been entrusted with the stories of people whose lives were forever altered by tragedy, acts of terror and acts of kindness. I have covered a papal visit, presidential inauguration, pandemic, riots and civil rights movement. I have even experienced aerial stunts in an F16 fighter jet, a physical feat rivaled only by my experiences with childbirth. Serving as a trusted source of information, comfort and good humor for my community has been the honor of my life.[13]

Bre'onna Richardson finds that on her first job in Macon, Georgia, her

> passion for journalism has strengthened…. I love telling stories that evoke a reaction from the community. For example, I covered a story about a local furniture store collecting donations for families impacted by Hurricane Laura.

Coverage of conscience coincides with journalists' motivations **143**

After my story aired, the owner of the store told me he received ample donations and support. It made me feel good knowing that I played a part in helping the community get involved.

She adds, "I love to tell stories that pull at people's heartstrings... . a story about a 9-year-old boy cutting grass for people with disabilities... . I love to tell stories and I love to make a difference."[14]

They all care

It's fair to say that journalists care. Let's look more closely at some of these persuasive stories.

After high school in China, Ren Gufeng enrolled in prestigious Tsinghua University's environmental engineering program. "During my freshman year," he recalls, "I became an avid reader for my campus newspaper and multiple Chinese language media outlets. I wanted to produce high-quality investigative journalism pieces like what the juniors and seniors did." So he became a reporter for the newspaper.

I began to realize that my true passion was in writing and talking with all kinds of people, instead of the lab work that my major required. Reporting was fun, while seeing my name appeared in bylines was simply exciting. I devoted nearly all my leisure time to my campus newspaper from sophomore to senior year.

However, he had to reckon with his parents.

I loved journalism, and my parents knew that. But when I told them that I should be a journalist in the future, they were shocked. They said environmental specialists will be one of the most needed professionals in the next decade to tackle China's environmental problems. More importantly, they put it blatantly: journalists earn little. That's true. Chinese journalists don't earn a lot compared with engineers (especially, computer engineers) and have to withstand heavy pressure from the government. However, I'm in my twenties, not fifties. I should have the luxury to pursue my passion, I thought.[15]

He went to the United States, took the first name Henry, earned a master's degree in journalism, and became a business reporter at Bloomberg News (the company that pays the best, well above average).

Jonathan Eig, a resourceful reporter and author now in his mid-forties, caught the bug early.

I was better at expressing myself on paper than out loud. I considered newspaper work romantic, thrilling, heroic ... . I was a product of the Watergate age, the era of Woodward and Bernstein in D.C., of Breslin and

144 The road to success redefined

Hamill in New York, of Royko, my favorite of them all, in Chicago. I remember reading *All the President's Men* and telling my parents that my kid brother's accusations that I had teased him were 'nothing but rumors and innuendo.' I had no idea what 'innuendo' meant. I wanted to speak truth to power... . I wanted to see my name in the paper—but, even more, I wanted to see my *words*. Up to about age fifteen, I entertained fantasies of being a professional baseball player. Since then it's been journalism all the way.[16]

Eig attended journalism school at Northwestern University, became a reporter for the *New Orleans Times-Picayune*, later the *Dallas Morning News* and *The Wall Street Journal*, wrote for *Vanity Fair, Chicago* and other magazines, and in recent years has written best-selling books about Lou Gehrig, Jackie Robinson, the inventors of The Pill, Al Capone and Muhammad Ali. Not to mention two children's books named for his daughter Lola. Next big biography: Martin Luther King, Jr.

Civic journalism, public journalism

Motivated by emotion, idealism and sometimes rationale, ethical journalists will not find it difficult to adopt the humanistic ethics of care. As the above stories suggest, most already have. In fact, for a time in the 1980s and 1990s several newspapers undertook imaginative and energetic civic initiatives that were very close to what the ethics of care might generate now. Their efforts were known as "civic journalism or" "public journalism." This idealistic movement was enthusiastically fostered by Jay Rosen of New York University, not a journalist but a principal booster of the media. A promotional pamphlet Rosen co-authored in 1993 declared that journalism faced multiple threats of "fraying of community ties, the rising disgust with politics, and a spreading sense of impotence and hopelessness among Americans frustrated by the failures of their democratic system." The pamphlet averred that "the press remains an influential force ... a unique franchise ... focusing daily attention on areas of common interest," and thus it should take the initiative to deal with public needs and problems, much as the Hutchins Commission had demanded.[17]

Several newspapers took the plunge. The *Ledger-Inquirer*, of Columbus, Georgia, a majority-black city that admittedly lacked civic attractions, with an economy in uneasy transition from textiles to service industries, was a notable innovator. The newspaper started by researching and publishing an eight-part series on the future of the city, addressing transportation bottlenecks, persistent low wages of some residents, lack of nightlife, a faltering school system, and "the perception that a local elite dominated city politics to the exclusion of others." The paper followed up by sponsoring a public meeting that drew three hundred people who talked for six hours. The editor, Jack Swift, then invited seventy-five "interested citizens" to a barbecue at his house, giving birth to a new civic organization with the editor himself in a leading role, and several task forces on various subjects. The paper thus made the transition from community observer to community leader. To address a persistent problem of race relations, Swift, who was white, teamed up with a black state court

Coverage of conscience coincides with journalists' motivations **145**

judge to host several small bi-racial barbecues at their homes. More community meetings. More stories in the paper. Jay Rosen later talked to Jack Swift about this sharp departure from journalism's traditional role. "The leap he talked about was toward a different ethic that could only be described using different words: democracy, community, citizenship, deliberation, public life."[18] Rosen's book doesn't bring the *Ledger-Inquirer* saga to a close, other than to explore how controversial it was in the newspaper profession.

Rosen goes on to describe similar community-focused initiatives by other newspapers: the *Wichita Eagle, Charlotte Observer, Dayton Daily News*, Akron *Beacon-Journal*. The *Beacon-Journal* also focused on improving race relations. First, it ran a series on racial differences. Then an editorial asked readers to pledge to do something across racial lines; an astonishing twenty-two thousand of its one hundred eighty thousand readers responded. Some one hundred seventy arts, religious, civic, social and educational organizations also stepped forward, so the paper signed them up for a new civic organization, which soon gained momentum and incorporated as a not-for-profit with its own leadership and active program. Black and white churches held joint prayer sessions and other gatherings, study circles coached participants on how to talk about race and a teen group coordinated workshops in high schools. For its enduring efforts the *Beacon-Journal* was awarded the 1994 Pulitzer Prize for Public Service. Rosen states, "It was the first such award for an initiative that could be called public journalism."[19]

Rosen also salutes several other newspapers that made concerted efforts in the 1990s to purposefully discern the needs and views of their readers, especially prior to elections—meetings large and small, polling, many background interviews with ordinary citizens and community leaders, more op-ed space for outside views—leading to major articles, focused especially on framing local issues that needed attention, written by political leaders and other residents, as well as the newspaper's editors.

Nevertheless, despite these flashes of fame, public journalism ran out of steam. "By 1997," Rosen writes, "I noticed that the name was already disappearing from use, even in the newsrooms where the idea had been most influential. People found they didn't need the title anymore, and they went back to calling their work 'good journalism.'"[20] He concludes that "public journalism meant trying to find a better answer... . Today, what we most need from journalists is their enlivened imaginations, as they try to picture a scene where democracy and citizenship are not in slow fade."[21]

Good journalism, with care

Attribute it to "democracy and citizenship" if you will, ethical news organizations responded abundantly to the exacerbation in 2020 of the corrosive societal threats of climate change, racial inequity and economic disparity caused by the Covid-19 pandemic, the resultant recession, and the angry furor over racial injustice triggered by the Minneapolis police killing of George Floyd and other

146 The road to success redefined

vicious assaults on other black citizens, several of them fatal, by white policemen. Much of this fine journalism may readily be characterized as in keeping with the ethics of care, if not in complete fulfillment of it—amelioration and solutions still needed.

A September 2020 search for "climate change" in *The New York Times* yielded a gargantuan eighty-two thousand seven hundred forty-one citations, including, for instance, "'Climate Change is Real,' Newsom Tells D.N.C. Amid Wildfires; Gov. Gavin Newsom of California addressed the Democratic National Convention remotely from near one of the wildfires burning across his state."[22] A similar search of *The Seattle Times* produced thirteen-thousand one hundred twenty-eight results, including "UN agency laments summer's 'deep wound' to Earth's ice cover."[23] Mentioned earlier, the online, not-for-profit news service Inside Climate News won a Pulitzer Prize for stories about an egregious pipeline spill of heavy Canadian petroleum into a river emptying into Lake Michigan. Inside Climate News was critical of President Trump's record on the environment, while reporting that "Biden's Early Climate Focus and Hard Years in Congress Forged His $2 Trillion Clean Energy Plan."[24]

As scores of wildfires raged in California in the summer heat, an unusually pervasive and destructive outbreak, the Associated Press noted—again—that they were aggravated by climate change:

> The state burns regularly because of fierce autumn winds, invasive grasses that act as kindling, fire-happy native shrubs and trees, frequent drought punctuated by spurts of downpours, a century of fire suppression, people moving closer to the wild, homes that burn easily, people starting fires accidentally or on purpose — and most of all climate change... . Dozens of studies in recent years have linked bigger wildfires in America to global warming from the burning of coal, oil and gas, especially because it dries plants and makes them more flammable... . [A] s the climate warms, snow melts earlier making for drier plants in the summer and the rains come later, extending fire season.[25]

The New York Times warned in September 2020: "Melting Glaciers Are Filling Unstable Lakes. And They're Growing." The story went on:

> Nearly freezing and often an otherworldly shade of blue, glacial lakes form as glaciers melt and retreat. These lakes are a source of drinking and irrigation water for many communities. But they can turn deadly in an instant when the rocks that hold them in place shift and send torrents of water coursing downstream... . That growth, largely fueled by climate change, means that such floods will likely strike more frequently in the future ...[26]

Turning to the seemingly eternal threat of racial inequity, a September 2020 search of the *Los Angeles Times* yielded fifty-eight thousand four hundred seventy-nine

Coverage of conscience coincides with journalists' motivations **147**

results, including "Rams players working on plan to address racial inequality; Rams team leaders, including Robert Woods and Jared Goff, are working with teammates to come up with a plan to address racial inequality."[27] A similar "racial inequity" search of *The Atlanta Journal-Constitution* produced one thousand two hundred fifty results, including "Workers protest racial inequality on day of national strike."[28]

In August 2020, a spectator's video showed a Kenosha, Wisconsin, white policeman shooting an unarmed black man named Jacob Blake seven times in the back at point-blank range, paralyzing him from the waist down, while seeking to arrest him. The Milwaukee Bucks professional basketball team, whose home arena is nearby and whose players, like the entire National Basketball Association, are predominantly black, erupted in fury. They refused to play their next game. Other athletes—in basketball, baseball, soccer, even tennis—followed suit. Basketball's most prominent star, LeBron James of the Los Angeles Lakers, tweeted angrily, "WE DEMAND CHANGE. SICK OF IT." The *Los Angeles Times* voiced support:

> How else to grab fans' attention, so lavished on their highlight dunks and three-point shots, and focus it instead on the injustice, the unrelenting violence that people of color face every day even in the midst of a so-called racial reckoning? How else to reach the masses of Americans who tune in to games but not to the problems confronting Black Americans?[29]

Disproportionate impact

Less confrontationally but more pervasively, it was widely recognized by the ethical news media throughout the Covid-19 pandemic that it was infecting—and killing—more people of color than whites, who were better able to work from home and control their personal interactions. *The New York Times* reported prominently in July that new data from the Centers for Disease Control and Prevention showed that

> Latino and African-American residents of the United States have been three times as likely to become infected as their white neighbors ... And Black and Latino people have been nearly twice as likely to die from the virus as white people, the data shows.[30]

Giving CDC data a more comprehensive sweep, The Marshall Project reported in August, "New data shows deaths from all causes—COVID and otherwise—have gone up 9 percent among White Americans, but more than 30 percent in communities of color."[31] *The Wall Street Journal* did a deep dive into other data and reported in August that

> For many minorities, the disease is killing them in the prime of their lives. Among people in the U.S. who died between their mid-40s and mid-70s since the pandemic began, the virus is responsible for about 9% of deaths. For

148 The road to success redefined

Latino people who died in that age range, the virus has killed nearly 25%, according to a *Wall Street Journal* analysis of death-certificate data collected by federal authorities.

The disproportionate impact on Latinos is "in part because their high representation in jobs ranging from health aides to meatpacking have made it harder for some of them to dodge the virus, and because many have poorer access to care, according to public-health experts."[32]

The *Washington Post* railed against apparent racial discrimination by a select high school in suburban Fairfax County, Virginia, whose public schools are about 10 percent black, according to the editorial.

THOMAS JEFFERSON High School for Science and Technology has offered admission to the class of 2024 to 486 students. Want to know how many of those students are black? Fairfax County officials won't say, but the number is so small — fewer than 10 — that officials claim its disclosure could lead to potentially personally identifiable information about individual students. That tells you all you need to know about the system's abject failure to expand educational opportunities to students of color.[33]

Call it "income inequality"

A random search in September 2020 of "income inequality," a more common phrase than the more comprehensive "economic disparity," in the *Chicago Sun-Times* yielded eight thousand three hundred thirty-nine mentions, including an op-ed contribution, "Yes, money can buy happiness, more so than ever. Today, money and happiness are more strongly related than in the past. One factor is income inequality, which has widened the gulf between the 'haves' and the 'have nots.'"[34] Searching "income inequality" in September 2020 at the *Houston Post* yielded two hundred eighty-one thousand four hundred seventy-one mentions, including an opinion piece, "Wanted: CEO to fight income inequality by cutting executive pay."[35]

CNN reported that during the pandemic and recession higher-income Americans, while still employed, reduced spending, "primarily because of health concerns," costing low-wage workers their jobs.

Rich Americans who curtailed their spending during the pandemic ended up costing a lot of low-wage workers their jobs, a trend that could hinder economic recovery, according to Harvard University research released Wednesday... . About 70% of low-wage workers in the most affluent ZIP codes in large cities became unemployed as compared to 30% in the lowest-rent ZIP codes, according to the report.... The cities with some of the biggest drops in small business revenue and low-wage worker hours included New Orleans, Louisiana; Washington, D.C.; Honolulu, Hawaii; and Miami, Florida... . The revenue drop was even sharper for businesses — such as restaurants and hotels — that rely on physical interaction.[36]

Coverage of conscience coincides with journalists' motivations **149**

The New York Times recognized a new category of economic have-nots: previously self-sufficient families that lost jobs and, to their shame and chagrin, were forced to fall back on food banks. A multi-page story headlined "America's New Needy" stated that

> [i]n one week in late July nearly 30 million Americans reported they did not have enough to eat, according to a government survey. Among households with children, one in three reported insufficient food, the highest level in the nearly two decades the government has tracked hunger in America, said Lauren Bauer, who studies food insecurity at the Brookings Institution.[37]

The Wall Street Journal reported on government and private commitments to community lenders that make loans to alleviate economic inequality aggravated by the pandemic and recession. The local lenders, the WSJ explained, are specialized small institutions. "Community development financial institutions, or CDFIs, are community-based banks, credit unions and investment funds that lend to home buyers, small businesses and others in rural, impoverished and minority communities." They received big influxes of new funds to lend from the federal Paycheck Protection Program and "multimillion-dollar investments from traditional lenders such as Goldman Sachs Group Inc. and Bank of America Corp., and new corporate supporters such as Netflix Inc." *The Journal* interviewed Sunyatta Amen, owner of tea and wellness stores in Washington, D.C., whose loan application had been turned down by a major bank, but who then obtained a loan from a community lender called Optus Bank. "With Optus, it was awesome. It was painless and I really salute them," Amen told *The Journal*.[38]

As we noted in Chapter 3, the San Francisco Public Press, an online not-for-profit, reported in mid-2020 that the crowded Tenderloin neighborhood, where many of the city's swollen homeless population live, experienced an above-average rate of Covid-19 deaths. "Every corner of life here is packed tight," reporter Christopher D. Cook wrote,

> sidewalks, streets, homeless tent encampments, apartment buildings and single-room-occupancy hotels, where residents have their own rooms but typically share bathrooms and kitchens. By far the most densely populated neighborhood in San Francisco, the Tenderloin is home to 45,587 people per square mile, almost 2.5 times the citywide density of 18,939 people per square mile. Neighborhood residents suffer the city's second-highest rate of COVID-19 infections — eclipsed only by the Bayview — and five times that of neighboring Nob Hill.[39]

In the midst of the pandemic and recession *The New York Times* editorialized for government payments to counter economic disparity: create a thousand-dollar savings account for every newborn, "in effect, a Homestead Act for the modern era, providing everyone with some means to pursue an education, buy a home or start a business." These "baby bonds" would be funded by "a modest increase in inheritance

150 The road to success redefined

taxation.... The combination would reduce the inequalities of wealth that exert a growing influence on American life."[40]

Squaring with the ethics of care

How do stories such as these—and there were many, many of them responding to the triple threat of pandemic, recession and racial turmoil—comport with the ethics of care? In a word, sublimely.

Let's look back at how the feminist philosophers, and latterly a few others, formulated the ethics of care in the last decades of the twentieth century. They explicitly rejected traditional rational moral philosophy, notably Immanuel Kant's "categorical imperative" of reasoned duty, looking instead to David Hume's more humane dictum: "Reason is, and ought only to be the slave of the passions, and can never pretend to any other office than to serve and obey them."[41] Philosopher Nel Noddings set out "a feminine view ... feminine in the deep classical sense—rooted in receptivity, relatedness, and responsiveness."[42] She advocated a "moral imperative," saying that women "approach moral problems not as intellectual problems to be solved by abstract reasoning but as concrete human problems to be lived and to be solved in living."[43] Carol Gilligan added: "While an ethic of justice proceeds from the premise of equality—that everyone should be treated the same—an ethic of care rests on the premise of nonviolence—that no one should be hurt."[44] Annette C. Baier wrote that she saw in David Hume a "sympathy and concern for others," a "downplaying of the role of reason and a playing up of the role of feeling in moral judgment."[45] Virginia Held declared that "the ethics of care attends to and values such moral emotions as empathy and a shared concern" and "is more suitable than traditional moral theories for dealing with many of the concerns of civil society."[46]

Of course, these feminist philosophers weren't writing about journalism, but their cogent, humane thinking is what journalism now needs. The ethics of care meets precisely the current needs of this profession and this society. The editorial decisions and the reporting efforts that went into the several articles and editorials cited previously in this chapter might well be founded in these philosophical writings expressing societal responsibility. The articles, mostly enterprise pieces rather than simply reporting on events, reflect the caring, the concern for others, expressed by the exponents of the ethics of care. Furthermore, the editorials and articles are entirely in accord with most journalists' professional motivations and with the profession's codes of ethics calling for facts, truth, accuracy, fairness, transparency and sensitivity. In other words, the best of journalism about the pandemic, the recession and the racial-justice furor is consistent with both journalistic codes of ethics and the ethics of care; there is no ethical conflict. We should add that this contemporary journalism reads as well like an apt response to the Hutchins Commission's declaration that journalists *must* meet the needs of our society.

So, if these several quite disparate threads are already in fact woven together in a smooth, strong and admirable cord, what's amiss? What's amiss is that American society still suffers from climate change, racial inequity and economic disparity, all

Coverage of conscience coincides with journalists' motivations **151**

exacerbated and emphasized by the pandemic, the recession and the racial furor triggered by police brutality. These egregious realities are simply unacceptable in a democratic republic based on the belief that government exists to solve the problems, to meet the needs, of the people who created it. With a robust embrace of the ethics of care—and the Hutchins Commission's mandate—ethical journalism has the power to persuade and even mobilize public opinion to demand effective government action to ameliorate, perhaps even eliminate?, America's unacceptable shortcomings.

Notes

1 Todd S. Purdom, "R. W. Apple, a Times Journalist in Full, Dies at 71," *The New York Times*, October 5, 2006, https://www.nytimes.com/2006/10/05/nyregion/05applecnd.html
2 Natalie Y. Moore, *The South Side: A Portrait of Chicago and American Segregation*, New York: St. Martin's Press, 2016, 169.
3 Tanja Babich, email response to the author, August 31, 2020.
4 Bre'onna Richardson, email response to the author, September 19, 2019.
5 Brian Stelter, *Hoax: Donald Trump, Fox News, and the Dangerous Distortion of Truth*, New York: One Signal Publishers Atria, 2020, 14–15.
6 Bill Kovach and Tom Rosenstiel, *The Elements of Journalism, Third Edition*, New York: Three Rivers Press, 2014, 272, 273.
7 Douglas Brinkley, *Cronkite*, New York: HarperCollins, 2012, 29.
8 Hannah Farrow, email response to the author, September 8, 2020.
9 Lincoln Academy of Illinois interview, 1995, www.youtube.com/watch?v=6XnjKsgN3pg
10 Bill Kovach and Tom Rosenstiel, op. cit. 277.
11 Todd S. Purdom, op. cit.
12 Dan Barry, "Jimmy Breslin, Legendary New York City Newspaper Columnist, Dies at 88," *The New York Times*, March 19, 2017, https://www.nytimes.com/2017/03/19/business/media/jimmy-breslin-dead-ny-columnist-author.html
13 Tanja Babich, op. cit.
14 Bre'onna Richardson, op. cit.
15 Henry Ren, email response to the author, September 1, 2020.
16 Jonathan Eig, email response to the author, August 30, 2020.
17 Jay Rosen, *What Are Journalists For?* New Haven: Yale University Press, 1999, 73, 74.
18 Ibid. 33.
19 Ibid. 97.
20 Ibid. 299.
21 Ibid. 297, 300.
22 *The New York Times*, "'Climate Change Is Real,' Newsom Tells D.N.C. Amid Wildfires. August 20, 2020," https://www.nytimes.com/search?query=climate+change
23 Associated Press, "UN Agency Laments Summer's 'Deep Wound' to Earth's Ice Cover. *The Seattle Times*, September 1, 2020," https://www.seattletimes.com/search/?query=climate%20change&sortby=mostrecent&page=1&perpage=20
24 Vernon Loeb, Marianne Lavelle and Stacy Feldman, Inside Climate News, undated, viewed September 4, 2020, https://insideclimatenews.org/tags/trump-vs-biden-whats-stake-climate
25 Associated Press, "Science Says: Climate Change, People Stoke California Fires," *The New York Times*, August 20, 2020, https://www.nytimes.com/aponline/2020/08/20/science/ap-us-sci-science-says-why-california-burns.html?searchResultPosition=4

152 The road to success redefined

26 Katherine Kornei, "Melting Glaciers Are Filling Unstable Lakes," *The New York Times*, September 2, 2020, https://www.nytimes.com/2020/09/02/science/global-warming-glacial-lakes.html?searchResultPosition=9

27 "Rams Players Working on Plan to Address Racial Inequality," *Los Angeles Times*, August 27, 2020," https://www.latimes.com/search?q=racial+inequity

28 "Workers Protest Racial Inequality on Day of National Strike," *The Atlanta Journal-Constitution*, July 2020, https://www.ajc.com/search/?q=racial%20inequity

29 "Editorial: Slogans and T-Shirts Aren't Working. The NBA Players' Strike Was the Most Powerful Message They Could Send," *Los Angeles Times*, August 27, 2020, https://www.latimes.com/search?q=editorial+August+27%2C+2020+NBA+players

30 Richard A. Oppel Jr., Robert Gebeloff, K.K. Rebecca Lai, Will Wright and Mitch Smith, "The Fullest Look Yet at the Racial Inequity of Coronavirus," *The New York Times*, June 5, 2020, https://www.nytimes.com/interactive/2020/07/05/us/coronavirus-latinos-african-americans-cdc-data.html?campaign_id=56&emc=edit_cn_20200707&instance_id=20074&nl=on-politics-with-lisalerer&regi_id=12942352&segment_id=32789&te=1&user_id=7d0e5105b76418ac21466ea00fa29497

31 Anna Flagg, Damini Sharma, Larry Fenn and Mike Stobbe, "COVID-19's Toll on People of Color Is Worse Than We Knew," The Marshall Project, with the Associated Press, August 21, 2020, https://www.themarshallproject.org/2020/08/21/covid-19-s-toll-on-people-of-color-is-worse-than-we-knew

32 Paul Overberg and Jon Kamp, "Covid-19 Deaths Skew Younger Among Minorities; Coronavirus Infections Take a Heavy Toll on Latino People in Their Prime Working Years, Data Show," *The Wall Street Journal*, August 17, 2020, https://www.wsj.com/articles/covid-19-deaths-strike-early-for-many-minorities-11597582801

33 Editorial, "A Virginia School Shows That Racial Inequities Aren't Confined to the Justice System," *The Washington Post*, July 27, 2020, https://www.washingtonpost.com/opinions/a-virginia-school-shows-that-racial-inequities-arent-confined-to-the-justice-system/2020/07/27/e8a95732-af75-11ea-8758-bfd1d045525a_story.html

34 Jean Twenge, "Yes, Money Can Buy Happiness, More So Than Ever," *Chicago Sun-Times*, July 9, 2020, https://chicago.suntimes.com/2020/7/9/21318790/income-inequality-money-can-indeed-buy-happiness-the-conversation

35 Chris Tomlinson, "Wanted: CEO to Fight Income Inequality by Cutting Executive Pay," *Houston Chronicle*. July 20, 2020. https://www.chron.com/search/?action=search&firstRequest=1&searchindex=solr&query=income+inequality

36 "Harvard Researchers: Rich Americans Cut Their Spending, Hurt Low-Income Jobs," CNN Wire, Fox40, June 17, 2020, https://fox40.com/news/business/harvard-researchers-rich-americans-cut-their-spending-hurt-low-income-jobs/

37 Tim Arango, photographs by Brenda Ann Kenneally, "America's New Needy: Vans Full of Families Lined Up for Food," *The New York Times*, September 4, 2020, A15–A19, https://www.nytimes.com/search?dropmab=false&query=Tim%20Arango%2C%20"America's%20New%20Needy%3A%20Vans%20Full%20of%20Families%20Lined%20Up%20for%20Food%2C&sort=best

38 Amara Omeokwe, "Renewed Focus on Race Triggers Surge of Interest in Community-Based Lenders," *The Wall Street Journal*, August 18, 2020, https://www.wsj.com/articles/renewed-focus-on-race-triggers-surge-of-interest-in-community-based-lenders-11597743000?mod=searchresults&page=1&pos=12

39 Christopher D. Cook, "What Crowding Looks Like During a Pandemic: Dismal Days in the Tenderloin," San Francisco Public Press, August 28, 2020, https://sfpublicpress.org/what-crowding-looks-like-during-a-pandemic-dismal-days-in-

the-tenderloin/?utm_content=Contact&utm_source=VerticalResponse&utm_medium=Email&utm_term=Neighborhood%20residents%20suffer%20the%20city%26rsquo%3Bs%26nbsp%3Bsecond-highest%26nbsp%3Brate%20of%20COVID-19%20infections%20%26mdash%3B%20eclipsed%20only%20by%20the%20Bayview%20%26mdash%3B%20and%20five%20times%20that%20of%26nbsp%3Bneighboring%20Nob%20Hill&utm_campaign=What%20Crowding%20Looks%20Like%20During%20a%20Pandemic%3A%20Dismal%20Days%20in%20the%20Tenderloin

40 Editorial, "America Needs Some Repairs. Here's Where to Start," *The New York Times*, July 2, 2020, https://www.nytimes.com/2020/07/02/opinion/sunday/income-inequality-solutions.html

41 David Hume, 2011, op. cit. 360.

42 Nel Noddings, 1984, op. cit. 1.

43 Nel Noddings, 2013, op. cit. 96.

44 Carol Gilligan, op. cit. 174.

45 Annette C. Baier, op. cit. 56.

46 Virginia Held, op. cit. 131.

13

THE CARING NEWSROOM

Diverse, purposeful, committed to results

With the ethics of care firmly in mind, journalists need to organize and operate differently to obtain the intended results—not just tell stories about societal problems that beggar democracy, but arousing public opinion to the point that elected officials and business leaders feel constrained to act, and act effectively, to ameliorate climate change, racial inequity and economic disparity. Reduce carbon emissions. Strengthen laws prohibiting racial discrimination. Shift taxation away from low-wage earners and toward the rich who can afford to pay without undermining their good lifestyle.

First, let's staff our newsroom

The spate of glaring—and sometimes fatal—police mistreatment of blacks that surfaced in 2020 beginning with the Minneapolis police killing of George Floyd informed the nation that law enforcement was often inequitable. Despite egregious violence that tarnished some demonstrations for police reform, the public emphatically expressed support for reforms such as mandatory wearing of body cameras by police officers.[1] The flagrant mistreatment also made it clear to white Americans—if it wasn't already apparent—that the black experience in society is different, sometimes tragically different, from the life experience of whites.

Ta-Nehisi Coates writes,

> In 2000, one in 10 black males between the ages of 20 and 40 was incarcerated—10 times that of their white peers. In 2010, a third of all black male high-school dropouts between the ages of 20 and 39 were imprisoned compared with only 13 percent of their white peers…. If generational peril is the pit in which all black people are born, incarceration is the trapdoor closing overhead.[2]

DOI: 10.4324/9781003140337-17

In the runup to the presidential election of 2020, the likely tendency of Latinos, now the nation's second largest ethnic group, was seriously misread. Their growing numbers in Florida and Texas, in particular, gave rise to speculation that those states might tip to the Democrats. But it wasn't even close. Those two states remained reliably Republican.[3] Perla Trevizo of Texas Tribune observed cogently afterward,

> the press, pundits and politicians at the national level still see immigration as the key issue for Latinos. If you want to win 'their' vote, talk about Dreamers, talk about citizenship, talk about the border. But just as for any other group, there are so many other issues that are important. More than 18% of the U.S. population is Hispanic—40% in Texas—yet we represent roughly 7% of the newsroom workforce, according to the News Leaders 2019 Diversity Survey. Latinos account for 10% of the staff at ProPublica, 21% at The Texas Tribune and 30% of our joint newsroom partnership.

She added:

> My hope is that once again, as journalists reflect on what we did well and what we can improve on, we remember that immigrants, border communities and people of color are not homogenous and we must engage them as readers, as voters, as residents, day in and day out, not just before an election. Only then will we, as a country, have a better understanding of who we are and what we represent. Only then will we stop covering immigrants, Latinos, rural communities, conservatives, Native Americans as something more than 'us' versus 'them.' Only then, will it be 'we.'[4]

Well stated

A commentary in trade publication *Editor & Publisher* by Evelyn Mateos focused on newsroom leadership, declaring "people of color make up only 18.8 percent of newsroom managers at both print/digital and online-only publications. Without this kind of representation, mistakes can slip through the cracks."[5]

It's simply indisputable that, given the vast differences in personal life experience of different ethnic groups, any news organizations that purports to cover a community needs a newsroom that reflects that diversity. As the executive editor of *The Arizona Republic*, Greg Burton, declared in a striking public statement in August 2020,

> we must build and sustain a workforce that is reflective of the diversity in the communities we serve… . A diverse and inclusive workforce helps us better connect and serve you, our readers and our community partners… . Now, as then, we're reckoning with an inequity of our own making. In America's newsrooms, African American, Latino, Native American and Asian journalists are underrepresented in the ranks of reporters, photographers, producers and editors; in sports, news and opinion; along the coasts and on the prairie.[6]

156 The road to success redefined

We'll have occasion to refer further to this forthright and ambitious statement by Burton, who is also the west regional editor of the extensive USA TODAY network of giant publisher Gannett Corp.

This lack of diversity has long been recognized in the journalism profession, and in schools of journalism, but not cured. As Bill Kovach and Tom Rosenstiel observe, "the newspaper industry failed to meet the goals" established over the years by the American Society of Newspaper Editors and others. Citing differing descriptions of their work by several journalists, the authors add: "There was already ample evidence that newsrooms lacking diversity were unable to do their jobs properly. They missed news. Their coverage had holes… . The myopia of traditional definitions of news is proof enough that personal perspective colors journalism."[7]

Consider Chicago, a city of 2.7 million, roughly one-third white, one-third black, one-third Latino. It has seventy-seven neighborhoods. Some are homogenous, some not. They vary greatly—in race, income, citizenship, crime, educational attainment, the presence of public institutions such as libraries, recreational amenities such as parks, playgrounds and beaches, theaters and other entertainment venues, social life, political and economic influence, and community leadership. Chicago newsrooms can hardly reflect all this diversity, but race, which cuts across all these characteristics, is a vital starter. It's also desirable, if not absolutely necessary, that a newsroom aspiring to be sensitive to local changes and problems employs at least some journalists who grew up in town, attended public schools, and know people—ordinary people.

So the question remains, as for years: how does a news organization recruit a diversity of qualified journalists? Or perhaps the first question is, how does the organization even *find* the candidates for such jobs? There's a potential source that's not well exploited: the more than one hundred historically black colleges and universities. Collectively, they award several thousand bachelor's degrees each year. Not many of those graduates take jobs in journalism, despite the fact that any academic major is appropriate background for news work. The journalism profession has not effectively communicated to these graduates that they're needed in journalism, and that the field now seeks a greater diversity of skills and interests than ever. Journalism needs an ethnic mix of enterprising newspaper reporters who like to write, television and radio reporters and producers who prefer the spoken word, still and video photographers and editors, social media practitioners, web site designers, producers and editors, documentarians, and on and on. Quite enough to engage the interests and skills of almost any college senior who's about to graduate without a clear idea of profession, or even a first job. And there are many of them, on every campus, particularly during the pandemic and recession.

Enter black colleges and universities

The nation's black colleges and universities—more than a hundred of them—have a role to play here. The institutions are represented by a Washington-based organization called NAFEO, the National Association For Equal Opportunity in Higher Education. It speaks for not only the thirty-nine private colleges and universities that are officially dubbed Historically Black Colleges and Universities, or HBCUs—such as Florida A&M, Howard, Wilberforce, Morehouse, Spelman, Tuskegee and Xavier—but forty-seven public colleges and universities, eighteen land-grant universities, nineteen other public universities, and still others with predominantly black enrollments. The career counselors in these colleges and universities know their seniors, their interests, their desires, their qualifications. But the news media need to inform them better, and continuously, of their needs for black journalists.

In U.S. colleges and universities—all of them—there are more than a hundred programs that teach journalism, from undergraduate majors and minors through bachelor's and master's degrees (plus a handful of doctoral programs for prospective college teachers). They, too, seek more minority students, and they have a role to play here. What's needed between the black institutions, the others teaching journalism, and news organizations is some sort of clearing house, an online database that informs black students of where they're wanted, with useful financial information such as salaries and scholarships. Many of the most prestigious master's degree programs are private—and expensive, upward of fifty thousand dollars.

One proposal to bridge these gaps would have universities with journalism master's programs offer small summer institutes for intensive reporting and writing instruction, free of tuition, to minority students from any college, but with emphasis on graduates of the predominantly black schools. These summer programs would award certificates for successful completion, and moreover, would offer the certificate-holders immediate admission in the fall to the master's degree program, again with free tuition. For the summer students who prefer to enter the job market immediately, the journalism schools' career offices would provide focused job search assistance, offering prospective employers a sweetener of paying half the student's first-year salary as a fellowship of the university. What might this cost the university? Depending on the size of the summer program, upward of half a million dollars a year, requiring an endowment of about fifteen to twenty million dollars. A lot of money. But there are today innumerable foundations, charities and philanthropists seeking to enhance opportunities for minorities, and what better way than this very precise and measurable opportunity? Optimistically, the money could be found by a university's well-honed fund-raising apparatus, and they all have them these days. Thus, the machinery and personnel for the financing and execution of these very ambitious but specific initiatives are all in place.

In the absence of determined, innovative and well-financed efforts like this, a caring newsroom will simply have to fall back on some sort of affirmative action, the effort to publicize job searches and other opportunities widely, with specific outreach to minority institutions, communities and publications. This is what most news organizations are already doing, often without satisfactory results. The pool of qualified applicants simply must be increased. Ultimately, it will fall to colleges, universities and employers to see to that somehow. They cannot simply sit back and accept applications.

"Here's my promise," wrote Greg Burton of *The Arizona Republic* in his 2020 declaration:

158 The road to success redefined

> By 2025, The Republic newsroom will look like Maricopa County, one of the fastest growing counties in the West, where people of color are 45% of the population.... The Republic is making significant progress. In 2016, journalists of color were 20% of The Republic's staff. Today, they are 34%. Of our managers, 28% are journalists of color. There are as many women at The Republic as there are men, at all levels.... The Republic and Gannett newsrooms across the country are recommitting to hiring, promoting and retaining journalists who reflect the diversity of the communities we cover.[8]

An important commitment. To be monitored. More on the *Republic's* newsroom shortly.

Organizing the caring newsroom

Assuming recruitment of enough minority reporters to make the staff resemble the community it covers, how would they be deployed? Should they cover a beat, the usual newsroom assignment, and if so, what are the beats to be covered? Madison wrote that a democratic republic serves the "public good."[9] The Hutchins Commission declared that the press "must supply the public need."[10] This is solid advice. How best to respond? Ordinarily, typical beats cover such important subjects as municipal government ("city hall"), police and crime ("cops"), schools, and business. But a better way to address the public need and serve the public good in a caring newsroom is by territory—both geographical territory and territories of local concern.

For instance, an apt geographical territory is a needy neighborhood, perhaps a source of crime and other human iniquities that cry out for remediation. In all municipalities except the very tiny, there are neighborhoods. They differ. In this regard, we should note that Jane Jacobs, the acerbic and influential critic of top-down utopian city planning, expressed doubts about differentiation by neighborhood. She looked instead to individual streets for the life of the city. Streets, she wrote in her monumental *The Death and Life of Great American Cities*, published in 1961, have "self-government" functions:

> to weave webs of public surveillance and thus to protect strangers as well as themselves; to grow networks of small-scale, everyday public life and thus of trust and social control; and to help assimilate children into reasonably responsible and tolerant city life.... The self-government functions of streets are all humble, but they are indispensable. In spite of much experiment, planned and unplanned, there exists no substitute for lively streets.[11]

She elaborated further:

> The street neighborhoods of a city have still another function in self-government, however, and a vital one: they must draw effectively on help when

The caring newsroom **159**

trouble comes along that is too big for the street to handle. This help must sometimes come from the city as a whole, at the other end of the scale.[12]

True enough. Nevertheless, for journalistic purposes, while keeping Jacobs' assessment in mind, it's convenient and useful to think of neighborhoods. A city's needs, and much of its news, are there.

As an example let's look again at Englewood, the low-income, high-crime, black neighborhood known for its hundreds of vacant lots and shrinking population on Chicago's South Side. The news coming out of Englewood is usually depressing. BlockClub Chicago, an online nonprofit newsroom focused on neighborhood news, reported this in August 2020 as protest demonstrations and sometimes egregious looting erupted all over the country in the aftermath of George Floyd's killing in Minneapolis:

> ENGLEWOOD — The widespread looting of Downtown was kicked off Sunday afternoon when police officers shot and wounded a Black man in Englewood, leading to angry confrontations, a flurry of social media posts and violence and destruction.[13]

Happily, there was more to this story. The *Chicago Tribune* identified one neighborhood resident, Joseph Williams, as a South Side "community activist," and reported that

> a college student's video of Williams talking about how he and other local volunteers defused tensions at the site of the police shooting Sunday in Englewood has garnered more than 125,000 views, with comments such as 'Good man right here' and 'If you want to know what's happened in Chicago, here is a great eye witness.'[14]

Furthermore, the *Tribune* added soon to the feel-good aftermath with an unrelated story:

> Englewood residents and organizers have big plans for the building at the intersection that unites the east and west parts of their community. It will be home to a Fresh Market grocery and food co-op, the first step of a redevelopment that aims to transform vacant lots and abandoned buildings into amenities that include the food store, a recycling operation, a health center, a business incubator, mixed-use housing, a job training site and a restaurant… . The hope is the final step will be the reopening of the Racine Green Line stop, a historic landmark that was shuttered some 25 years ago, a decision that for residents symbolized disinvestment along racial lines — abandonment that made Englewood synonymous in Chicago with poverty, lack of opportunity and high crime. The idea has the backing of local Ald. Stephanie Coleman, 16th.[15]

160 The road to success redefined

There's a ton of learning in these stories of bad and good news in forlorn Englewood. First, Englewood is a neighborhood in great need. Second, even in despair there are beacons of light and hope that deserve encouragement and financial support. Third, it took a tragedy to wring some good news out of Englewood. Fourth—not entirely evident—no further news emanated from Englewood at that time. Radio silence.

But troubled Englewood has visible amenities: a warm and fuzzy public library, a post office, a large community college situated on a handsome green campus, a large police station, a new public high school, a lively bank branch, and, with city help, a new Whole Foods supermarket and a nearby Starbucks at a major intersection.

Englewood also has important human assets. Aisaha Butler, an indefatigable booster, founded and heads a neighborhood organization called Residents Association of Greater Englewood, or RAGE, though it exhibits more love than anger. RAGE sponsors an endless succession of upbeat community meetings encouraging activity and development. A tiny, federally supported Community Development Corporation, or CDC, tucked away on the fourth floor of the aging bank building, schools, advises and provides a shared office to first-time entrepreneurs such as Eugene Shelby, founder and sole employee of a chicken sausage company that sells to local grocery stores and restaurants. Milam and Sullivan Sausage Company keeps overhead low by contracting out the actual production and other necessary business functions, a strategy that proved especially shrewd when the business was hit by the pandemic. A not-for-profit called Growing Home, Inc. operates a large and impressive, year-round organic farm on two contiguous mostly vacant blocks in Englewood, selling its abundant produce at attractive prices in its own farm store, while employing and training each year about fifty unskilled young people, mostly formerly incarcerated, who move on to jobs in food service, restaurants and other food-related businesses. A local group calling itself the Rowan Trees Garden Society & 4-H Club has for more than thirty years taken advantage of the community's abundant vacant lots to turn some of them into gardens, according to the organization's secretary, the Reverend John Ellis. The first such conversion, next door to Ellis's town house where he can keep an eye on it, was supported financially by Home Depot and the Chicago Botanic Garden, and features a handsome, glistening white gazebo, cedar-bordered walkways and meticulous landscaping. It's open to the community for scheduled events.

So, you might wonder, with such assets, why does Englewood suffer high crime and a steady drain of its population, now (counting adjacent West Englewood) down by more than half to sixty thousand from its peak one hundred sixty thousand several decades ago, its residents earning currently a median income of only twenty-four thousand dollars?[16]

Two reasons stand out. Nearby jobs have dried up. Chicago's fabled stockyards, also located on the city's South Side, closed years ago, and a once-vigorous steel industry, located on the South Side and just over the Indiana line nearby, is greatly reduced from its one-time second-in-the-nation peak. The second reason, recalling Jane Jacobs' admonition of necessary influence on City Hall, is that for many decades Chicago's large City Council, made up of an alderman from each of the

The caring newsroom **161**

city's fifty wards, has chosen to virtually disenfranchise the voters of Englewood. While the current population of about sixty thousand would be an ideal size for a single ward in the city of 2.7 million, the aldermen instead have chopped the neighborhood higgledy-piggledy into portions of no fewer than five wards, actually six if you count a tiny slice of still another ward. As a local publication pointed out in 2020,

> For decades wards have chiseled their way into the Greater Englewood area — composed of both Englewood and West Englewood … The community has been a part of five wards since the'70s. Today, the 6th, 15th, 16th, 17th and 20th Wards, along with a small portion of the 3rd Ward, divide through the community area.[17]

Furthermore, none of the six aldermen lives in Englewood. Thus, no alderman takes responsibility for the welfare of Englewood, the six instead focusing their energies on their adjacent neighborhoods.

So who should look out for poor, neglected Englewood, the stepchild of Chicago politics? The news media! This is the essence of the ethics of care: to reach out to those in need, with a determination to make a positive difference in their lives. In the administration of a new mayor, Lori Lightfoot, there's evidence that City Hall is already listening to Englewood and similar needy communities. She announced in October 2020 a planned investment of public and private funds totaling an impressive seven hundred fifty million dollars in businesses, housing and other economic developments in depressed neighborhoods of the South and West Sides. Of course, the news media duly reported this eye-catching announcement.[18]

Though neither the mayor nor the press said it, such business support by government is appropriate for several reasons, even though it benefits private enterprise. A healthy street, a healthy community requires prosperous, profitable local businesses—restaurants, bars, shops selling clothing, athletic gear, personal electronics and so forth, services such as laundries, electronics repairs, package delivery, copying and printing—places to walk and bike to. And, importantly, the community needs those business opportunities to increase personal income and wealth. Pursuing the ripple affect further downstream, schoolchildren need family income to prosper academically, according to a persuasive 2020 book by a veteran of education research and legislation. "A major reason the schools are so challenged today is that half of the enrollment are children from low-income families," declares Jack Jennings, founder of a nonprofit called the Center on Education Policy, a Washington education research organization, and previously a subcommittee staff director and then general counsel of the House of Representatives Committee on Education and Labor.

> The problems that poor families have not only can overwhelm them, but can also frustrate good teaching and learning… . The best way to increase a child's success is to increase the family's income, educational level, and type of employment… A better economy may be the only way to bring about better schools.

162 The road to success redefined

Therefore, Jennings advises,

> school reformers ought to spend at least as much time working on good economic and social policies as on school improvement. That is how the parental backgrounds of students can be strengthened. Once they are improved, students should do better in school.

He adds a dour observation about "the uneven growth of wages," an imbalance we have mentioned previously. "From 1979 to 2018," Jennings states, "the bottom 10th percentile saw a 4 percent increase in real wages, the middle percentile saw a 14 percent increase, and the top 90th percentile received a 56 percent bump."[19]

Yes, the press reported Mayor Lightfoot's nine-figure announcement about economic development. But what about the follow-through? The news media sometimes fail to write the results as well as they report arresting announcements of flashy government programs. It's necessary to follow such investments as they devolve. How is the money allocated? Who gets it? How much? Why? Then, perhaps a year later, what are the results? Have the businesses succeeded? Are local owners and employees benefitting? Has the promised housing been built and occupied? Why, or why not? What does it mean for individual residents, for their families, for the community? A "horizontal" beat reporter covering Englewood and similar needy communities as well, must dig for these stories, whether of despair or hope.

For a current illustration of a geographically territorial beat, we refer again to the noteworthy statement in 2020 by *The Arizona Republic* executive editor. He announced the addition of "a reporter to focus on economic and educational gaps in south Phoenix, a region with more than 200,000 people, many of them African American or Latino."[20]

Besides a geographical beat, other territorial beats in a caring newsroom should address a territory of concern, i.e., a broad subject or problem that needs continuing coverage. Such beats exist now in some newsrooms. The *Chicago Tribune*, for instance, has a features reporter,

> Alison Bowen, who covers immigration, family dynamics and health. Jaclyn Cosgrove, the *Los Angeles Times* county government reporter, focuses primarily on human services including mental health, child welfare, homelessness, criminal justice reform and indigent care. Donnelle Eller covers agriculture, the environment and energy for the *Des Moines Register*.

And, to salute *The Arizona Republic* once more, Editor Burton's statement noted

> a new reporting initiative on housing and homelessness. For the next three years, this team will explore our state's opportunity divide, especially as low income and rural Arizonans struggle to survive.... For more than a year, we have reemphasized coverage of Arizona's Indigenous communities. We now have two reporters dedicated to covering the state's 22 tribes and environmental

The caring newsroom **163**

concerns on tribal lands. These journalists ensure we not only reflect Arizona but also tell its peoples' story.[21]

The caring newsroom in operation

The work of a typical newsroom radiates from a daily editorial conference. Typically, the editor or news director convenes it and discusses with his sub-editors or lead reporters, the city editor or assignment editor, for instance, what's in the pipeline for that day, and then decides what stories will be displayed on page one or lead the evening broadcast. They'll also discuss and assign longer-term stories and investigations.

In the caring newsroom, the decision discussion must be broad, probably fluctuating from day to day to include reporters with ideas, for their own beats or for the newsroom more broadly. Especially if most reporters of color are young and of limited experience, while the editors are mostly older and white, this requires some thought. To take full advantage of the differing perspectives of the diversity of reporters, the newer reporters must be heard. This is not to suggest that they should be obnoxious or loud to attract attention and support for their story ideas, but their voices must be part of the decision-making process. In any newsroom, this is critical—critical for the life of the community. Journalists decide every day what they'll cover, and those decisions set the agenda for public discourse in the community. No politician, no pillar of the community, can make his or her case without the megaphone of the news media.

Bill Kovach and Tom Rosenstiel, veteran reporters and editors, have a good sense of the internal dynamics of a newsroom that might well be called caring, as least as far as it goes. Here's their take:

> We need our journalists to feel free, even encouraged, to speak out and say, 'This story idea strikes me as racist,' or 'You're making the wrong decision,' or 'I want to raise a concern about something on the site.' Only in a setting in which all can bring their diverse viewpoints to bear can the news have any chance of accurately anticipating and reflecting the increasingly diverse perspectives and needs of American culture. Simply put, those engaged in news must recognize a personal obligation to differ with or challenge editors, owners, donors, advertisers, and even citizens and established authority if fairness and accuracy require they do so. That engagement must be constructive in order to be effective, not self-serving, egoistic, or designed to create pyrotechnics. In turn, those who run news organizations, whether large institutions or small Web experiments, must encourage and allow staff to exercise this personal obligation.[22]

What's missing, however, in this excellent statement is the affirmative aspect of the ethics of care. What should those in the caring newsroom talk about? Not just events or trends or pain or problems or shortcomings or needs in the community— all legitimate stories—but reach higher to enhancements, ameliorations, solutions, and how to achieve them. That's the distinction of the caring newsroom.

164 The road to success redefined

For instance, coverage of community concerns and needs must include both private and public actions that are being proposed and debated to deal with those subjects. Are local churches or other community organizations taking helpful action. Are city council members or state legislators getting into the act? What are their plans? If none, why? If they voice no proposals or ideas, reporters should keep calling them, monthly or maybe even weekly if the need is dire. The politicians won't appreciate stories that portray them as useless or unconcerned. This is journalistic ethics of care in action.

Then, as plans or actions are announced, as with Mayor Lightfoot's big proposal for Chicago's needy neighborhoods, it's necessary for the news media to follow the money, report where it goes and what it accomplishes, if anything. The taxpayers are owed this follow-up. Too much public money is misplaced or even lost.[23]

Finally, the caring newsroom should from time to time assess the state of a needy neighborhood or other local concern. Are things improving, or not? Crime? Jobs? Parks? Public transportation? Schools? What's been accomplished, and what more needs to be done? What do academic experts and government officials have to say about your findings? How do the residents feel?

The caring newsroom must also reach out imaginatively and continuously to the community—to give readers confidence in the journalists and their methods, to solicit ideas and opinions about the daily product, to broaden personal connections on both sides of current issues, and to assess both the quality of the product and the state of the community. For instance, the *Minneapolis Star-Tribune* hosts community events to showcase the work of their journalists, to explain why the journalists do certain stories and how they report them, to tell why they're currently seeking information through data analysis or freedom of information requests, and to explicitly solicit more information from their readers. Once a year, the paper presents a community impact report, and each quarter it brings in young readers to inform them about the function of a newspaper and to get feedback.

So this is the ethics of care in action, for the mission of journalism is to cover action—or, if necessary, lack of it.

Notes

1 Nolan D. McCaskill, "Americans Agree on Police Reforms That Have Divided Washington, New Poll Shows; Large Majorities Favor Policing Proposals Included in Bills That Have Stalled in Congress," Politico, July 14, 2020, https://www.politico.com/news/2020/07/14/americans-agree-police-reforms-360659
2 Ta-Nehisi Coates, *We Were Eight Years in Power*, New York: One World, 2017, 231, 271.
3 Arian Campo-Flores and Elizabeth Findell, "Latino Voters Drifted from Democrats in Florida and Texas," *The Wall Street Journal*, November 5, 2020, https://www.wsj.com/articles/latino-voters-drifted-from-democrats-in-florida-and-texas-11604582691
4 Perla Trevizo, "The Myth of the Latino Vote and What Newsrooms Must Learn from 2020," Texas Tribune, with ProPublica and the *Houston Chronicle*, November 10, 2020, https://www.propublica.org/article/the-myth-of-the-latino-vote-and-what-newsrooms-must-learn-from-2020

The caring newsroom **165**

5 Evelyn Mateos, "To Solve Journalism's Diversity Problem, Change Must Start at the Top," *Editor & Publisher*, July 9, 2020, http://www.editorandpublisher.com/stories/to-solve-journalisms-diversity-problem-change-must-start-at-the-top,166761

6 Greg Burton, "From the Republic Editor: Our Pledge for a Newsroom That Reflects Our Diverse Community," *The Arizona Republic*, August 20, 2020, https://www.azcentral.com/story/news/arizona-republic/2020/08/20/staff-diversity-arizona-republic-newsroom/5603177002/

7 Bill Kovach and Tom Rosenstiel, *The Elements of Journalism, Third Edition*, New York: Three Rivers Press, 2014, 161, 162, 163.

8 Greg Burton, op. cit.

9 James Madison, Federalist 10, *The Federalist Papers*, op. cit. 71, 80, 101.

10 *A Free and Responsible Press*, op. cit. 131.

11 Jane Jacobs, *The Death and Life of Great American Cities*, New York: Vintage Books Edition, 1992, 119, 120; originally published by Random House, Inc., New York, 1961.

12 Ibid. 119–20.

13 Jamie Nesbitt Golden and Maxwell Evans, "Police Shot a Black Man in Englewood. Then Misinformation Spread Like Wildfire," BlockClub Chicago, August 11, 2020, https://blockclubchicago.org/2020/08/11/police-shot-a-black-man-in-englewood-then-misinformation-spread-like-wildfire/?mc_cid=d9b7910203&mc_eid=50e880ab47

14 Nara Schoenberg, "In the Wake of Englewood Police Shooting, a Father of 5 Goes Viral on Twitter with a Heartfelt Video Highlighting Role Activists Played in Defusing Tensions between Neighbors and Police," *Chicago Tribune*, August 10, 2020, https://www.chicagotribune.com/lifestyles/ct-life-englewood-shooting-social-media-08102020-20200810-3u3ncrapevgjngcmpsqhtxnjwa-story.html

15 Annie Sweeney, "In Another Troubled Time, Englewood Continues Efforts to Transform," *Chicago Tribune*, August 14, 2020, https://www.chicagotribune.com/news/criminal-justice/ct-englewood-jobs-young-men-20200814-3bwfz2maxrbgpjl5spua42eo4u-story.html

16 U.S. Census Bureau, "These Figures Combine Englewood and Its Neighbor West Englewood."

17 Marissa Nelson, "What Englewood's Irregular Ward Boundaries Mean for Residents," 14EAST, January 24, 2020, http://fourteeneastmag.com/index.php/2020/01/24/englewood-irregular-ward-boundaries/

18 Lauren Zumbach, "Mayor Lori Lightfoot Announces Neighborhood Investment Plan with $10 Million from BMO Harris Bank," *Chicago Tribune*, October 21, 2020, https://www.chicagotribune.com/business/ct-biz-chicago-mayor-lori-lightfoot-neighborhood-investment-bmo-harris-20191021-nrvhjgbyfbcu3iotjxenijbwqe-story.html

19 Jack Jennings, *Fatigued by School Reform*, Lanham, MD: Rowman & Littlefield, 2020, 123, 124, 125.

20 Greg Burton, op. cit.

21 Ibid.

22 Kovach and Rosenstiel, op. cit. 273.

23 For a recent example, see Aaron Gregg and Yeganeh Torbati, "Pentagon Used Taxpayer Money Meant for Masks and Swabs to Make Jet Engine Parts and Body Armor," *Washington Post*, September 22, 2020, https://www.washingtonpost.com/business/2020/09/22/covid-funds-pentagon/

CONCLUSION

The challenge for a caring journalist is clear: produce enough stories that illuminate racial inequity, economic disparity and climate change (and perhaps other ills that threaten the quality of our democracy) to enlighten and mobilize public opinion to bring sufficient pressure on politicians, business leaders and other policy makers so they will move the ball perceptibly toward the goal of improvement and ultimately resolution. These subjects are not boring. There are innumerable, truly unlimited ways of illuminating their manifestations.

For instance:

The BBC reported in September 2020 of a "daring plan to save the Arctic ice with glass." The story explained that a proposal by the

> California-based non-profit Arctic Ice Project appears as daring as it is bizarre: to scatter a thin layer of reflective glass powder over parts of the Arctic, in an effort to protect it from the Sun's rays and help ice grow back. 'We're trying to break [that] feedback loop and start rebuilding,' says engineer Leslie Field, an adjunct lecturer at Stanford University and chief technical officer of the organisation.[1]

Or, consider that in September 2020, National Public Radio reported that "implicit bias" training required of New York City police personnel had changed minds but "not necessarily behavior." The story pointed out that such training was being required in many police departments after the appalling rash of police killings of blacks during 2020 and previously, so researchers were anxious to learn what the results of the training were in the nation's largest police force of thirty-six thousand officers. The researchers found that police became more aware of racial disparities in enforcement actions, and that was encouraging.

DOI: 10.4324/9781003140337-18

Conclusion **167**

But then the researchers examined data about NYPD officers' actions on the job before and after the training. Specifically, they looked at a breakdown of the ethnic disparities among the people who were arrested and had other kinds of interactions with those officers. And in those numbers, they found no meaningful change.[2]

The NYPD was striving for change, for improvement, which is certainly commendable. But the ethics of care demands more. It demands evidence of change, of progress, of improvement. An important advocate of such improvement, which sounds like an application of the ethics of care, is promoted vigorously and imaginatively by a not-for-profit called the Solutions Journalism Network. Co-founded by accomplished journalists and authors Tina Rosenberg (a Pulitzer Prize winner), David Bornstein and Courtney Martin, the organization advocates and trains journalists to seek stories that demonstrate progress ameliorating social problems. Their philosophy does not explicitly embrace the ethics of care but sounds very much like it.

The Solutions Journalism database of thousands of commendable stories contains such caring examples as those above and these:

A publication of University of Georgia journalism students reported in October 2020 that in Athens, Georgia, two women seeking to ease the pain of the pandemic had created and found financing for an "Athens Community Fridge." "Located in the parking lot of Caledonia Lounge, at the corner of Pulaski and West Clayton Street, it provides free, fresh food and produce to all members of the community." A volunteer called it a "community care approach." She was quoted, "At the end of the day, you have to take are of the people around you. It's up to us to look out for our own community." To fund the food purchases local businesses conducted raffles and sales, and a tattoo parlor raised more than four thousand four hundred dollars from sales of three-hundred-dollar gift certificates; it split the proceeds between Athens Community Fridge and the Athens Mutual Aid Network. A student reporter camped out by the fridge, and

> met a man named Joseph, who was choosing between a packaged meal prepared by Campus Kitchen and a pre-made salad. The fridge 'really makes a difference,' says Joseph. 'I always go to pre-made meals because I don't have a kitchen to cook food.'[3]

WHYY, the NPR station in Philadelphia, reported in October 2020 that a cluster of immigrant African entrepreneurs were helping each other out during the pandemic. Without bank lines, shopkeepers and other business owners for years had each contributed a thousand dollars a month to a fund to provide business loans. The story went on,

> When the pandemic hit, the club decided to prioritize its struggling business owners. In April, Kamara [Korkor Kamara, owner of Kamara African Foods] got a payout, known as a 'hand' — of about $24,000. She used the money to pay down debt and order a new shipment of goods from Africa. 'I felt happy, I felt relief,' Kamara said. 'If anybody said, "Do you have fufu?" I can say 'Yes.'[4]

168 The road to success redefined

To provide some guidance and perhaps some regularity to pursuit of caring journalism, consider this:

A journalist's code of caring ethics

A caring journalist believes that every person—

- Has an innate right to life, liberty and the pursuit of happiness, as stated in our Declaration of Independence.
- Has a right to decent housing, adequate nourishment, health care, personal safety and education.

A caring journalist believes that this independent profession—

- Is essential to our democracy, as protected by the First Amendment to our Constitution.
- Is intended to serve the public good, as stated in the Federalist Papers.
- Is obligated to respond to public need, as stated by the Hutchins Commission.
- Is privileged and therefore responsible to the public.

A caring journalist recognizes that practitioners of this special profession—

- Have a unique opportunity to make a difference.
- Must adhere to the high standards of the Code of Ethics of the Society of Professional Journalists [or other journalism code of ethics], independently seeking facts and balance, telling the truth accurately, fairly and transparently, and holding public officials to account.

A caring journalist understands that the Ethics of Care—

- Imposes obligations on all people to assist and support family members, friends, neighbors and others in need.
- As applied to society as a whole, deems such infirmities as racial inequity, economic disparity and climate change unacceptable threats to our democracy.
- Is fairly and appropriately recognized as applicable to responsible, ethical, independent journalism.
- Obligates journalists to go beyond reporting events, problems and societal needs, to seek solutions, to mobilize public opinion and resultant public and private remedial action, and then to report the sufficiency of results.
- Is now a personal professional commitment.

———————

Yes, we *can* make the world a better place.

Notes

1 Katarina Zimmer, "The Daring Plan to Save the Arctic Ice With Glass," BBC, September 23, 2020, https://www.bbc.com/future/article/20200923-could-geoengineering-save-the-arctic-sea-ice?utm_source=Solutions+Story+Tracker
2 "Martin Kaste, "NYPD Study: Implicit Bias Training Changes Minds, Not Necessarily Behavior," National Public Radio, September 10, 2020, https://www.npr.org/2020/09/10/909380525/nypd-study-implicit-bias-training-changes-minds-not-necessarily-behavior?utm_source=Solutions+Story+Tracker
3 Kate Ross, "Athens Community Fridge Changes How People Seek, Provide Aid: For Everybody, Owned By Nobody," Grady Newsource, University of Georgia, October 22, 2020, https://gradynewsource.uga.edu/athens-community-fridge-changes-how-people-seek-provide-aid-for-everybody-owned-by-nobody/?utm_source=Solutions+Story+Tracker
4 Miles Bryan and Jarred Cruz, "'We Stand Very Strong': Community Sharing Helps African businesses in Philly Stay Afloat during COVID-19," WHYY, October 8, 2020, https://whyy.org/articles/we-stand-very-strong-community-sharing-helps-african-businesses-in-philly-stay-afloat-during-covid-19/?utm_source=Solutions+Story+Tracker

APPENDIX

Selected journalism codes of ethics

Associated Press Statement of News Values and Principles
https://www.ap.org/about/news-values-and-principles/

Center for Public Integrity Journalistic Ethics
https://publicintegrity.org/about/editorial-policies/

Chicago Tribune Code of Editorial Principles
http://www.trbas.com/media/media/acrobat/2017-04/70017931280960-25200546.pdf

Dow Jones & Company Code of Conduct
https://www.dowjones.com/code-conduct/

Los Angeles Times Ethics Guidelines
https://www.latimes.com/la-times-ethics-guidelines-story.html

Marshall Project Code of Ethics
https://www.themarshallproject.org/about/code-of-ethics

National Public Radio Ethics Handbook
https://www.npr.org/ethics/

The New York Times Ethical Journalism
https://www.nytimes.com/editorial-standards/ethical-journalism.html

ProPublica Code of Ethics
https://www.propublica.org/code-of-ethics

Radio Television Digital News Association Code of Ethics
https://www.rtdna.org/content/rtdna_code_of_ethics

Society of Professional Journalists Code of Ethics
https://www.spj.org/ethicscode.asp

TEGNA Ethical Journalism
http://www.tegna.com/wp-content/uploads/2019/03/TEGNA-2018-Social-Responsibility-Highlights-1.pdf

Texas Tribune Code of Ethics
https://www.texastribune.org/about/ethics/

Washington Post Policies and Standards
https://www.washingtonpost.com/news/ask-the-post/wp/2016/01/01/policies-and-standards/

BIBLIOGRAPHY

Abernathy, Penelope Muse, "News Deserts and Ghost Newspapers: Will Local News Survive?," Hussman School of Journalism and Media, University of North Carolina, 2002, https://www.usnewsdeserts.com/reports/news-deserts-and-ghost-newspapers-will-local-news-survive/the-news-landscape-in-2020-transformed-and-diminished/vanishing-newspapers/

Abernathy, Penelope Muse, "The Loss of Newspapers and Readers," The Expanding News Desert, Hussman School of Journalism and Media, University of North Carolina, https://www.usnewsdeserts.com/reports/expanding-news-desert/loss-of-local-news/loss-newspapers-readers/

Baier, Annette C., *Moral Prejudices: Essays on Ethics*, Cambridge and London: Harvard University Press, 1994.

Bates, Stephen, *An Aristocracy of Critics: Luce, Hutchins, Niebuhr, and the Committee That Redefined Freedom of the Press*, New Haven and London: Yale University Press, 2020.

Bentham, Jeremy, *An Introduction to the Principles of Morals and Legislation*, Dumfries & Galloway: Anodos Books, 2019; originally published 1780.

Binder, Sarah A., "Going Nowhere: A Gridlocked Congress," Brookings Institution, December 1, 2000, https://www.brookings.edu/articles/going-nowhere-a-gridlocked-congress/

Brandeis, Louis, dissenting in part, *Louis K. Liggett Co. v. Lee*, 288 U.S. 517 (1933).

Brinkley, Douglas, *Cronkite*, New York: HarperCollins, 2012.

Brueggemann, Walter, *Virus as a Summons to Faith: Biblical Reflections in a Time of Loss, Grief and Anxiety*, Eugene, OR: Cascade Books, 2020.

Case, Anne, and Angus Deaton, *Deaths of Despair and the Future of Capitalism*, Princeton: Princeton University Press, 2020.

"CEOs Now Earn 320 Times as Much as a Typical Worker," Economic Policy Institute press release, August 18, 2020, https://www.epi.org/publication/ceo-compensation-surged-14-in-2019-to-21-3-million-ceos-now-earn-320-times-as-much-as-a-typical-worker/

Chernow, Ron, *Alexander Hamilton*, New York: Penguin Group (USA) Inc., 2004.

Coates, Ta-Nehisi, *We Were Eight Years in Power*, New York: One World, 2017.

Cohen, Adam, *Supreme Inequality: The Supreme Court's Fifty-Year Battle for a More Unjust America*, New York: Penguin Press, 2020.

Commission on Freedom of the Press, *A Free and Responsible Press: A General Report on Mass Communication: Newspapers, Radio, Motion Pictures, Magazines, and Books*, Chicago: The University of Chicago Press, 1946.

Bibliography 173

Damore, David F., Robert E. Lang and Karen A. Danielsen. *Blue Metros, Red States: The Shifting Urban-Rural Divide in America's Swing States*, Washington: The Brookings Institution, 2021.

Economic Policy Institute, "Raising America's Pay," June 4, 2014, https://www.epi.org/publication/raising-americas-pay-summary-initiative/

Emanuel, Rahm, *The Nation City: Why Mayors Are Now Running the World*, New York: Alfred A. Knopf, 2020.

Federal Election Commission, "Statistical Summary of 24-Month Campaign Activity of the 2015–2016 Election Cycle," March 23, 2017, https://www.fec.gov/updates/statistical-summary-24-month-campaign-activity-2015-2016-election-cycle/

Figueres, Christiana, and Tom Rivett-Carnac, *The Future We Choose: Surviving the Climate Crisis*, New York: Borzoi Books, Alfred A. Knopf, 2020.

Gao, Pengjie, Chang Lee and Demot Murphy, "Financing Dies in Darkness? The Impact of Newspaper Closures on Public Finance," Hutchins Center Working Paper #44, Hutchins Center on Fiscal & Monetary Policy, Brookings Institution, September 2018, https://www.brookings.edu/wp-content/uploads/2018/09/WP44.pdf

Gazzaniga, Michael S., *The Ethical Brain*, New York and Washington: Dana Press, 2005.

Gilligan, Carol, *In a Different Voice: Psychological Theory and Women's Development*, Cambridge and London: Harvard University Press, 1982.

Goldstein-Rose, Solomon, *The 100% Solution: A Plan for Solving Climate Change*, Brooklyn and London: Melville House, 2020, 52, 59.

Hall, Mark D., "James Wilson: Presbyterian, Anglican, Thomist, or Deist? Does It Matter?," in Daniel L. Dreisbach, Mark D. Hall, Jeffry H. Morrison, eds., *The Founders on God and Government*, Lanham, MD: Rowman & Littlefield, 2004.

Hamilton, Alexander, Federalist 9 and 71, *The Federalist Papers*, New York and London: Penguin Books, 1961.

Hare, Kristen, "The Coronavirus Has Closed More Than 50 Local Newsrooms across America. And Counting," Poynter Institute, September 9, 2020, https://www.poynter.org/locally/2020/the-coronavirus-has-closed-more-than-25-local-newsrooms-across-america-and-counting/

Held, Virginia, *The Ethics of Care: Personal, Political, and Global*, Oxford and New York: Oxford University Press, 2006.

Herman, Arthur, *How the Scots Invented the Modern World*, New York: Three Rivers Press, 2001.

Holthaus, Eric, *The Future Earth: A Radical Vision for What's Possible in the Age of Warming*, New York: Harper One, 2020.

Homeland Security Digital Library, National Advisory Commission on Civil Disorders: Summary of Report, 1968, https://www.hsdl.org/?abstract&did=35837

Horowitz, Juliana Menasche, Ruth Igielnik and Rakesh Kochhar, "Most Americans Say There Is Too Much Economic Inequality in the U.S., But Fewer Than Half Call It a Top Priority," Pew Research Center, January 9, 2020, https://www.pewsocialtrends.org/2020/01/09/trends-in-income-and-wealth-inequality/

Hossain, Mohammad Delwar, and James Aucoin, "The Ethics of Care as a Universal Framework for Global Journalism," *Journal of Media Ethics*, 33:4, 2018, 198–211, published online Nov. 1, 2018, https://www.tandfonline.com/doi/abs/10.1080/23736992.2018.1509713

Hume, David, "A Treatise of Human Nature," in *The Essential Philosophical Works: David Hume*, Ware, Hertfordshire: Wordsworth Editions Limited, 2011.

Jacob, Mark, "The Arkansas Gamble: Can a Tablet and a Print Replica Rescue Local News?," Local News Initiative, Medill School of Journalism, Media, Integrated Marketing Communications, Northwestern University, January 13, 2020a, https://localnewsinitiative.northwestern.edu/posts/2020/01/13/arkansas-democrat-gazette-tablet/

174 Bibliography

Jacob, Mark "8 Reasons Why Email Newsletters Are a Game-Changer for Local News," Local News Initiative, Medill School of Journalism, Media, Integrated Marketing Communications,Northwestern University,November 9,2020b,https://localnewsinitiative. northwestern.edu/posts/2020/11/09/newsletters-eight-reasons-why/index.html

Jacobs, Jane, *The Death and Life of Great American Cities*, New York: Vintage Books Edition, 1992; originally published by Random House, Inc., New York, 1961.

Jennings, Jack, *Fatigued by School Reform*, Lanham, MD: Rowman & Littlefield, 2020.

Kant, Immanuel, *Groundwork of the Metaphysics of Morals*, trans. Thomas Kingsmill Abbott, Monee, IL, 2020; originally published 1785.

Kennedy, Dan, "A Murder, a Media Frenzy, and the Rise of a New Form of Local News," NiemanLab, published by the Nieman Foundation at Harvard, June 5, 2013, excerpted from Kennedy's book, *The Wired City: Reimagining Journalism and Civic Life in the Post-Newspaper Age*, University of Massachusetts Press, 2013.

Kosar, Kevin, "A Permanent Committee to Improve Congress," *Politico Magazine*, 2019, https://www.politico.com/interactives/2019/how-to-fix-politics-in-america/gridlock/

Kovach, Bill, and Tom Rosenstiel, *The Elements of Journalism, Third Edition*, New York: Three Rivers Press, 2014.

Krugman, Paul, "The Rich, the Right, and the Facts," *The American Prospect*, Fall 1992, in Paul Krugman, *Arguing with Zombies: Economics, Politics, and the Fight for a Better Future*, New York: W.W. Norton & Company, 2020.

Kuttner, Robert, *Can Democracy Survive Global Capitalism?* New York and London: W.W. Norton & Company, 2018.

Kuttner, Robert, *The Stakes: 2020 and the Survival of American Democracy*, New York and London: W.W. Norton & Company, 2019.

Levine, Phillip B., and Robin McKnight, "Three Million More Guns: The Spring 2020 Spike in Firearms Sales," Brookings Institution, July 13, 2020, https://www.brookings.edu/blog/up-front/2020/07/13/three-million-more-guns-the-spring-2020-spike-in-firearm-sales/

Levitsky, Steven, and Daniel Ziblatt, *How Democracies Die*, New York: Broadway Books, 2018.

Locke, John, *An Essay Concerning Human Understanding*, quoted in A. John Simmons, *The Lockean Theory of Rights*, Princeton: Princeton University Press, 1992.

Madison, James, Federalist 10 and 14, *The Federalist Papers*, New York and London: Penguin Books, 1961.

McCombs, Maxwell E., and Donald L. Shaw, "The Agenda-Setting Function of Mass Media," *The Public Opinion Quarterly*, 36: 2, Summer 1972.

McIntosh, Kriston, Emily Moss (both of The Hamilton Project), Ryan Nunn (Federal Reserve Bank of Minneapolis) and Jay Shambaugh, *Examining the Black-White Wealth Gap*, Washington: The Brookings Institution, February 27, 2020, https://www.brookings.edu/blog/up-front/2020/02/27/examining-the-black-white-wealth-gap/

McManus, John H., *Market-Driven Journalism: Let the Citizen Beware?* Thousand Oaks, CA and London: Sage Publications, Inc., 1994.

Meacham, Jon, *The Soul of America: The Battle for Our Better Angels*, New York: Random House, 2018.

Mishel, Lawrence, and Jori Kandra, "CEO Compensation Surged 14% in 2019 to $21.3 Million, n.d.

Moellendorf, Darrel, *The Moral Challenge of Dangerous Climate Change: Values, Poverty, and Policy*, Cambridge and New York: Cambridge University Press, 2014.

Moore, Natalie Y., *The South Side: A Portrait of Chicago and American Segregation*, New York: St. Martin's Press, 2016.

Bibliography   175

Noddings, Nel, *Caring: A Relational Approach to Ethics and Moral Education*, 2013 edition, Berkeley and Los Angeles: University of California Press, 2013. First published 1984, original title *Caring: A Feminine Approach to Ethics and Moral Education.*

Pew Research Center on Journalism and Media, "For Local News, Americans Embrace Digital But Still Want Strong Community Connection," March 26, 2019, https://www.journalism.org/2019/03/26/for-local-news-americans-embrace-digital-but-still-want-strong-community-connection/

Pickard, Victor, *Democracy without Journalism? Confronting the Misinformation Society*, New York: Oxford University Press, 2020.

Piketty, Thomas, *Capital in the Twenty-First Century*, Cambridge, MA: Harvard, 2014.

Rosen, Jay, *What Are Journalists For?* New Haven and London: Yale University Press, 1999.

Rubado, Meghan E., and Jay T. Jennings, "Political Consequences of the Endangered Local Watchdog: Newspaper Decline and Mayoral Elections in the United States," *Urban Affairs Journal*, April 3, 2019, https://doi.org/10.1177/1078087419838058

Sampson, Robert J., *Great American City: Chicago and the Enduring Neighborhood Effect*, Chicago and London: University of Chicago Press, 2012.

Schaeffer, Katherine, "The Highest-Earning 20% of Families Made More Than Half of All U.S. Income in 2018," Pew Research Center, February 7, 2020, https://www.pewresearch.org/fact-tank/2020/02/07/6-facts-about-economic-inequality-in-the-u-s/

Schudson, Michael, *Discovering the News: A Social History of American Newspapers*, New York: Basic Books, 1978.

Schudson, Michael *Why Democracies Need an Unlovable Press*, Cambridge and New York: Polity Press, 2008.

Schwartz, Nelson D., *The Velvet Rope Economy: How Inequality Became Big Business*, New York: Doubleday, 2020.

Shierholz, Heidi, "Many Workers Have Exhausted Their State's Regular Unemployment Benefits," Economic Policy Institute, September 24, 2020, https://www.epi.org/blog/many-workers-have-exhausted-their-states-regular-unemployment-benefits-the-cares-act-provided-important-ui-benefits-and-congress-must-act-to-extend-them/

Sinclair, Upton, *The Jungle*, New York: Modern Library, 2002.

Singer, Peter, *Ethics in the Real World: 82 Brief Essays on Things That Matter*, Princeton: Princeton University Press, 2016.

Slote, Michael, *The Ethics of Care and Empathy*, London and New York: Routledge, 2007.

Smith, Richard Norton, *The Colonel: The Life and Legend of Robert R McCormick*, New York: Houghton Mifflin, 1997.

St. John, Jeffrey, *Constitutional Journal: A Correspondent's Report from the Convention of 1787*, Ottawa, IL: Jameson Books, Inc., 1987.

Starr, Paul, *The Creation of the Media: Political Origins of Modern Communications*, New York: Basic Books, 2004.

Stelter, Brian, *Hoax: Donald Trump, Fox News, and the Dangerous Distortion of Truth*, New York: One Signal Publishers Atria, 2020.

Stone, Geoffrey R., and David A. Straus, *Democracy and Equality: The Enduring Constitutional Vision of the Warren Court*, New York: Oxford University Press, 2020.

Sullivan, Margaret, *Ghosting the News: Local Journalism and the Crisis of American Democracy*, New York: Columbia Global Reports, 2020.

Urofsky, Melvin I., *The Affirmative Action Puzzle: A Living History from Reconstruction to Today*, New York: Pantheon Books, 2020.

Vanacker, Baastian, and John Breslin, "Ethics of Care: More Than Just Another Tool to Bash the Media?," *Journal of Mass Media Ethics*, 21: 2–3, 2006.

176 Bibliography

Waldman, Steven, and the Working Group on the Information Needs of Communities, *The Information Needs of Communities: The Changing Media Landscape in a Broadband Age*, Washington: Federal Communications Commission, 2011.

Ward, Stephen J. A., *Ethics and the Media: An Introduction*, Cambridge and New York: Cambridge University Press, 2011.

INDEX

Page numbers followed by n indicate notes.

Abaco Islands 34; ABCChicago anchor
  Tanja Babich, 141, 142; determinedly
  entered the news business, 132
Abernathy, Penelope (Penny) Muse 61n59,
  104, 110n1
Abraham 74
Abraxane 109
Adelson, Sheldon 109
Affirmative action 13
Affirmative Action Puzzle: A Living History
  from Reconstruction to Today 19n9
Affordable Care Act 55
Agricultural Adjustment Administration 55
Akron, Ohio 140
Alcorn, Chauncey 60
Alexander Hamilton 60n15, 138n6
Ali, Muhammad 144
All the President's Men 144
Amazon.com, Inc. 109
Amazon River basin 37
American Bible Society 49
American Independent Party 131
American Journalism Review 102n15
American Prospect, The 30n4
American Society of Newspaper Editors 156
Anchorage, Alaska 66
Annenberg School for Communication 106
Anniston Star 120
Anonymous sources, avoiding (usually):
  Associated Press 95; Los Angeles Times 95;
  Washington Post 94
Anti-Loan Shark Bureau see Chicago
  TribuneAppeal to Reason 130

Applebaum, Anne 44
Apple, R. W. ("Johnny"), Jr. 140, 142, 151n1
Arbery, Ahmaud 14
Arctic National Wildlife Refuge 136
Arguing with Zombies: Economics, Politics,
  and the Fight for a Better Future
  30n4, 41n1
Arango, Tim 31n20, 152n37
Aristocracy of Critics: Luce, Hutchins,
  Niebuhr, and The Committee That
  Redefined Freedom of the Press, An
  86n53
Aristotle 47, 53
Arizona Republic, The: executive editor's
  statement on newsroom diversity of
  155–58, 162
Arkansas Democrat-Gazette: loaned iPads
  to all subscribers 106
Around the World in Eighty Days 129
Articles of Confederation 45
Asia 39; Associated Presson California
  wildfires 146, 151n25; code of ethics of
  7, 89, 91, 93–95, 133, 138n18; on
  disparity of white and black wealth
  20n21; on fabrications in USA TODAY
  98, 102n13; founding of 116; on loss of
  earth's ice cover 151n23; on police
  officer charged with George Floyd's
  death 19n12; on racial disparities of
  Covid-19 infections 152n31
Athens Community Fridge 167, 169n3
Athens Mutual Aid Network 167
Atkin, Emily 108

178 Index

Atlanta Journal-Constitution, The: search of "racial equity" results 147; on workers' protest over racial inequality 152n28

Atlantic, The: on building a multiethnic democracy 44; "Why Obama Fears For Our Democracy" 60

Aucoin, James 81, 84n49

Aurora, Colorado 15

Austin, Texas 114

Axios Media: on carbon tax 39, 43n23; publishes subscription newsletters 109

Ayers Family Foundation 120

Ayers, Josephine 120, 123n11

Ayrshire 48

Babich, Tanja 141, 142, 151n3, 151n13

Badger, Emily 139n29

Bahamas 34

Baier, Annette C.: admirer of David Hume 73, 78, 84n6, 85n25, 85n30–85n31, 150, 153n45; criticizes "great moral theorists" such as Immanuel Kant 77–78, 85n28, 85n29; fears for feminist moral philosophers without tenure 85n32; salutes Carol Gilligan 77

Baier, Bret 137

Bank of America Corp. 149

Barry, Dan 102n11, 151n12

Barstow, David 102n11

Bass, Paul 119

Bates, Stephen 82, 86n53–86n58

Bauer, Lauren 149

Bauer, Shane 115, 122n6, 133, 138n20

Bay Citizen 121

Bayview 149

BBC: on reflective glass powder experiment in Arctic 166, 169n1; on shooting of black man in Kenosha, Wisconsin 19n14

Beacon-Journal, Akron: won Pulitzer Prize for public journalism initiative 145

Beacon, The 109

Bentham, Jeremy 8, 10n2, 99

Bergstresser, Charles 8

Berman, Mark 20n18

Bernstein (Carl) 143

Berry, Dr. Susan 139n32

Better Government Association 132

Bezos, Jeff 109

Biden, Joe: supported by voters concerned about racial inequity in 2020, 17; supported by urban voters in 2020, 66; won narrow Congressional approval of pandemic-relief bill 67; Fox called Arizona for him in 2020, 137; said climate change aggravated wildfires 137; New York Times op-ed by member of Biden-Harris transition team 14, 19n11

Billionaires 109

Bill of Rights see ConstitutionBinder, Sarah A.

Birmingham, Alabama 66

Birney, Fred 141

Bishops' War 47

Black Lives Matter 15

Blair, Jayson 97

Blake, Jacob 147

BlockClub Chicago: on neighborhood coverage by 113, 122n2; on start of looting in downtown Chicago 159, 165n13

Bloomberg News: Code of Ethics of 7, 88, 91, 95, 97; reporter Gufeng (Henry) Ren 140, 143

Bly, Nellie 129

Bomey, Nathan 110n5

Border Patrol (U.S.) 121

Bornstein, David 167

Boston College 108

Boston Globe, The 109

Boston, Massachusetts 127

Boston Red Sox 109

Boudinot, Elias 49

Bowen, Alison 162

Boyd, Gerald 98

BP 39

Bradley, Teresa and Marvin 100

Brandeis, Louis 21

Brandeis University 53, 55

Brazil 37

Breakthrough Institute 39

Breitbart News: on commentator's criticism of Biden on wildfires 137, 139n32

Breslin, Jimmy 142, 143, 151n12

Breslin, John 81

Brinkley, Douglas 151n7

British Crown 49

Broad Foundation, Eli and Edythe 122

Brookings Institution: on Congressional gridlock 67n3, 68n11; on cost of newspaper closures 59, 62n61; on economic disparity by race 24, 31n10; on firearms sales 44, 60n5; on hunger during pandemic 149; on legislative accomplishments 63–64; on urban-rural political divide 66

Brueggeman, Walter 81

Bryan, Bob 67n5

Bryan, Miles 169n4

Buchanan, George 47

Buchan, James 50

Index **179**

Buffalo, New York 32n29, 37
Buford, Talia 20n22
Bui, Quoctrung 139n29
Bureau of Indian Education (U.S.) 16
Bureau of Prisons (U.S.) 117
Burton, Greg 155, 157–58, 165n6, 165n20
Bush, George H.W. 64
Bush, George W. 63
Business Insider: on Congressional gridlock 67n5
Butler, Aisaha 160
Bzdak, Zbigniew 122n1

Cahokia 21
Caledonia Lounge, Athens, Georgia 167
CalMatters: on California homelessness 118–19, 123n8; founding, financing and staffing of 118
Calvin, John 47
Campo-Flores, Arian 164n3
Campus Kitchen *see* Grady NewsourceCanada 107
Can Democracy Survive Global Capitalism? 61n47
Capital in the Twenty-First Century 30n3
Capone, Al 133
Caring: A Feminine Approach to Ethics and Moral Education 10n6
Caring: A Relational Approach to Ethics and Moral Education 10n6
Caring newsroom 161–64
Carlson, Tucker 137
Carson, Rachel 36
Carter, Jimmy 63
Case, Anne 25, 31n14, 53, 61n40
Categorical imperative 8
Catholic Church 47
CBS: determinedly entered the news business 132; on future anchorman Dan Rather's first-grade newspaper 140; on future legendary anchorman Walter Cronkite's early attraction to journalism 141; on "60 Minutes" coverage of Mirage Tavern investigation 133
Census Bureau (U.S.) 118; on disproportionately black homelessness in California 118–19; on growing disparity of earnings 24; on shrinking population and low median income in Englewood 165n16
Center for Investigative Reporting: Bay Citizen merged into 121; founding and finances of 116; prizes won by 116–17

Center for Public Integrity: code of ethics of 96; donors of, not immune from coverage by, if warranted 89; modest fund-raising by 117
Center on Education Policy 162
Centers for Disease Control and Prevention (U.S) 15, 100, 147
Ceylon 129
Chaidez, Alexandra 122n2
Chalkbeat: founding and financing of 117
Charles I 47
Charlotte, North Carolina 66
Charlotte Observer: as initiator of a community-focused undertaking 145
Chattanooga, Tennessee 8
Chavis, Lakeidra 122n1
Chernow, Ron 48–49, 60n15, 138n6
Chicago: Austin 12, 16; Chicago Housing Authority 13; City Council 160–61; crime 12; crime statistics by police district 19n5; Englewood 12, 13, 16, 158–61, 165n13–165n17; Garfield Park 16; Ida B. Wells Drive 138n8; Lawndale 16; Lightfoot, Lori, Mayor 29, 165n18; police 11; Robert Taylor Homes 13; South Shore 13; South Side 13, 140, 161; Streeterville 12; Upton Sinclair's meat-packing exposé 130; Washington Park 13; West Side 13, 161
Chicago (magazine) 144
Chicago Botanic Garden 160
Chicago News Cooperative 113
Chicago Sun-Times: Mirage Tavern investigation 1977, 132–33; on money can buy happiness 152n34; search of "income inequality" results 148
Chicago Tribune: code of ethics of 7, 90; on Covid-19 impact 16, 20n25; on depressed neighborhood of Englewood 159, 165n14–165n17; on economic disparity 20n21, 29, 32n27; has reporter covering immigration, family dynamics and health 162; on lockups of school children 112, 122n1; on Mayor Lightfoot's announcement of development plan 165n17; ombudsman column and Anti-Loan Shark Bureau drew attention 132; opposed to Mayor Thompson's re-election 133; on weekend shootings, especially of children 12, 19n6
China 40
Christian Science Monitor: founding of 116
Chronicle of Higher Education, The: former editors of, founded Open Campus nonprofit 117

180 Index

Church of England (in America) 49
Cimini, Kate 123n8
Citizens United v. Federal Election
  Commission, 558 U.S. 310 (2010) 57,
  61n56
City Bureau: on mortgage disparities by
  Chicago neighborhood 17, 21n30
City Club of Chicago 32n27
Civilian Conservation Corps 55
Civil War 11, 14, 54
Cleveland, Ohio 66
Clinton, Bill 63, 64
CNN: on collaboration of President Trump
  and Fox News, in Brian Stelter book
  136–37; on economic disparity 26,
  31n18; on firearms sales 44, 60n4; on
  reduced spending by higher-income
  Americans costs low-wage jobs 148,
  152n36; on Texas officer charged with
  murder 19n16–20n16
Coates, Ta-Nehisi 154, 164n2
Cochrane, Emily 68n13, 68n14
Codes of ethics (generally; *see* individual
  companies or publications) 1, 2, 10,
  87–88, 101, 170–71
Cohen, Adam 28
Cohen, Jodi S. 122n1
Coleman, Stephanie 159
Coleman, William 128–29
College of New Jersey 48, 49, 50
Colonel: The Life and Legend of Robert R.
  McCormick, The 138n16
Columbia University 120
Columbus, Georgia 144
Commission on Freedom of the Press
  (Hutchins Commission): cites mandatory
  duties and responsibilities of press 83,
  86n53; criticizes contemporary
  journalism 83, 86n55; declares press must
  assume community objectives 84, 86n57,
  135, 138n23; declares press must supply
  the public need 84, 86n60, 101, 103n20,
  150–51, 158, 168; issued report 1946: *A
  Free and Responsible Press* 21n33, 86n52,
  138n23, 165n10; lectures press on need
  to ameliorate antagonisms of "social
  islands" 18–19, 134–35; members of
  86n52; origin and leadership of 82;
  quoted by Jay Rosen on addressing
  public needs and problems 144; Stephen
  Bates's history of 82; threatens
  government regulation 83, 86n56, 107,
  135, 138n26
Committee on Education and Labor (U.S.
  House of Representatives) 161

Community Development Corporation
  (CDC) 160
Community development financial
  institutions (CDFIs) 149
Company reputation, safeguarding of, in
  codes of ethics: Bloomberg 92; Dow
  Jones & Co. 91–92; Juan Williams fired
  by NPR 92; National Public Radio 92
Compassion & Choices 91
Conflicts of interest, striving to avoid, in
  codes of ethics: Associated Press 89;
  Bloomberg News 88; Center for Public
  Integrity 89; *Los Angeles Times* 89; *New
  York Times, The* 89; Texas Tribune 89;
  Wall Street Journal, The (Dow Jones &
  Co.) 89–90; Watkins, Ali 89; Winans, G.
  Foster 89
Congress: creation of, by Constitutional
  Convention 45; deemed most
  dysfunctional, 2011–2014, 67n1; gridlock
  of 63–68, 67n2–67n7; passed Bill of
  Rights 128; passed legislation proposed
  by President Roosevelt 55; passed
  monumental pandemic-relief bill 2021,
  67; years of one-party or two-party
  control of 63
ConocoPhillips 39
Constitutional Convention 45, 50,
  51, 60n8
Constitutional Journal: A Correspondent's
  Report from the Convention of 1787,
  60n8
Constitution, U.S.: Bill of Rights of 11, 128;
  drafting of, in 1787, 45, 51, 128; effective
  1789, 51; Eighteenth Amendment of 133;
  First Amendment of 18, 58; preamble of
  52; Sixth Amendment of 9; Thirteenth
  Amendment of 11
Consumer Reports: founding of 116
Continental Congress 49
Cook, Christopher D. 27, 31n22, 149,
  152n39–153n39
Cooke, Janet 98, 102n12
Cook, Lisa D. 14, 19n11
Cornell University 38
Corrections Corporation of America
  (now CoreCivic) 115, 133
Cosby, William 127
Cosgrove, Jaclyn 162
Council of Economic Advisers 39
Covenanters 47–48
Covid-19 pandemic 1, 12, 14, 15, 17, 26–27,
  29–30, 31n19, 32n28, 38, 44, 66, 105,
  110n5, 119, 136, 145, 147, 149, 152n31–
  152n32, 152n39, 169n4

Index 181

Creation of the Media: Political Origins of Modern Communications, The 137n1–138n5
Cromwell, Oliver 47
Cronkite 151n7
Cronkite, Walter 141
Cruz, Jarred 169n4

Dallas Morning News 144
Dallas, Texas 66
Damore, David F. 66, 68n11
Danielson, Karen A. 66, 68n11
Dayton Daily News: as initiator of a community-based undertaking 145
Death and Life of Great American Cities, The 158, 165n11, 165n12
Deaths of Despair and the Future of Capitalism 31n14, 53, 61n40
Deaton, Angus 25, 31n14, 53, 61n40
Declaration of Rights (Virginia's) 128
Democracy: challenged by pandemic 59; explained in Constitutional Convention and Federalist Papers 45–46, 50–51; hampered by political gridlock 63–68; impaired by wage stagnation 55–56; influenced by David Hume 48-51; needs growing income 53–54; praised by Alexis de Tocqueville 52–53; Scottish and Presbyterian influence 47–51; threatened 44–62
undermined by news shrinkage 58–59
Democracy and Equality: The Enduring Constitutional Vision of the Warren Court 19n2
Democracy in America 52–53, 60n33
Democracy Without Journalism? confronting the misinformation society 110n8–110n10
Democratic National Convention 11
Department of the Interior (U.S.) 136
DePaul University 32n28
DesMoines, Iowa 66
DesMoines Register: has reporter covering agriculture, environment and energy 162
Detroit, Michigan 3, 141
Diane Rehm Show, The 91
Discovering the News: A Social History of American Newspapers 138n7
Dow, Charles 8
Dow Jones & Co. (The Wall Street Journal): Code of Ethics of 89, 91–92; new performance records of 110n4
Dreisbach, Daniel L. 60n27

14EAST: on division of Englewood into six wards 165n17
Eau Claire Leader-Telegram 30, 32n31
Eau Claire, Wisconsin, 30
Eckes, Barbara 30
Economic Policy Institute: on CEO compensation 24, 30n8, 56; on pay disparity 23–24, 25, 30n4, 30n5, 30n6, 31n13, 32n30, 61n48–61n49, 61n51; on regional differences in workers' compensation 55–57, 61n52
Economist, The: on climate policy 38, 42n18, 42n19, 42n20, 43n21
EDF Renewables 39
Edison Research 17
Editor & Publisher: on paucity of newsroom leadership of color 155, 165n5
Eig, Jonathan 140, 141, 143–44, 151n16
Elements of Journalism, Third Edition, The 10n4, 131, 138n12, 151n6–151n7
Eller, Donnelle 162
Ellis, John 160
Emanuel, Rahm 27–28, 32n23, 42n5
Energy Poverty: How to Make Modern Energy Access Universal? 42n8
England 129
Englewood see Chicago
Environmental Protection Agency (U.S.) 136
Epoch Times, The: on FBI's finding missing cell phone 137, 139n33
Equal Employment Opportunity Commission (U.S.) 93
Essay Concerning Human Understanding, An 10n5
Essential Philosophical Works: David Hume, The 10n8
Ethics and the Media: An Introduction 138n21
Ethics in the Real World: 82 Brief Essays on Things That Matter 86n59
Ethics of care: based on philosophy of David Hume 10, 71–73; compatible with contemporary journalism standards of ethics 99–101; complements existing codes of ethics 71–86; disputing rational moral philosophy 9–10, 47, 71; formulated by—; Nel Noddings 73–74; Carol Gilligan 74–77; Annette C. Baier 77–78; Virginia Held 78–80; Michael Slote 80; illustrated by previous news coverage 80, 81–82; reasons for journalism's adopting 3; as similar to other professionals'

182 Index

philosophical views 81; summary of this book 2
Evans, Maxwell 165n13
Ewing, Maura 20n18
Exxon 39

Fabrications by journalists: Brian Williams, NBC 98; Jack Kelley, USA TODAY 98; Janet Cooke, *Washington Post* 98; Jayson Blair, *The New York Times* 97–98; Ruth Shalit, *The New Republic* 98 Stephen Glass, *The New Republic* 98Facebook 107, 121
Fairfax County, Virginia 148
Fan, Andrew 21n30
Fandos, Nicholas 67n5, 68n13
Farrow, Hannah 141
Fatigued by School Reform 165n19
Federal Communications Commission: 2011 report on decline of local news organizations 113, 122n3
Federal Deposit Insurance Corporation 55
Federal Election Commission 57–58, 61n57
Federal Emergency Relief Administration 55
Federalist Papers: on advantages of a democratic republic 50; on legislative checks and balances 63; on Madison's concerns about factions 50, 60n26; on support for new government for the public good 17, 21n32, 30, 45, 50, 52; writing of 45–46
Federalist Papers, The, Clinton Rossiter, ed. 60n6, 67n1
Federal Meat Inspection Act 130
Federal Reserve: created 54; former chairs of 39; on rising household net worth 25
Federal Reserve Bank of Minneapolis 31n10
Feldman, Stacy 138n28, 151n24
Fenn, Larry 20n24, 152n32
Figueres, Christiana 35, 42n6, 42n9
Findell, Elizabeth 164n3
First Amendment *see* Constitution
Flagg, Anna 20n24, 152n31
Flavelle, Christopher 42n15
Flitner, Emily 102n3
Florida A&M 157
Floyd, George 1, 14, 15, 19, 20, 44, 113, 145, 154, 159
Folkenflik, David 102n8
Food and Drug Administration (U.S.) 55, 118
Food banks 149
Forliti, Amy 19n12

Fortune: former writer Polina Marinova's newsletter 108; on hidden reports to FDA of injuries and device defects 118
Founders on God and Government, The 60n27
Fox News: application of code of ethics of 101n1; Brian Stelter's description of Fox-Trump relationship 136–37, 151n5; fallout caused by Fox's early call of Arizona for Joe Biden 139n31; increasing partisanship leading to top cable ratings 136; Juan Williams' offensive comments to Bill O'Reilly, on 92
Fox40: on harm to low-income workers caused by rich Americans' spending cutbacks 31n18, 152n36
Franklin, Benjamin 48, 51, 127, 128
Franklin, James 127
Franklin, Tim 108–09
Frank, Robert H. 38–39, 43n22
Free and Responsible Press, A *see* Commission on Freedom of the PressFreedman, Lisa
Freedom of Information Act 100
Free Speech and Headlight, The 129
Fresh Market 159
Friedman, Benjamin M. 53–55, 61n41
"Friend of the People" 132
Frosch, Dan 21n29
Future Earth: A Radical Vision for What's Possible in the Age of Warming, The 41n2, 42n6

Gannett Corp.: as publisher of USA TODAY 98, 156; second quarter 2020 financials of 105, 110n5
Gao, Pengjie 62n61
Gates Foundation, Bill and Melinda 115, 118
Gazzaniga, Michael S. 81
Gebeloff, Robert 20n23, 100, 152n30
Gehrig, Lou 144
Geophysical Research Letters 34
George Fox University 60n27
Ghosting the News: Local Journalism and the Crisis of American Democracy 31n16
Gilligan, Carol: as advocate of non-violence, that no one should be hurt 150, 153n44; as pioneer author of ethics of care 73–74; studies of pregnant women, and of young educated women and men, by 74–77, 85n15–85n24
Glasgow, Scotland 48

Index **183**

Glass Steagall Act 55
Glass, Stephen 98
Glater, Jonathan D. 102n11
Goff, Jared 147
Goldberg, Jeffrey 3
Golden Age 3, 7
Golden, Jamie Nesbitt 165n13
Goldman Sachs Group Inc. 149
Goldstein-Rose, Solomon 40, 41, 43n26
Google 107
Gorner, Jeremy 19n6, 20n25
Graduate School of Journalism, Columbia University 120
Grady Newsource, University of Georgia: on Athens Community Fridge 132, 169n3
Grand Rapids, Michigan 100
Great American City: Chicago and the Enduring Neighborhood Effect 19n7
Great Depression 3, 7, 21, 54–55
Great Lakes 36
Great Recession of 2007–09, 13, 23, 55
Great War 3, 7
Green, Bill 102n12
Green, Emily 116
Gregg, Aaron 165n23
Grim, Ryan 89
Grist: on minimal restoration of coal-despoiled lands 115
Gross domestic product 14
Groundwork of the Metaphysics of Morals 10n1
Growing Home, Inc. 160
Grynbaum, Michael M. 101n2, 102n3

Haberman, Maggie 139n31
Hall, Mark D. 60n27
Hamill (Pete) 144
Hamilton, Alexander: advocating legislative checks and balances, other innovations 63, 67n1; agreed with Madison that republican government purpose is the public good 18–19, 21n32; author of Federalist Papers 46, 60n6, 63, 67n1; biography of 60n15; birth and youth 48–49; in Constitutional Convention 46founder of *New-York Evening Post* 128–29; supportive of republican government 46, 60n6
Hamilton, Andrew 127
Hamilton, James 48
Hamilton Project, The 31n10
Hannity, Sean 137
Harder, Amy 43n23

Hare, Kristen 110n2
Harpur, Robert 49
Harvard 13, 15, 26, 31n18, 53, 55, 119, 148
Hassan, Carma 19n16–20n16
Hayes, Steve 108
Hearst, William Randolph 7
Held, Virginia: challenges news media to imagine alternatives not within the market 80, 85n41; contrasts care ethics with dominant rational moral theories 78–79, 85n34, 150, 153n46; on David Hume 73, 84n7; declares care is more than simply charity 79, 85n35; describes ethics of care as a must, not just an aspiration 79, 85n40; as ground-breaking author 78, 85n33; sees justice and health care fitting into caring relations 79, 85n36–85n39
Hellman, Warren 121
Henry, John 109
Herman, Arthur 47, 60n9, 60n14–60n15, 60n29
Hewlett Foundation, William and Flora 122
Historically black colleges and universities 156–57
Hoax: Donald Trump, Fox News, and the Dangerous Distortion of Truth 139n30, 151n5
Holthaus, Eric 34, 40, 41n2, 43n28
Home Depot 160
Homelessness 27, 29, 31n21, 118, 119, 162
Homestead Act 149
Honolulu, Hawaii 148
Horberry, Max 42n17
Horowitz, Juliana Menasche 30n1
Hossain, Mohammad Delwar 81, 85n49
House of Representatives: creation of, by Constitutional Convention 45
Housing and Urban Development, Department of 119
Houston Chronicle: on cutting executive pay 152n34; on "myth of the Latino vote" 164n4
Houston Post: search of "income inequality" results 148
Houston, Texas 66, 141
Howard (University) 157
How Democracies Die 15, 31n12, 61n46
How the Scots Invented the Modern World 60n9
Huffington Post 89
Hume, David: on admitting possibility of error 72; as a leading author, in Scottish Enlightenment 10n8, 60n12; as a philosophical source of U.S. Constitution

184 Index

46–47; embraced by Nel Noddings 74; as familiar to James Wilson 51; on importance of life experience 72; intellect admired by James Madison 50; on passions over reason 48, 71–72, 84n1–84n5, 150, 153n41; as philosophical inspiration of ethics of care 10, 10n8, 71; on religion of John Knox 47–48; on welcoming discussion 73; writings introduced to Alexander Hamilton 49–50
Humphrey, Hubert 131
Hungary 57
Huntsman, Paul 120
Hurricane Dorian 34
Hurricane Katrina 121
Hurricane Maria 34
Hussman, Walter E., Jr. 106
Hutcheson, Francis 40
Hutchins Commission *see* Commission on Freedom of the Press

Igielnik, Ruth 30n1
Independent Institute 109
Indianapolis, Indiana 66
Indian Health Service 17
Individual rights 9
Ingraham, Laura 137
Inside Climate News: on anti-environment actions of Trump Administration 136, 138n28; on Biden climate-change proposals 151n24; on Exxon's pioneering but secret research on climate change 118; on Pulitzer-Prize-winning investigation of Michigan oil spill 118, 146; on silence of Republican leaders on perils of climate change 135, 138n27
Inslee, Jay 37
Institute for Housing Studies at DePaul University 32n28
Institute for Nonprofit News 113
Intergovernmental Panel on Climate Change 41, 42n10
Internal Revenue Service: advantages of obtaining IRS recognition as "charitable" 114
Internal Revenue Code section 501(c)(3) 114, 122n4
International Energy Agency 42n8
Interstate Highway System 54
Introduction to the Principles of Morals and Legislation, An 10n2
Investigative Reporters and Editors 117

Investment prohibitions, in code of ethics of: Associated Press 90; *Chicago Tribune* 90; *Los Angeles Times* 90; *New York Times, The* 90; ProPublica 90; TEGNA 90; *Washington Post* 90

Jacob, Mark 110n6
Jacobs, Jane 158, 160, 165n11–165n12
James, LeBron 147
Jefferson, Thomas 128
Jennings, Jack 161–62, 165n19
Jennings, Jay T. 62n60
Jensen, Elizabeth 102n6
Jim Crow 11, 13, 54
Johnson, Akilah 20n22
Johnson, Gabe 21n29
Johnson, Lyndon 11, 54
Jones, Edward 13
Journalism profession: the caring newsroom 154–65; daily decisions on what to cover determine public discourse and influence public actions 131; elements of, Kovach and Rosenstiel 9, 10n4; ethical and moral aspects of, Kovach & Rosenstiel 141, 142, 151n6, 151n10; ethics of care can undergird more purposeful coverage of democracy's debilities 3, 41, 59; functions in a democracy, Michael Schudson's list 135; Jay Rosen: reach beyond rational to "set mind and soul in balance" 82, 85n51; journalists' motivations and satisfactions reflect idealism and caring 141–44; loyalty to citizens, Kovach & Rosenstiel 131, 138n12; newspapers shrinking 58–59; solutions journalism accords with the ethics of care 167–68
Journalist's code of caring ethics, A 167
Journal of Mass Media Ethics: on ethics of care in journalism 85n48
Journal of Media Ethics: on ethics of care in journalism 85n49
Jungle, The 130, 138n10

Kaiser Family Foundation, Henry J. 118
Kaiser Health News: on hidden reports of deaths and injuries from device defects 118; on manufacturers' confidential reports to FDA of device defects 118
Kalamazoo River 188
Kamara, Korkor 167–68
Kames, Lord 50
Kamp, Jon 152n32
Kandra, Jori 30n8, 61n51; Kant, Immanuel challenged by care ethicists

Index 185

generally 99, 150; challenged by David Hume 47; challenged by Nel Noddings 9–10, 77; known for his "categorical imperative" 8, 10n1, 71, 150
Karni, Annie 139n31
Kaste, Martin 169n2
Kelley, Jack 98
Kelly, Meg 139n34
Kenneally, Brenda Ann 31n20, 152n37
Kennedy, Dan 123n9
Kenosha, Wisconsin 14, 19n14, 147
Kerner Commission 11
Kerner, Otto Jr., 11
Kessler, Glenn 139n34
King's College 49
Knight Foundation, John S. and James L. 115, 122
Knox, Hugh 48–49
Knox, John 47
Kochhar, Rakesh 30n1
Kolbert, Elizabeth 36
Kormann, Carolyn 36
Kornei, Katherine 152n26
Kosar, Kevin 65, 67n8
Kovach, Bill 9, 10n4, 131, 138n12, 141, 142, 151n6, 151n10, 156, 163, 165n7, 165n22
KQED *see* National Public Radio
Krugman, Paul *see The New York Times*
Kurtis, Bill 142
Kuttner, Robert 53, 55, 57, 61n47, 61n53, 61n56

Lai, K.K. Rebecca 20n23, 100, 152n30
Lake Michigan 118, 146
Langer, Emily 102n12
Lang, Robert E. 66, 68n11
Las Vegas Review-Journal 109
Lavelle, Marianne 138n27, 138n28, 151n24
Lawless, Jennifer 65, 67n9
Ledger-Inquirer, The 144–45
Lee, Chang 62n61
Levenson, Michael 20n17
Levine, Phillip. B. 60n5
Levitzky, Steven 15, 18, 20n20, 21n34, 25, 31n11, 55, 61n46
Lewin, Tamar 102n4
Lightfoot, Lori 29, 32n27, 161
Lincoln Academy of Illinois 151n9
Liptak, Adam 102n11
Livingston, William 49
Lockean Theory of Rights, The 10n5
Locke, John 9, 10n5, 47, 99
Loeb, Vernon 138n28, 151n24
Lord Protector 47

Los Angeles 27, 118
Los Angeles Lakers 147
Los Angeles Times: code of ethics of 7, 90, 91, 93, 95; editorial support for NBA players' strike 152n29; on homelessness 2, 31n21; Pulitzer Prize of 116; purchased by Patrick Soon-Shiong 109; on "racial inequity" search result 146–47; on Rams' players addressing racial inequality 152n27; subscriptions to 105
Louis K. Liggett Co. v. Lee, 288 U.S. 517, 580 (1933), Brandeis, J., dissenting in part 30n2
Louisville, Kentucky 14
Loury, Alden 21n30
Loyola University Chicago 81
Lustgarten, Abrahm 36, 42n11
Luther, Martin 47
Lutton, Linda 21n30

MacArthur Foundation, John D. and Catherine T. 113, 122
Mackrael, Kim 32n29
Macon, Georgia 141, 142
Madison, James: as admirer of intellect of David Hume 50; as author of Federalist Papers 17, 21n31, 46, 60n7, 60n26, 60n32; early years and education 50; on republican form of government 46–47, 50; as supportive of a democratic republic to serve the public good 17–18, 52, 60n32, 165n9
Mahr, Joe 20n25
Marantz, Andrew 44, 60
Maricopa County, Arizona 158
Marin County, California 36
Marinova, Polina, 108
Market-Driven Journalism: Let the Citizen Beware? 110n7
Marshall Project: code of ethics of 94; on Covid-19 deaths 16, 20n24; on parental rights terminations of incarcerated parents 117; on racial disparities in Covid-19 infections 147, 152n31; shared Pulitzer Prize for false rape story 177; on sparse federal usage of elderly early release 117
Marshall, Thurgood 117
Martin, Courtney 167
Mason, George 128
Mateos, Evelyn 155, 165n5
Mather, Cotton 127
McCann, Allison 42n16
McCaskill, Nolan D. 164

186 Index

McClain, Elijah 15
McCombs, Maxwell E. 131, 138n13
McConnell, Mitch 66, 67n7, 68n13
McCormick, Robert R. 132, 133
McIntosh, Kriston 31n10
McKay, Rich 19n15
McKenzie, Hamish 108
McKibben, Bill 36
McKnight, Robin 60n5
McLaughlin, Eliott C. 19n16–20n16
McManus, John H. 106, 107, 110n7
Meacham, Jon 11, 14, 19n1, 19n10, 57, 61n55
Mecina, Tony 108
Medicare and Medicaid 54
Medill School of Journalism, Media,
  Integrated Marketing Communications,
  at Northwestern Universit 108, 110n6,
  138n17
Memphis, Tennessee 129
Miami, Florida 66, 148
Michaels (store) 9, 30
Michigan State University 14
Microsoft 39
Midwest 38
Migliozzi, Blacki 42n16
Milam and Sullivan Sausage Company 160
Mill, John Stuart 47, 99
Milloy, Steve 137
Milwaukee Bucks 147
Milwaukee, Wisconsin 15, 37, 100
Minneapolis, Minnesota 14, 15, 119
Minneapolis Star Tribune: hosts community
  events 164; Joel Kramer, former publisher
  of, and wife Laurie, as MinnPost
  founders 119
MinnPost: founding and financing of 119
Mirage Tavern investigation *see* Chicago
  Sun-Times
Mishel, Lawrence 30n8, 61n51
Mnuchin, Steven 66
Moellendorf, Darrel 35, 42n8
Moore, Natalie 140, 151n2
Moral Challenge of Dangerous Climate
  Change: Values, Poverty, and Policy,
  The 42n8
Moral Consequences of Economic Growth,
  The 53–54, 61n41
Morehouse 157
Morrison, Jeffry H. 60n27
Moss, Emily 31n10
Mother Jones: on fund-raising by 115; on
  private-prison mismanagement 115,
  122n5, 133
Mueller, Robert 137
Murphy, Demot 62n61

Nance, Malcolm W. 44
Nation City: Why Mayors Are Now
  Running the World, The 32n23, 42n5
National Advisory Commission on Civil
  Disorders 11
National Association For Equal
  Opportunity in Higher Education
  (NAFEO) 156
National Association for the Advancement
  of Colored People 129
National Basketball Association 147
National Covenant 47
National Election Pool 17
National Hurricane Center 34
National Public Radio: appropriations for,
  seen as contentious 107; broadcaster of
  prize-winning "Reveal" podcasts 116;
  code of ethics of 91, 92, 102n5–102n8;
  fund-raising success of 115; member
  stations of; KQED, 116; WAMU-FM, 91;
  WBEZ, 17, 21n30, 116, 140; WHYY,
  167, 169n4; WNYC, 116; on police bias
  training and results in New York 166–67,
  169n2
National Shooting Sports Foundation 44
Native Americans 16, 20n28
NBC: anchor Brian Williams suspended by
  98, 102n16; determinedly entered the
  news business 132
Nelson, Marissa 165n17
Netflix 117, 149
Nevis 48
New England Courant 127
New Haven (Connecticut) Independent: on
  murder of Yale graduate student 119
New Orleans, Louisiana 66, 121, 148
New Orleans Times-Picayune: author
  Jonathan Eig was reporter 144; exposed
  police violence after Hurricane
  Katrina 121
New Republic: former writer Emily Atkin
  makes "six figures" from climate change
  newsletter 108
Newsletters 108–09
Newsom, Gavin 146, 151n22
Newspapers, Golden Age of: *Chicago
  Sun-Times* Mirage Tavern investigation
  1977, 132–33; 1,700 daily newspapers in
  mid-20th century 132
New York (city) 49, 100, 127, 129
New Yorker, The: on climate change 36; on
  "democracy hangs in the balance" 44; on
  Washington "power grab" 59
New-York Evening Post 128–29
New York (magazine), 108

New York Society Library 49
New York Times, The: on carbon tax 43n22;
on climate change 33, 36, 37, 40, 41n5,
42n13, 146, 152n26; code of ethics of
88–89, 90, 95; on Congressional gridlock
and dysfunction 64–65, 66–67, 67n4,
67n7, 68n13; contract with Chicago
News Cooperative 113; early history of
7, 13; on economic disparity 25, 26, 28,
31n11, 136, 139n29; on elite "velvet rope
economy" 28, 32n24; on food banks and
their unexpected clients 26, 31n20, 149,
152n37; on Fox's early call of Arizona for
Biden 139n31; hired Brian Stelter to
cover news media 141; Jimmy Breslin,
obituary of 151n12; on killing of black
man in Illinois 20n17; on *The New
Republic* writer frauds 102n14; op-eds 14,
15, 18, 19n5, 20n20, 23, 38; on passage of
major pandemic-relief bill, 2021, 68n14;
Paul Krugman opinion columns 23, 30,
33, 41, 174; proposals to alleviate
economic disparity 28–29, 32n26,
149–50, 153n40; on racial disparities in
Covid-19 infections 15–16, 20n23,
100–01, 103n19, 147, 152n30; on racial
inequity 12, 14, 18, 19n11; on reporter
Jayson Blair fraud 102n11; reporter R.W.
("Johnny") Apple, Jr., obituary of 140,
142, 151n1; rising subscriptions to 105,
110n3; on sparse federal usage of elderly
early release 117; Special Section: "Out
of work in America" 32n31; Special
Section: "The Amazon Has Seen Our
Future" 37, 42n12; on suspension of
Brian Williams by NBC 102n16; on
Times reporter in leak case 101n2, 102n3;
on trial of WSJ reporter for fraud 102n4;
on wildfires 42n14, 42n15, 42n16,
42n17, 151n22
New York Times Magazine, The: on climate
change 36, 42n11
New York University 144
New York Weekly Journal 127
New York World: early history of 13; built
circulation with stunts and investigations
132; on Nellie Bly's around-the-world
trip 129; on Nellie Bly's insane asylum
exposé 129
New Zealand 73
News Corp. 110n4
Newsletters 108–09
Nieman Foundation at Harvard
(NiemanLab) 123n9
Nixon, Richard 15, 131

Nobel Prize 23, 25, 33, 39, 53
Nob Hill 149
Noddings, Nel: challenges Immanuel Kant
74; expresses a distinctly feminine view
9–10, 10n6, 150, 153n42–153n43; as a
pioneer in formulating ethics of care
73–74, 84n9, 84n10; quoted in epigram,
1; stated objective is goodness, not moral
rectitude 73
Nordhaus, Ted 39, 43n25
North, the 37
Northwest, the 37
Northwestern University 106, 108, 110n6,
138n17
Not-for-profit journalism: described
112–23; encouraged by Victor Pickard
106; newspapers, 119–20; ProPublica as
successful nonprofit 108, 120–22;
Pulitzer Prizes won by 120; *Salt Lake
Tribune* converted to nonprofit 105–06;
state or local focus of many nonprofits,
118–19
Novak, Robert D. 140
Nunn, Ryan 31n10

Oakland, California 109
Obama, Barack: as author of Affordable
Care Act 55; as enjoying Democratic
majority in Congress for only two years
63; as fearing for democracy 44, 60n3
Ochs, Adolph 13
Omeokwe, Amara 152n38
Open Campus: founding of 117–18, 123n7
Oppel, Richard A. Jr. 20n23, 100, 103n19,
152n30
Optus Bank 149
O'Reilly, Bill 92
Orlando, Florida 66
O'Shea, James 113
Overberg, Paul 152n32

Page, Lisa, 137
Paris Agreement 34–36, 41, 41n5,
42n5–42n6
Parlapiano, Alicia 139n29
Parliament 47, 128
Paycheck Protection Program (PPP) 149
Peabody (Prize) 116
Pelosi, Nancy 66, 68n13
Pennsylvania Gazette, The 127
Pentchoukov, Ivan 139n33
Pew Research Center: on citizen
dependence on local newspapers 58,

188   Index

61n58; on economic inequality 22, 24, 31n9
Phoenix, Arizona 162
Philadelphia, Pennsylvania 51, 127, 167–68, 169n4
Pickard, Victor 106–07, 110n8
Piketty, Thomas 30n3
Pill, The 144
Pine Ridge, South Dakota 17
Plagiarism, as prohibited in codes of ethics of: Associated Press 95; Bloomberg 95
Plessy v. Ferguson 54
Plot to Destroy Democracy: How Putin and His Spies Are Undermining America and Dismantling the West, The 44
Plotkin, Mark J. 37, 42n12
Plumer, Brad 42n13
Plumer, Brian 42n13
Pratt, Gregory 32n27
Pogrebin, Robin 102n14
Poland 57
Political activity prohibitions, in codes of ethics of: Associated Press 90–91; Dow Jones (The Wall Street Journal) 90; National Public Radio 91; New York Times, The 90
Politico: on police reforms 164n1; reporter Hannah Farrow 142
Politico Magazine: on Congressional dysfunction 65, 67n8
Poynter Institute for Media Studies: on pandemic's quickening of newspaper closures 105, 110n2
Poynter, Nelson 119–20
Presbyterian Church 47
Presbyterians: in early New York and New Jersey 49
Popovich, Nadja 42n13, 42n16
Presser, Lizzie 16, 20n26
Price, Jonathan 14
Princeton University 25
ProPublica: on amputation epidemic among blacks 20n26; code of ethics of 91; contributors to 108, 110n11; on Covid-19 infections 15, 20n22; on education of Native students 20n28; established first regional bureau, in Chicago 122; founding and financing of 120–22; Latino share of newsroom workforce of 155; on lockups of school children 112–13; on "myth of the Latino vote" 164n4; on shared Pulitzer Prize for false rape story 117; as winner of eight Pulitzer Prizes 120

Public Broadcasting Service: appropriations for, seen as contentious 107; member station of; on successful fund-raising by 115–16; WGBH 116
Public (civic) journalism 144–45
Pulitzer, Joseph 7, 120, 129, 132
Pulitzer Prize 44, 98, 116, 117, 120–21, 133, 138n8, 138n11, 167
Purdom, Todd S. 151n1, 151n11
Pure Food and Drug Act 130

Racial inequity 1, 2, 3, 11–21
Racine Green Line 159
Radio Television Digital News Association: code of ethics of 7, 8, 9, 101
Raines, Howell 98
Rainey, Malik 32n29
Ramsey, Ross 114
Rams (Los Angeles) 147, 152n27
Rather, Dan 140
Rational moral philosophy 1, 2
Rawls, John 99
Rehm, Diane 91
Reinhard, Scott 42n16
Ren, Gufeng (Henry) 140, 143, 151n15
Report of the National Advisory Commission on Civil Disorders: Summary of Report 19n3
Republican National Convention of 2020, 135
Residents Association of Greater Englewood (RAGE) 160
Reuters: on charges in shooting of black jogger 19n15
Reynolds, Glenn Harlan 64, 67n6
Richards, Jennifer Smith 122n1
Richardson, Bre'onna 141, 142–43, 151n4, 151n14
Richardson, Heather Cox 108
Richmond, Virginia 37
Rivett-Carnac, Tom 35, 42n6, 42n9
Rizzo, Salvador 139n34
Robinson, Jackie 144
Rochester, New York 37
Rockefeller Brothers Fund 118
Rocky Mountain News: failure of nonprofit successor of 114
Roll Call: on Congressional dysfunction 63, 67n1
Rolling Stone 108
Roosevelt, Franklin D. 55
Roosevelt, Theodore 130
Rosen, Jay 82, 85n51, 144–45, 151n17–151n21

Rosenberg, Tina 167
Rosenstiel, Tom 9, 10n4, 131, 138n12, 141, 142, 151n6, 151n10, 156, 163, 165n7, 165n22
Rossiter, Clinton 60n6, 67n1
Ross, Kate 169n3
Roundtree, Richard 92–93, 102n9, 102n10
Rowan Trees Garden Society & 4-H Club 160
Royko (Mike) 144
R Street Institute 65
Rubado, Meghan E. 62n60
Russia 57

Sacramento, California 118
Salt Lake City, Utah 106
Salt Lake Tribune, The 105–06, 120
Sampson, Robert J. 13, 19n7
San Diego County 26
San Diego Union 109
Sandler, Herbert and Marion 120
San Francisco, Callifornia 16, 36, 116, 121, 129, 149
San Francisco Public Press: on attacks against Asian-Americans 16, 20n27; on Covid-19 deaths in the Tenderloin neighborhood 149, 152n39; founding and financing of 119; on homelessness 27, 31n22, 119
Santa Clara University 106
Schaeffer, Katherine 31n9
Schiller, Vivian 92
Schoenberg, Nara 165n14
Schudel, Matt 102n12
Schudson, Michael 128, 133, 138n7, 138n22
Schwartz, Nelson D. 28, 32n24
Scotch Presbyterian Church (St. Croix) 48
Scotland 46, 51
Scottish Catholicism 47
Scottish Enlightenment 10, 47, 49, 51
Scottish Kirk 47
Seattle, Washington 37, 115
Seattle Times: "climate change" search result of 146; on loss of earth's ice cover 151n23
Securities and Exchange Commission 55
Sellers, Frances Stead 20n18
Senate: creation of, by Constitutional Convention 45; Intelligence Committee of 88
Serkez, Yaryna 37, 42n14
Shalit, Ruth 98
Shambaugh, Jay 31n10
Shane, Scott 102n3

Sharma, Damini 20n24, 152n31
Shaw, Donald L. 131, 138n13
Shaw, Randy 123n12
Shelby, Eugene 160
Shell 39
Shepard, Alicia C. 102n15
Shepherd, Katie 20n18–20n19
Shierholz, Heidi 32n30
Sinclair, Upton 130, 138n10–138n11
Singapore 129
Singer, Peter 84
Sixth Amendment see Constitution
Slavery 8, 11, 13
Slote, Michael: believes ethics of care values reason 80, 85n44; describes ethics of care as a total or systemic human morality 80, 85n42; on "Humean moral-sentimentalist tradition" 73, 84n8; says "empathy is crucial to moral motivation" 80, 85n43
Smialek, Jenna 31n11, 31n17
Smith, Adam 10, 47, 50, 51
Smith, Evan 114
Smith, Mitch 20n23, 100, 152n30
Smith, Richard Norton 138n16
Social Security Act 55
Social media, in code of ethics of: Center for Public Integrity 96; National Public Radio 95–96
Society of Professional Journalists : code of ethics of 7, 8, 9, 101, 133, 138n19; on its awards to San Francisco Public Press 119
100% Solution: A Plan for Solving Climate Change, The 43n26
Solutions Journalism Network 167
Somaiya, Ravi 102n16
Soon-Shiong, Patrick 109
Soth, Alex 19n4
Soul of America: The Battle for our Better Angels, The 19n1, 61n55
Southern Horrors: Lynch Law in all its Phases 129
South Side: A Portrait of Chicago and American Segregation, The 151n2
Special Report: Global Warming of $1.5{\circ}C$ 42n10
Spelman 157
Stakes: 2020 and the Survival of American Democracy, The 61n53
Stanford University 73
Starbucks 160
Starr, Paul 127, 128, 132, 137n1, 138n9, 138n15
St. Croix 48
Steel, Emily 102n16
Steiger, Paul 121

190 Index

Steinberg, Jacques 102n11
Stelter, Brian 136, 139n30, 141, 151n5
St. John, Jeffrey 60n8, 60n30
St. Louis Beacon 114
St. Louis, Missouri 66
St. Louis Post-Dispatch, The: publisher of, also publisher of *New York World,* established Pulitzer Prizes 120
St. Louis Public Radio 114
Stobbe, Mike 20n24, 152n31
Stolberg, Sheryl Gay 67n4, 67n7
Stoll, Michael 119, 123n10
Stone, Geoffrey R. 11, 19n2
Stop AAPI Hate 16
St. Petersburg Times *see* Tampa Bay Times
Straus, David A. 11, 19n2
Streeterville *see* Chicago
Substack 108
Suez Canal 129
Sullivan, Andrew 108
Sullivan, Margaret: as author of book on newspaper shrinkage 31n16, 59n1; on Fox News ethics 101n1; on loss of local newspapers 44, 59n1; on *The New York Times* coverage of economic disparities 25
Sullivan, Tim 19n12
Supreme Court: advocated by James Wilson 51; on affect of its *Citizens United* decision 57; creation of, by Constitutional Convention 45; James Wilson appointed to the first Court by President Washington 60n29; on supporting economic disparity 28, 32n25; on supporting efforts to remedy racial inequity 13; Warren Court and civil rights, 1950s and 1960s 11
Supreme Inequality: The Supreme Court's Fifty-Year Battle for a More Unjust America 32n25
Sutton, Joe 19n16–20n16
Sweden 107
Sweeney, Annie 19n6, 20n25, 165n15
Swift, Jack 144–45

Taibbi, Matt 108
Tampa Bay Times, The (formerly The St. Petersburg Times): intern Hannah Farrow 141; ownership of, transferred to Poynter Institute for Media Studies 106, 119–20; on WTSP's dismissal of anchorman 92–93, 102n9–102n10
Tampa-St. Petersburg, Florida 92
Taylor, Breonna 14
TEGNA Corp.: code of ethics of 8, 90, 92–93

Ten Days in a Mad-House 129
Tenderloin 27, 31n22, 149
Tennessee Valley Authority 55
Tesla 39
Texas Tribune: code of ethics (corrections) of 94; creation of 114–15; imaginative fund-raising by 115; Latino share of newsroom workforce of 155; on minimal restoration of coal-despoiled lands 115; on misuse of civil asset forfeitures 115; on "myth of the Latino vote" 164n4; not beholden to contributors to 89
Thirteenth Amendment *see* Constitution
Thomas Jefferson High School for Science and Technology 148
Thompson, Stuart S. 37, 42n14
Thornton, John 114
Tocqueville, Alexis de 52, 60n33
Tomlinson, Chris 152n35
Torbati, Yeganeh 165n23
Toronto, Ontario 141
Towson University 141
Tracy, Marc 110n3
Treasury (U.S.) 39
Treatise of Human Nature, A 10n8
Trevizo, Perla 155, 164n4
Trossman, Mindy 132–33, 138n17
Trump, Donald: administration of 13, 116; altered hurricane map 34; announced withdrawal from Paris accord 34, 41n5, 135; capitalized politically on stagnant wages 2016, 55; close collaboration with Fox 136, 141; criticized for Congressional gridlock 64; criticized for immigration restrictions 38; as critic of "fake news" 84, 120; election seen as symptom of "rot" in U.S. systems 107; favored additional pandemic relief 67; lost 88 of 100 most populous counties 2016 66; low support of, in 2016 exit poll 17; swept lowest-wage states in 2016, 56–57
Tsinghua University 143
Turkey 57
Tuskegee 157
TVNewser 141
Twenge, Jean 152n34
Twenties, the 7
Twilight of Democracy: The Seductive Lure of Authoritarianism 44

Unicorn Riot 109
United Kingdom 107
United Nations 34
United Nations Framework Convention on Climate Change 42n6

Index **191**

United States 34, 40
University of Georgia 167
University of North Carolina Hussman School of Journalism and Media: on newspaper closings 58, 61n59, 104, 110n1
University of Missouri-St. Louis 114
University of Pennsylvania 106
University of Pittsburgh 73
University of South Alabama 81
University of Tampa 141
University of Virginia 65
Urban Affairs Review: on declining coverage of California newspapers 59, 62n60
Urban-rural political divide: Nevada gun-control tussle 66; as seen by Brookings Institution analysis 66, 68n11
Urofsky, Melvin I. 13, 19n8
USA TODAY: on Congressional gridlock 64, 67n6; on declining revenue of parent Gannett Corp. 110n5; Principles of Ethical Conduct for Newsrooms of 98, 102n13; west regional editor of network of 156
Utility (utilitarianism) 2, 7, 8, 99

Vanacker, Bastiaan 81
Vancouver, British Columbia 37
Vanity Fair: author Jonathan Eig previously wrote for 144
Varn, Kathryn 102n9
Velvet Rope Economy: How Inequality Became Big Business, The 32n24
Vice News: Pulitzer Prize of 116
Virginia Commonwealth University 13
Vox Media, Inc. : as owner of The Verge, New York magazine, other media 110n12; reduced staff 2020, 108

Waldman, Steven 122n3
Wales, Jimmy 109
Wallace, George 131
Wallace, Mike 133
Wallace, Tim 42n16
Wall Street Journal, The: on carbon tax supporters 39, 43n24; code of ethics of 7, 13, 89; on disparities in health care costs 26, 31n19; on drift of Latino vote away from Democrats in Florida and Texas 164n3; early history of 7; on ignoring "fake climate debate" 43n25; on impact of Covid-19 on minorities in Buffalo 28, 32n29; on killing of Breonna Taylor

19n13; on loans by Community Development Financial Institutions (CDFIs) 149, 152n38; Paul Steiger, former managing editor of, as first editor of ProPublica 121; on racial disparities in Covid-19 infections and deaths 147–48, 152n32; reporter Jonathan Eig 144; rising total subscriptions of 105, 110n4; on transfer of Indian Health Service doctor 17, 21n29
WAMU-FM see National Public Radio
Ward, Stephen J. A. 133, 138n21
Warren, Earl 11, 28
Washington, D.C. 39
Washington Post: code of ethics of 7, 90, 93, 94, 96; on Colorado man dies after police stop 20n19; on conviction of reporter for fraud 102n4; on Diane Rehm and The Diane Rehm Show 91; on Fox News ethics 101n1; on Janet Cooke fraud investigator, obituary of 102n12; on misuse of Pentagon appropriations 165n23; on protests in Philadelphia 20n18; purchased by Jeff Bezos 109; subscriptions to 105; on small number of black students offered admission to select high school 148, 152n33; on threat to democracy 44; on 20,000+ Trump falsehoods 137, 139n34
Watkins, Ali 88–89
Waukegan, Illinois 14
WBEZ see National Public Radio
Weaver, Christopher 21n29
Weber, Mr. 17
Weekly Standard, The: former reporter Tony Mecia writes newsletter on business 108
Wells, Ida B. 128, 138n8
Wenus, Laura 20n27
West Coast 37
West Indies 48
West, the 37, 137
We Were Eight Years in Power 164n2
WGBH see Public Broadcasting Service
What are Journalists For? 85n51
Whelan, Robbie 31n19
Whole Foods 160
Why Democracies Need an Unlovable Press 138n22
WHYY see National Public Radio
Wichita Eagle: initiated community-focused undertaking 145
Wikipedia 109
WikiTribune 109
Wilberforce 157
Williams, Brian 98
Williams, Joseph 159

192 Index

Williams, Juan 92, 102n8
Wilson, James: active and influential delegate to Constitutional Convention 51, 60n29; appointed to first Supreme Court by President George Washington 60n29; birth and immigration from Scotland 51
Winans, G. Foster 89, 102n4
Winfield, George 29–30
Wired City: Reimagining Journalism and Civic Life in the Post-Newspaper Age, The 123n9
Wiseman, Paul 20n21
Witherspoon, John 49, 50
Witte, Griff 20n18
13WMAZ 141
WNYC see National Public Radio
Women's Lunatic Asylum on Blackwell's Island, New York 129
Woods, Alden 20n28

Woods, Robert 147
Woodson, Bob 65, 67n10
Woodson Institute 65
Woodtiger Fund 122
Woodward (Bob) 143
Works Progress Administration 55
World War I 131
World War II 3, 7
Wright, Will 20n23, 100, 152n30
WTSP Tampa-St. Petersburg 92

Xavier (University) 157

Zeller, Shawn 67n1
Zenger, John Peter 127
Ziblatt, Daniel 15, 18, 20n20, 21n34, 25, 31n12, 55, 61n46
Zimmer, Katrina 169n1
Zumbach, Lauren 165n18